THE MATILDA EFFECT

FIONA CRAWFORD

MELBOURNE
UNIVERSITY
PRESS

MELBOURNE UNIVERSITY PRESS
An imprint of Melbourne University Publishing Limited
Level 1, 715 Swanston Street, Carlton, Victoria 3053, Australia
mup-contact@unimelb.edu.au
www.mup.com.au

First published 2023
Text © Fiona Crawford, 2023
Images © various contributors, various dates
Design and typography © Melbourne University Publishing Limited, 2023

A catalogue record for this book is available from the National Library of Australia

Cover design by Philip Campbell Design
Typeset by Sonya Murphy, Adala Studio
Cover image by Rachel Bach/By the White Line
Printed in Australia by McPherson's Printing Group

9780522878004 (paperback)
9780522878035 (ebook)

For the Matildas, both known and unknown

CONTENTS

KEY TERMS, ACRONYMS AND INITIALISMS

ACL	anterior cruciate ligament
AFC	Asian Football Confederation
AFLW	Australian Football League Women's
AIS	Australian Institute of Sport
AWSA	Australian Women's Soccer Association
CBA	collective bargaining agreement
FA	Football Australia
FFA	Football Federation Australia
FIFA	Fédération Internationale de Football Association
FIFPRO	Fédération Internationale des Associations de Footballeurs Professionnels
IOC	International Olympic Committee
NIAG	National Indigenous Advisory Group
NPLW	National Premier Leagues Women's
NWSL	National Women's Soccer League (2012–present)
NZHRC	New Zealand Human Rights Commission
PFA	Professional Footballers Australia
USMNT	US Men's National Team
USWNT	US Women's National Team
VAR	video assistant referee

WNSL   Women's National Soccer League (Australia;
          1996–2004)
WSA   Women's Soccer Australia (2000–03)
WUSA   Women's United Soccer Association (US women's
          football league 2000–03)

Football/soccer
This book uses the term football, which is most commonly used around the world, and which is reflected in governing bodies' nomenclature.

National governing football bodies, leagues and teams
Australia's governing football bodies have undergone some name changes in recent times, and have also gone from women's only and men's only to women's and men's. As much as possible, the names used reflect the relevant bodies' names at that time. However, although the Australian Women's Soccer Association (AWSA) was briefly known as Women's Soccer Australia (WSA) in the early 2000s, the book mostly uses AWSA as that is the most recognised name and the one interviewees used throughout.

Australian and New Zealand governing football bodies
- Australian Soccer Federation (men's football association pre-1995)
- Australian Women's Soccer Association (1974–2000)
- Soccer Australia (1995–2003/04)
- Football Federation Australia (FFA) (2005–20)
- Football Australia (FA) (2020–present)
- New Zealand Football/NZ Football
- Women's Soccer Australia (2000–03)

Australian and New Zealand national leagues/teams
- Australian Women's National Soccer League (WNSL) (women's football league 1996–2004)
- A-League (Australian men's football league 2004–21)
- W-League (Australian women's football league 2008–21)

- A-League Men's (Australian men's football league 2021/22–present)
- A-League Women's (Australian women's football league 2021/22–present)
- National Premier Leagues Women's (the tier below A-League Women's 2014–present)
- Football Ferns (New Zealand national women's football team)
- Matildas (Australian national women's football team)
- Socceroos (Australian national men's football team)

US national leagues/teams
- Women's United Soccer Association (WUSA) (women's football league 2000–03)
- National Women's Soccer League (NWSL) (women's football league 2012–present)
- US Men's National Team (USMNT)
- US Women's National Team (USWNT)

INTRODUCTION

C LAD IN KHAKI King Gee shirts and shorts and platinum-blonde wigs, and moving through the crowd with enthusiastic strides, seven women collectively known as 'The Croissants' unleashed their inner gregariousness at the 2019 FIFA Women's World Cup. Their 'Croc-*Kerr*-Dile Hunter' costumes, an all-round crowd hit, were a reference to star Matildas striker Sam Kerr and Australian crocodile hunter and larger-than-life character Steve Irwin.

'We just wanted to dress up and do something funny and iconically Australian and recognisable,' the Croissants say of the outfits' transformative, extroversion-inducing powers. 'When we're just in our civilian clothes, everyone's real nervous. But when you put on that Steve costume, you become something else ... It's a newfound confidence in costume.'

Those seven women were keen to show their support for women's sport. 'For some bizarre reason, we named ourselves the Croissants because we were going to France. In reality, we should have done something Australian,' they say. Also: 'Half of us don't actually like croissants.'

While the Croissants' efforts earned them a standing ovation at a 2019 Women's World Cup pre-match pub gathering, those efforts did come with some attendant challenges—the first being negoti-ating with French security to bring their prop inflatable crocodile into the stadium. Whether or not French security got the Steve Irwin gag or were simply confused by seven women wearing tradie outfits and skew-whiff wigs was unclear. What *was* clear was that the crocodile was contraband.

But, fuelled by determination, beer and jet-lag-induced delirium, these sports-loving women weren't going to be prevented from cheering on their team. So they sought first to negotiate with the security guards and then to outwit them. 'I think we deflated it, shoved it down somebody's shirt, and went back,' they say of the crocodile. 'The guards said, "We can see it—it's in your shirt." We were like, "We don't know what you're talking about."' Eventually, they and the crocodile made it into the stadium, at which time the crocodile was promptly reinflated.

After the Matildas lost that sudden-death Round of 16 match on penalties, dejected fans trickled out of the stadium and the city of Nice. 'That next morning we woke up and everyone was super flat,' the Croissants say. But then one of their members issued a pep talk: 'Guys, we can be disappointed, but we're here for women's sport in general. We're going to pick teams and we're going to support them.'

Step one was to select teams and prep country-specific cos-tumes. For Italy, they strung yarn 'meatballs' from hats and wore shirts emblazoned with 'Pay me in pasta'. For the United States, they scoured regional fabric and craft stores and hostel bathrooms to assemble iconic Statue of Liberty togas and torches. Lucy Gilfedder ('Gilf'), a product designer by day, was head of costumes. She baulked when her fellow Croissants suggested the Statute of Liberty. 'I said, "No, it's not going to work—we can't find the materials." We were in the middle of nowhere. We had no idea where anything was, and you can't ask people, "Hey, what's the equivalent of Spotlight?"'

Eventually the Croissants found green fabric that matched the Statue of Liberty's oxidised copper, then sourced empty toilet rolls and tissue paper to make the torch and flames. 'After that it was on,' they say. 'We stayed up to 4 a.m. cutting fabric that night. [We] will never forget it. We were cutting for *hours*.'

Brought together by a mutual love of women's football (soccer), the Croissants individually and as a group embody what it is to be a contemporary women's football fan. Intelligent, resourceful and self-effacing, they strike a balance of feminism and fandom. Acutely aware of the issues pervading women's football, they are in awe of the sacrifice it takes for players to succeed. But more than anything, they are positive, enthusiastic, welcoming supporters of the game. ('We have such respect for that US team. As a whole it has done such groundbreaking things for women's sport in general, as well as obviously the equal-pay advocacy,' the Croissants explain.)

The Croissants and their crocodile would be asked to pose for photos while they were weaving their way through the 2019 Women's World Cup crowds. They happily obliged. One photo request came from a fellow Australian millennial. She was wearing a yellow T-shirt with 'Australia' stencilled on it that she'd purchased from the official merchandise stand. (The woman had actually been after a Matildas jersey and was musing on the missed commercial opportunity, because the merchandise stand only had 'Australia' shirts. But the Croissants had no knowledge of that. To them, she was simply a fellow fan.) The photo took but a moment, then the woman tweeted the picture and, as did the Croissants themselves, melted back into the crowd as she made her way to her seat.

Few knew who that woman was or why she was there, and her name may not be instantly recognisable to people beyond her work circles. A London-based human-rights lawyer and Rhodes scholar, Jennifer Robinson has worked on countless significant human-rights cases but is perhaps best known to ordinary Australians as one of the lawyers who represents actor Amber Heard and WikiLeaks founder Julian Assange. There to turn her legal mind to the human-rights issues hampering women's football—including the effects of missed commercial opportunities on the games' financial viability, prize money and player remuneration—Robinson's presence spoke of the gravity and entrenched nature of the human-rights issues with which women's football grapples.

* * *

Whether played out in front of record-breaking crowds or (as they were in their first few iterations) in relative anonymity, Women's World Cups are pinnacle, quadrennial events in the football calendar. They are also litmus tests for social and cultural issues, attitudes and change. From tackling gender-based discrimination to challenging homophobia to normalising women's participation in sport, Women's World Cups are about more—much more—than football.

There's the complexity of being the best women's football team in the world and better than your male counterparts and having to sue your federation on gender discrimination grounds. Of being denied the opportunity to play until, and only as long as, you were needed to make up the numbers. Of being allowed to occupy only a space that is 'not men's'. (Hello, gender-delineated '*Women's* World Cup' compared with the default male ownership of the term 'World Cup'.) Of the open slights when social media trolls suggest women can't play football, and the more insidious ones when male administrators overlook you. Of grappling not just with time and training constraints, but also with crippling successive season-ending knee injuries, denigration, homophobic trolling and lack of pay parity as you attempt to forge a football career. Of not being able to see it—a role model—in order to be it, but also finally being able to see it and be it and inspire your peers, your predecessors and the next generation too.

There's a lot to Women's World Cups—exhilarating highs offset by achingly low lows, and the wearying weight of women's rights advocacy to carry during and in between. Mostly, though, informed and brought together by a history and throughline of human-rights activism, there are stories of truly astonishing women (and some men). Individually and collectively, they have advanced the women's game and women's rights and accomplishments in innovative, inspiring, often invisible, non-linear but life-changing ways.

I asked many of the people I interviewed for this book when they became aware of the Women's World Cup and that it was something they could become a part of. Some said it was 1999, with the tournament's breakout success and US player Brandi Chastain's iconic shirtless penalty-winning celebration. For others, as it was for me, it was 2007 and the Matildas' initial taste of World Cup success. Combined with the fact that SBS TV broadcast every 2007 Women's World Cup match, which was then cemented by the release of the *Never Say Die* documentary and the W-League launch, the 2007 tournament indeed marked a turning point in results and awareness of Australian women's football.

More common was that the interviewees knew there was a Men's World Cup and aspired to play in it courtesy of a youthful obliviousness to the fact it wasn't open to them because of their gender. Many were for a long time unaware there was a Women's World Cup or even a national women's football team. This was despite the fact that they were skilled enough at football to be considered for selection for one or both—lack of visibility, access and opportunity have historically stymied Australian women's football. Pitted against men's football, it's always been overshadowed or, at best, an afterthought.

That experience is familiar not just to the modern Matildas but to other Matildas throughout history. Nineteenth-century abolitionist and women's rights activist Matilda Joslyn Gage, who was denied entry to medical school on account of being a woman, observed that men often maligned, overlooked or even usurped women's expertise and achievements.[1] Gage herself was largely lost to history until science historian Dr Margaret W Rossiter stumbled across her tale—in an Australian article, of all things.[2] As a Yale History of Science student, Rossiter noticed that women scientists were absent from scientific history. Her lecturers informed her that this was because there were no contributions to mention. Certain that couldn't be accurate, Rossiter researched, wrote and published not one but three books detailing women's previously omitted or camouflaged scientific work.[3] She also coined, on the basis of Gage's observation of the phenomenon of writing women out of scientific history, the term 'the Matilda Effect'.[4]

The Matilda Effect's premise is that women's scientific contributions have been forgotten, omitted or misattributed to the nearest male.[5] (The Nobel prize is the classic example of this. Just fifty-nine Nobel prizes—less than 10 per cent of the total—have been awarded to women since the prize's 1901 establishment; fifty-eight if you consider that Marie Curie received the award twice.[6])

While the Matilda Effect principle is firmly entrenched in the science, the experiences, principles and themes that underpin it are arguably quite recognisable to those working in women's sport. In Australia and Aotearoa New Zealand, as well as around the world, women's football and women's football players and administrators have long had to contend with being denied recognition for their work or having it devalued. That invisible handbrake has undoubtedly been applied to women's football, which has operated with the tension of lack of funding and lack of opportunity, at best, holding it in stasis.

But as we approach the 2023 Women's World Cup, such Matilda Effect-adjacent experiences are shifting and lifting. More successful, more accessible and voted most beloved national team in 2019, and the only Australian women's sporting team operating on a truly global scale, the Matildas are being recognised for their achievements within and beyond Australia. As advocates for equal working conditions and pay, as well as unrivalled role models for women and girls, they have changed the women's sports landscape. And in 2023, when Australia and Aotearoa New Zealand co-host the Women's World Cup, the Matildas will no longer be a curtain-raiser or a footnote in history: they'll be the main event and story.

1

1988:
BE SO GOOD THEY
CAN'T IGNORE YOU

AT THE 1986 FIFA Congress in Mexico City, 'mother of
Norwegian football' Ellen Wille asked FIFA for a Women's
World Cup.[1] It wasn't an unreasonable request. Women had been
advocating for such a tournament for some time, and the equivalent
men's tournament, first held in 1930, had been running quadrenni-
ally for more than fifty years.

Wille had strategised her speech before heading to Mexico,
including the fact that it would best be delivered by a woman. It
wasn't good enough that women's football wasn't considered or
mentioned in FIFA's documents, Wille argued when she addressed
the room full of more than 100 men: it was, she said, time for
women to have their own World Cup.

FIFA had periodically teased the possibility of staging a
Women's World Cup, with women's football advocates and players
having their hopes raised and dashed countless times. ('FIFA was
toying with the women, I think,' says former football administrator
Heather Reid AM.) But 1986 was the first time FIFA officially
committed. Two years later, China hosted the FIFA Women's
Invitational Tournament, which was, for all intents and purposes, a
pilot Women's World Cup.

There had technically been a pilot-pilot Women's World Cup in Mexico in 1971, but it had been independently organised rather than FIFA-endorsed. (Notably, that tournament demonstrated that the 'No one would be interested in women's football' line male administrators had traditionally peddled was inaccurate: an estimated 100,000 people attended the opening match; more again attended the final between Mexico and Denmark.[2])

Five incarnations of a third international invitational tournament, the Mundialito (Spanish for 'the little World Cup'), which played out between 1981 and 1988, likely also applied pressure to FIFA to take ownership of the space. Taiwan had been angling for a Women's World Cup too, staging an independent equivalent and showing up geopolitical and football rival China. 'Taiwan was at the forefront of Asian women's football competitions, for whatever reasons, whether it was political to say, "Up yours, China—we're going to set the scene,"' Reid says. Not that Australians were necessarily across the finer details of the tournament backstory and wider geopolitical machinations. It was former Matilda Moya Dodd, who has Chinese heritage, who unpacked the rivalry between the two countries for Reid while the team was travelling on a bus in Taiwan in 1987.

So whether FIFA read the room, sought to vanquish the competitor tournaments, realised there might be an untapped audience for and/or money in women's football, or a combination of all three, 1988 became the auspicious year the Women's World Cup unofficially officially kicked off.

★ ★ ★

The year 1988 was a big one for Australia showcasing itself internationally. With the tagline 'Together We'll Show the World', the popular Expo '88 spotlit Australia's (and Aotearoa New Zealand's) ability to host a world-class show. Its New Zealand pavilion contained wooden sheep-shaped stools visitors could straddle; the floor tilted to reflect and immerse audiences in the on-screen action as the visitors watched a short film. The Australian pavilion featured a boat ride with a concealed mechanical crocodile that leapt out, jaws snapping, at a predetermined but entirely unanticipated moment that successfully scared people every. single. time. Showcasing Australia in a much less publicised way, but befitting the 'Together We'll Show the World' tagline, was an assembly of Australian national women's team football players and administrators just beginning their careers.

Forbes would name Moya Dodd the seventh most powerful woman in world sport in 2018. (The *Australian Financial Review* and Westpac had named her the overall winner of their '100 Women of Influence' awards two years before that.) But thirty years earlier, in the lead-up to 1988, Dodd was an Adelaide-based, tomboyish Asian-Australian teenager who just wanted to play football. Dodd, whose introduction to gender inequality had occurred at school when she discovered boys were allowed to play sport on the oval three days a week compared with girls' two, knew little of the behind-the-scenes manoeuvres required to convince FIFA to stage the venerated pilot event. She was, as she puts it, 'just a player who was hoping to get that letter in the mail [to tell me I'd been selected for the team]. I mean, literally going to the letterbox every day.'

That letter did eventually arrive. It was typed and sent by Reid, the woman who would later be one of the (if not the) modern matriarchs of Australian women's football. In 1988, Reid was a newly minted sports management graduate in Canberra cutting her teeth in football administration. A self-described 'young upstart', she was brimming with ideas to elevate women's football 'from the kitchen table to the boardroom'. She had been a mature-age student, having completed her sports management degree in 1983, and was seeking to help and learn about the world game while transitioning from a previous job as a secretary. Handily, she could type and do short-hand, filing and bookkeeping—skills transferable to her fledgling sports administration career. Australian Women's Soccer Association (AWSA) president Elaine Watson OAM's response to Reid's interest in the game was, as Reid puts it, 'Wow, have I got a job for you.'

Hired as the AWSA National Executive Director in 1986, Reid was tasked with setting up the organisation's office at ACT Sports House, a repurposed primary school in the inner-northern Canberra suburb of Hackett. From that office, which the AWSA shared with the ACT Women's Soccer Association, she prepared the very letters players like Dodd were making trips to their letterbox for. 'That was me writing individually to every player,' Reid confirms. Her responsibilities included 'notifying players of selection or non-selection and how they had to pay for the privilege of being in the national team, which included travel and accommodation expenses as well as their tracksuits and other items'.

Reid typed that correspondence on a Brother Super 7800 electric golf-ball typewriter—one she still has—and created template letters for efficiency. (She used to switch golf balls to vary the fonts for different documents.) 'I would write to them all, and then I'd have to write to them all again to tell them their travel details,' she says. Australia Post and a telephone with an inbuilt fax machine were the primary communication channels. 'I'd come into the office in the morning and there'd be this roll and roll and roll of paper on the floor from something Elaine had faxed to me the night before, or something from overseas, replies from players ...'

Reid's start in the national executive director role was relatively rocky. 'I started in February '86, and three weeks later—there'd been a dispute with New South Wales women's football and the AWSA bubbling away for a little while—I was being told the five New South Wales players weren't going to New Zealand for the Oceania Cup in March. They didn't want to pay the money; many didn't have the money. So in my mind now I see this as the first attempt at a strike or a boycott of a tour [long before the 2015 Matildas strike]. In the end, they did withdraw. The board wasn't happy, and Elaine particularly wasn't happy. I was instructed to talk to coach Fred Robins about replacing the players. We were going ahead.'

The withdrawal of the New South Wales players meant five new selections, with later Matildas greats Julie Murray, then fifteen years old, and Dodd, just turned twenty, getting their breaks. It effectively launched the careers of two players who would make substantial on- and off-pitch contributions to the game. But Reid didn't know that at the time. Her primary concern was that, having been the messenger, she found herself the unanticipated focal point of media attention. She was fifteen workdays into the job.

Decisions by the board and the fallout from 1986 led to New South Wales not participating in the 1987 national championships, which doubled as a national team selection tournament. That meant the players were also technically ineligible for the 1988 national team and therefore the pilot Women's World Cup. But after intervention from the New South Wales [men's] Soccer Federation and from the coaches, perhaps because the point had been made or because the players were too valuable to exclude long term, New South Wales returned to the fold. So in 1988, Australia sent a truly national team to FIFA's inaugural women's world football tournament.

★ ★ ★

Australia had not been playing at international level long—in the vicinity of a decade—when the 1988 tournament unfolded. The team had few resources and minimal preparation time to work with, so it made do with a little to prove a lot. Players trained in isolation, sometimes in parking lots with car headlights providing the only light, and met up with teammates when they converged for the tournament itself. 'We trained on a pitch for maybe a week before we left,' Murray says, 'so we had a week's preparation. I guess you have to bear in mind that everyone had work, I had school, that sort of stuff.'

'The stage that women's football was at, this was next-level stuff for all of us. It was just the beginning of how it could look. It was very inspiring,' says the inaugural Matildas captain, Julie Dolan, of training together as a team for more than a few days. 'We all thought, *Wow, if we could all get together much more often, how good would that be?*' But players hailed from locations as disparate as New South Wales and South and Western Australia. 'So it was very diffi-cult in those days to finance any kind of camp like that,' Dolan says. 'And most of the officials, well, I know the coach himself would have had to take time off work to attend.'

On one level, the players who attended the 1988 trial tourna-ment didn't know what they were in for. On another, they knew how essential it was to prove that not only were they skilful, but that a Women's World Cup had merit as a sporting and commercial concept. Likewise, in some ways they knew they were making history; in other ways not.

'I kind of did. It was exciting,' Reid says. 'But it was also a lot of banging your head against the wall. Because you'd go away to these [non-FIFA] tournaments and come back full of excitement and with more knowledge and world connections … There had been a lot of talk since the 1970s that FIFA was going to give us a World Cup, but, of course, we know that didn't happen until they actually ran the tournament themselves as a precursor in China '88. I often say this was just FIFA testing to see if we deserved a World Cup.'

No, not really, Dolan says when asked if she was aware she was making history. 'You have a sense of how important it is, but when that momentum isn't behind you, you sometimes wonder whether it will get any legs—you know, whether the pilot World Cup will turn into something else, or whether we will go back and keep trying to build … I didn't really have a sense of what would happen in the future, probably because of the lack of momentum behind women's football back at home. Everyone just tried so, so hard all the time. That hasn't changed. People are still trying very, very hard to make the most of it.'

To participate in the tournament, the Australian players each paid A$850. Those fees covered such costs as domestic airfares to attend the pre-tournament Australian training camp, and team tracksuits. For Dodd, who had only recently started working full time, it represented weeks' worth of pay. 'I was allowed to pay in two instalments,' she says. 'I think I coughed up $400 and $450, something like that … That was a fair bit of money to cough up when you're on about the $300 a week I was taking home.'

Being a woman footballer in and around 1988 was indeed an expensive and hard slog: in addition to paying fees out of their own pockets, they were constantly fundraising to cover costs for national championships and national team participation. 'We were forever organising raffles,' Dolan says. 'I had a few casino nights that I had to run by the local constabulary.' The casino nights were, she says, 'much more lucrative than the lamington drives'. Other fundraising efforts were more miss than hit, particularly in Sydney, compared with Dolan's other community in northern New South Wales. 'I can remember going to a bowling club and saying to the manager, "Can I come through and sell tickets to the patrons to raise money, because I'm playing for Australia." He [absentmindedly] said no. So sometimes it was great; sometimes it was a slap in the face. But those were the days.'

Employment situations proved equally tricky. 'Generally they were pretty good. But at times, it was easier for me to leave the job,' Dolan says. Some employers were, for example, outwardly and vocally supportive but 'That sometimes wasn't backed up by having a job to come back to or donating any funds to the cause.' (There's at least one newspaper article documenting such sacrifices—it outlines how Dolan was refused leave from a travelling salesperson job and would, if she couldn't find anyone to cover for her, be forced to resign.)

Meanwhile, Dodd, who was a judge's associate at the time, scored brownie points from the other associates by forgoing, and covering for them during, their university graduation ceremony. 'So they all owed me, and when I went away, they covered for me,' she explains. 'I wanted to take two or three weeks off. We didn't know how far we would go in the tournament. My workplace gave me one week off as special leave because I was playing for Australia, and the rest I took as unpaid leave. I have payslips that show me being docked. That was life as a Matilda.'

Reid and academic Marion Stell, who co-wrote *Women in Boots*, a book about Australian women's football in the 1970s (published in 2020), point out that it's the aggregate of such employment challenges that was the concern: it's not just a few hundred or even a few thousand dollars of lost wages for the time you're away—it's the additional time it takes to find another job.[3] So sacrificing financial security to pursue football hampered players visibly and invisibly, both short and long term. 'Oh, absolutely,' Dolan confirms. 'That has a cumulative effect, essentially, because I found myself at twenty-eight and all I had was a pair of old business suits—everybody else had a mortgage. You have to really reassess at that point and think, *OK, here I am, I've got nothing behind me—what should I do next?*' But as she acknowledges of the playing experience, 'You ask any of the Matildas and they probably wouldn't change it.'

★ ★ ★

Having scraped together the fees to participate in 1988, the players left and returned with little fanfare, no ticker tape, and almost no awareness among the general public. But what they were going to and what they achieved laid the groundwork for subsequent Women's World Cups.

The figures proved impressive for a first-time tournament: twelve national teams spanning all six confederations participated; 375,780 spectators turned out for it, with an average match attendance of 14,453. Between them, the teams scored 81 goals—an average of more than 3 per match.[4] Norway won, perhaps a fitting full-circle outcome given that it was their delegate who'd most recently directly tabled the idea. (To be fair to New Zealand, they and many others had also been advocating for a Women's World Cup for some years. Australia was invited as Oceania's representative. The Football Ferns' omission remains, as New Zealand's 'Mrs Football', Barbara Cox MBE, notes, 'a sore point'.)

Problematic, though, and controversial, was that the 1988 unofficial Women's World Cup matches and the subsequent 1991 official ones were planned to be only eighty minutes long—something former US player April Heinrichs famously quipped may have been because FIFA was worried that women's ovaries would fall out if they played the full ninety minutes.[5] Murray recalls that clearly: 'Like, did they really think our ovaries would fall out? Just bizarre.' The ostensible reasoning was a carryover from decades of flawed medical opinion about 'protecting' women—protection that was more likely motivated by a desire to protect the men's game from perceived competition. Irrespective of its concealed motivation, such reasoning had underpinned bans on women playing football around the world. In the same vein, the tournament regulations did not specify which size ball should be used. Organisers eventually went with the Size 5 ball—the standard size all footballers, women or men, were used to—but it was galling that there was even discussion about using a Size 4 ball. The eighty-minute matches, however, stood.[6]

Travelling from Australia to China involved flying to Hong Kong, then to China—all up, a trip in the vicinity of twenty-four hours. 'It took a bloody long time to get there,' Dodd says, after trying to calculate the travel time of various legs. (That's before she recalled flying with then-Chinese-monopoly CAAC Airlines, which at the time had a disquieting safety track record that included multiple hijackings, a crash into a mountain, and a collision with a bomber while taxiing.) 'And when we arrived, I remember the local organising committee met us and said, "Would you like to go to the hair salon?" We were like, "Er, not really." But they kept offering. They must have heard that Western women liked hair salons—they had organised a salon where you could get your hair cut and blow-dried.' After a few days of this, the Australians thought it would be rude to continue declining the invitation, so Dodd and a few teammates agreed to check it out. Unexpectedly, the salon was underground—a location that gave the players pause—but it turned out to be legitimate. 'So I got my hair cut,' Dodd says. 'I used to have my part in the centre of my head. They moved it to the side and cut it, and it was much shorter at the back. I thought, *Whatever*. I've kept it on the side ever since. It's my souvenir, having my part shifted.'

Reid's recollection of the event differs slightly: she thinks the offer may have had less to do with catering to Western predilections than with the Australians' hair being a little scraggly. 'If you look at the profile photos of the Chinese players, they all had the same bowl haircut. Very few of them had long hair,' she says. 'And you look at the profile photos of the Australians and the Americans, in particular … You know, we're talking 1980s hairstyles.'

In terms of the tournament itself, there was an impressive opening ceremony that featured flower-waving children and a Chinese dragon-lion.[7] 'That's when we got our first walking-out uniform,' Murray recalls. 'When we'd travelled before, we just wore tracksuit pants. Here we got this white skirt, pants and blazer outfit, I think the night before we left to go to China. Mine was way too big.'

Also, Murray says, 'We had tracksuits that were fleece-lined for a 38°C China summer, so it was pretty hectic.'

Dodd recalls the white suits, too. They were markedly different from the bottle-green trousers and jackets of previous tours that had made the players look like they 'had visited the army disposals store … Of course, nothing fitted properly because we were never fitted properly. A bunch of stuff just turned up and everybody scrambled to get the best fit, and you might trade around so at least everyone could have something to wear, quite often too big, sometimes too small …'

The uniform challenges extended to the playing kits. 'On the eve of the first match against Brazil, we were sewing shorts,' Murray says. 'I don't think I was, because I'm not very good at sewing. Definitely someone else was doing mine,' she laughs.

'More often than not, we didn't get the gear from suppliers or sponsors until the night before or a couple of days before,' Reid explains. 'They often didn't have any embellishment. We didn't have any names of players on the back, for a start, because the AWSA had to keep the uniforms for future tours. The players didn't get to keep them—they were part of the AWSA stock. We had to account for them every June in the stocktake. So when the tracksuits arrived and they didn't have Australian badges, I handed out the badges and either myself or Elaine or somebody else would sew them on to the tracksuits. We were rushed and had to ask the players to help sew the badges on. Otherwise, I would have been sitting on a plane sewing badges on to twenty-five tracksuits.'

The rice cooker Dodd famously traditionally took on tour to ensure the team had enough carbs didn't attend the 1988 tournament. Dodd did, however, learn the words for 'steamed rice' before she went so she knew what to request. 'We asked for bread and they didn't know,' Murray says. 'We got this thick, sweet bread. They tried very hard, but of course they didn't have any Western influence. We'd get pork buns and all that sort of stuff for breakfast.' Not that she minded—they were all foods she liked.

Murray recalls that some of the players hired bikes and went for a ride. 'Remember, this is pre–Tiananmen Square as well. There's not too much Western stuff going on,' she says. 'We got caught on a roundabout and couldn't get off. There were thousands of people [traversing the roundabout], and I remember laughing about getting killed before we'd played our first match.'

To get to that first match, the team was escorted by a cavalcade of police cars blaring their sirens. 'I think it took us about three hours, four hours, to get there instead of eight. The traffic just parted—it was like parting the Red Sea,' Murray says. 'The police were up the front [with megaphones] saying "Get off the road" while our bus travelled along. Everyone was off the side into the rice paddies and all sorts of stuff.' The team felt relatively special until they saw a funeral procession, including the coffin, move aside.

The printed program was equally unforgettable. It featured an eclectic mix of tournament regulations, team profiles and full-page ads for men's underwear and pharmaceuticals. The latter variously claimed to remove inflammation and clear toxic material, and would likely not have passed tournament drug-testing protocols.

So few Australians of Chinese heritage have represented Australia in football that it was significant for her to be playing there. The team liaison person quickly realised Dodd's familial background and one morning excitedly told her she was in the paper. 'I was like, "Oh?" She showed it to me and I said, "Can you read it to me?"' Dodd had purportedly granted the paper an interview in which she indicated she was happy to be back in her mother's home country and hoped to perform well. 'After that newspaper article, I became a point of interest and people at the matches were pointing at me in the stands, and even the soldiers wanted me to sign things like their uniform hats. I had a brief fifteen minutes of fame. Even funnier, when we left, we left by train ... and as we were lining up to go through the passport checks, I got hauled out of the line. They wanted to see me separately and they checked my passport and looked me up and down. Everyone thought it was hilarious, but I was like, "No, I have an Australian passport. I'm Australian, and I'm leaving."'

At tournament's end, a few of the players attempted to keep their uniforms, stocktake requirements be damned. There's some conjecture as to whether the heist involved shirts or shorts, but either way it came to light after some players found kit on their beds—kit they had not sourced for themselves. An investigation determined that some of the New South Wales players had distributed it. The rationale was that if everyone had some, 'no one would dob them in'. As tour leader, Watson informed the team that no questions would be asked if the uniforms were returned to her room, stat. But half the kit was still missing by the time the team was at the train station, so manager Stephanie Quinn ordered the players to open their bags on the platform. The pilfered kit was located and grudgingly returned.[8] Apparently the coaches had been complicit: they were sympathetic to the players' disappointment that they couldn't keep their uniforms as a souvenir. But, as Watson wrote in her tournament report, some of the players had been shouting drinks back at the hotel, which Watson later realised 'should have made us suspicious'. You only had to show your room key to run up a tab, and they were using coach John Doyle's. She noted that Doyle's sympathy may have waned when he had to pay his account.[9]

That wasn't the last of it, though. Another whole bag of gear was missing on arrival in Australia, and the uniforms were only returned after the AWSA asked its New South Wales equivalent to apply pressure to the New South Wales players. The AWSA flag, which had cost A$167, was also poached and never returned.

★ ★ ★

Uniform hijinks aside, the 1988 tournament was important for myriad reasons, not least because it was a chance for the national team to properly test itself against its international peers. Australia made history as the first team to kick the ball at the first-ever FIFA women's football world tournament. The team also pulled off an upset win against the benchmark-setting Brazil.

'That first game is quite historical,' Dodd says. It wasn't the official opening match, but it unofficially was because it kicked off earlier in the day. 'The first kick-off that was ever taken in women's football under a FIFA-organised match was by Australia—Janine Riddington and Carol Vinson—against Brazil in June 1988. That was the first-ever game we played in. It was not only our first FIFA match, but also FIFA's first match of women's football that it organised itself. And we won 1–0, much to our amazement.' Their and the much-favoured Brazilians' amazement, if we're honest. The win came courtesy of Riddington's spectacular long-range chip over the Brazilian keeper. As Watson notes in her book *Australian Women's Soccer: The First 20 Years*, the win was so important it was 'recognised by a telegram from Prime Minister Bob Hawke'.[10]

'I can't remember if all the teams were in the same hotel, but certainly the Brazilian team was in ours,' Dodd says. 'We'd see them around, and we had to play them in our first match, which was a hugely challenging idea because Brazil had such a formidable reputation in football and who were we from down under? We had no tapes of them playing, no footage. We didn't know what we were in for. One of the coaches snuck off to have a peek at them at training before we played them. There's a bit of a code [about not watching opponents' training sessions]. Well, anyway, he did it.' The intel was that the Brazilians played a 4–2–4 formation, with the weakest players at the back. The thinking was 'If we can get to the end of the field, we've got a chance of scoring. But we're going to have to defend like Trojans. So even when in full attack, we had to be prepared to scramble and defend.'

That the Australians did. (Defender Anissa Tann so put her body on the line that she ended up with a broken arm.) 'We were obviously happy and relieved that we'd come to a tournament and been able to hold our own, we hadn't been outclassed, and we'd actually taken three points off Brazil, which put us in a position to potentially make the quarter-final,' Dodd says. 'So we were thrilled but absolutely exhausted. The emotional energy you expend on that sort of occasion—not just on the match, but the whole occasion— is enormous. I remember sitting around that night and Jo Millman, who was always good for a laugh, said, "I'm going to write all my postcards tonight." You know, nothing but good news. Could there ever be a better day to?

'Some people wanted to phone home, of course, but the phone lines in China were limited. The way you made a call home was you rang reception and booked a call, then they rang back when they had the call for you. I think there were so few phone lines out of the hotel that they couldn't actually carry many calls at once. People were getting calls back at two o'clock in the morning from home—you can imagine their parents being woken in the middle of the night by someone on the phone saying, "There's a call for you," and they'd be thinking, *Oh my god, what's happened?* and there's some excited Matilda on the other side—who's also just been woken up in the middle of the night by the operator—telling them we just beat Brazil.'

That win set up a rivalry that continues to this day. 'It's always a good game with us and Brazil,' Dodd says, 'because Brazil are crowd-pullers. Women's football needs Brazil, I always think. We need the big countries like Brazil with a lot of tradition and a lot of support—well, a lot of a following, put it that way—and a big reputation …' She's alluding to the fact that Brazil, a country steeped in men's football tradition, banned women from playing football between 1941 and 1979. Despite the Brazilian women players' impressive talent, they received—receive—scarcely any support or funding. 'For us to knock them off in the first game [was extraordinary],' Dodd says. 'We've had a lot of battles over the years, and they've gone both ways: we've won a few and they've won a few. It all started in 1988.'

Unlike most matches from that era, this match is preserved for posterity and publicly available on YouTube. 'When it's a FIFA tournament, generally you get cameras,' Dodd explains. 'That's the difference it makes to have a global governing body running the tournament.' (Reid recalls that, at the time, 'I had to beg for money to purchase videotapes of games and then share those with SBS and other networks. We had the tapes copied and made available for players and others to purchase.')

'On one of the anniversaries of '88—2020, so thirty-two years since that match—we got a bunch of ex-Matildas of that era together and watched it online,' Dodd says. 'We were basically all watching it at the same time. Some people fell behind, so we'd all stop and restart it again … We were on Zoom together, but we were each watching it individually on YouTube.'

'It was sort of surreal,' Murray says of watching that replay. 'A little bit surreal in that I was playing in that match. It was eons ago. I'm one of the old people now as opposed to being young and spritely.'

Goalkeeper Theresa Deas (née Jones) didn't get a chance to play against Brazil—Toni McMahon was the first-choice keeper at the time. 'As my memory serves me, emotionally I was frustrated, but full of anticipation to get my chance at a starting spot,' Deas says. 'However, I do remember the excitement of being on tour with a talented group of players that I had a great deal of respect for, having played with and against them at many national championships.' She also recalls the Brazilians as 'having big and bold personalities both on and off the pitch'.

That Brazil win propelled the Australians into the quarter-finals, but that's where their tournament ended. Deas was selected as the goalkeeper in what would turn out to be her last game for the Matildas. 'To be in the Starting XI against a formidable China was very daunting, not just because they were fast and technical foot-ballers and this was the quarter-final, but because our team was without previous Starting XI players who were benched for curfew violations,' Deas explains. China won that match 7–0, but, impres-sively, Deas and her teammates managed to hold off 50 other direct shots the Chinese team made on goal.

The Brazil match may have been the high point of the team's on-pitch results, but Australia made advances off the pitch too. Reid, for example, made connections that would prove fruitful both immediately and across her career. Two such contacts helped her link up with Danish club Fortuna Hjørring FC and Swedish club Malmö FF. Malmö later became the first European team to visit Australia for a three-match series, as part of the Matildas' preparation for the Oceania qualification tournament for the 1991 Women's World Cup. Reid leveraged the Fortuna Hjørring connection into obtaining the first-ever overseas contracts for Australian women footballers, for Murray and Vinson. Alison Leigh Forman would debut for the Matildas in 1989 and obtain a Fortuna Hjørring contract in 1992; she made 283 player appearances for the club and has lived in Denmark ever since, working with Fortuna Hjørring in playing and administration positions.

There's not as much footage available of Australia's subsequent pilot Women's World Cup matches, but they played Norway and

Thailand in their remaining group-stage games. Coach John Doyle was sent off during the Thailand match for coaching in a manner officials deemed too loud and enthusiastic. 'He ended up being the only person on the other side of the stands,' Murray says. 'You could just see him, this dot, this male figure in a green Aussie tracksuit … still barking out orders.'

The 3–0 loss to Norway wasn't what the Australians were after, but Murray has in recent years developed a new appreciation for the Norwegian players' efforts on and off the pitch: 'I was playing against Heidi Støre, who was obviously one of the best centre midfielders in the world at that time, and captain of Norway. She stands over six foot [183 centimetres]. I don't know if you know my size, but I'm not close to six foot … It was sort of another welcome to football, to international football. But to be honest, I only properly realised in the last few years that Støre and some of those players were really instrumental in getting that particular World Cup—I won't say going, but in terms of all the rules, because FIFA wanted less minutes in the halves and smaller balls. I had no idea up until a couple of years ago. So, really great credit to all those players who tried to say, "No, no, no, we are not accepting that. We'll play football for 45-minute halves and play with Size 5 [ball]."'

★ ★ ★

It's worth noting that the Men's World Cup never really went through a trial phase: it was deemed something worth staging and applying the FIFA branding to straight away. Regardless, by executing the 1988 tournament well and making do with or without regulation ninety-minute matches, the women who participated demonstrated the golden rule that invariably underpins success: be so good that they can't ignore you. Without grounds for kyboshing the event—for example, nobody's ovaries fell out—FIFA ran a women-specific refereeing course in Norway in 1989 to develop referees' skills and experience, and also earmarked a 1991 return to host nation China for the first official FIFA Women's World Cup.

2

1991: LEGIT NOW

I F 1988 WAS the unofficial first, 1991 was the official first, albeit with that honour being applied retrospectively. It was named the rather convoluted 'First FIFA World Championship for Women's Football for the M&M's Cup'. (M&M's manufacturer, Mars, was the sponsor, a perk of which was that players received a packet of M&M's on their hotel pillows each night.) The tournament was rebadged a World Cup only once it proved a legitimate success. So, viewed in relation to 1988, the women didn't just have to prove themselves worthy of a Women's World Cup, they had to prove themselves twice. Regardless, 1991 finished what 1988 had started, demonstrating that a FIFA-endorsed, FIFA-run tournament for women was feasible, much-supported, and warranted.

The Australians had to watch it from afar, though, as New Zealand pipped them at the Oceania qualification round. It didn't need to be that way. As qualification tournament hosts, Australia set the draw. That meant they could—*should*—have scheduled the tournament in a manner that gave them the best qualification chance. 'We could have chosen to play Papua New Guinea first, ease our way in,' Heather Reid explains. Coach Steve Darby instead elected to gain insight into how New Zealand played. 'We said, "We've played

New Zealand a dozen times since 1978 or 1979. We know how they play,"' Reid says, but Darby wasn't swayed. So Australia started the tournament in the stands, watching New Zealand take on Papua New Guinea.

The Football Ferns defeated Papua New Guinea 16–0, setting a high benchmark the Australians spent the rest of the tournament chasing. They and New Zealand each defeated the other 1–0, cancelling out the results, and Australia needed to beat Papua New Guinea 20–0 to secure the coveted Women's World Cup spot. The eventual 12–0 scoreline was a pummelling but still 8 goals short, so New Zealand booked that first Women's World Cup berth. (Reid documents the result clinically in the AWSA's July 1991 *Far Post* newsletter cover story. Her opening line is: 'The national team will not be going to China for the 1st World Cup.' In a layout that speaks volumes, the inside cover contains an advertisement inviting applications for a new Matildas coach.)

'There's no football god who decides what's fair and allocates things accordingly. You just get what you get, and you need to make the most of it,' Moya Dodd says pragmatically of the outcome, which clearly still stings. 'We had a huge chance in '91 and missed out on goal difference in a very strange tournament that involved two fairly strong and equal teams and one team that lost all its games by significant margins. That team was Papua New Guinea. And if you look at their scores, they lost by less each time they played.' Papua New Guinea's final match, against Australia, yielded the team's best result. 'So that's how the cookie crumbles,' Dodd continues. 'It was hugely disappointing, because we had some great players of that era who would have done well on the world stage, I think.'

Still, not qualifying for the 1991 tournament was, Reid says, 'devastating' and 'a massive wake-up call for Australia'. Encapsulating 1991, Julie Murray says, 'We didn't go, the US won, which actually, when you look at it, really catapulted the US Women's National Team [USWNT] out of this world, because US men's football hadn't really, and still hasn't really, done anything at the international level. So that was probably a really good indicator that a country like the US could take football globally to a higher level just because of what they were able to do as a team. For us, it was back to the drawing board.'

★ ★ ★

While Australia didn't go to the tournament, Reid did. ('I was able to convince the ABC to give me accreditation' is how she puts it.) Under ABC Radio auspices, she was the lone Australian media representative among the 600 journalists who covered the event. She was also likely the first-ever Australian with media accreditation at a Women's World Cup.

Reid still has the notebook she kept throughout the tournament. Notes in her neat cursive handwriting include where she jotted down the ABC telephone number and 'Tracey'. That was Tracey Holmes, the ABC reporter who would go on to become the first woman host of ABC Radio's sports show *Grandstand*. Reid relayed tournament reports to Holmes and ABC Radio through faxes and phone calls. On one page, Reid tracked her expenses and stipend: $64.50 spent faxing Australia, $79 for insurance, $500 to cover costs such as ironing and food. Another of her notes hints at the expense of international phone calls in pre-internet days: 'Decided to pay to call home.'

'Here's a little scribble from Elaine [Watson],' Reid shows me. (Watson has vascular dementia and her memory isn't what it used to be, so every glimpse of her rich life and contribution to football is precious. She continued to be actively involved in the women's game up to her mid-seventies, when the onset of her illness saw her withdraw her participation. She currently lives in an aged-care facility where staff ensure she watches the Matildas whenever possible as they know the joy it brings her to see 'her girls' play. That gesture represents invaluable recognition. It's thanks in large part to Watson's tireless, decades-long contributions that the Matildas are as accomplished as they are today.)

Another page provides particular insight into male administrators' prevailing attitudes. 'This is the final press conference, and I'm getting ready to ask a question,' Reid says. She directed her question to FIFA president João Havelange and David Will, who was chairman of the

Referees Committee. 'Do you think it would be possible to have a women's exhibition game at the 1994 Men's World Cup, especially if the US wins today's final, as that country is hosting the 1994 World Cup and the '96 Olympics, in order to continue to improve the worldwide interest in women's football?' (This was before women's football was in the Olympics.) The answer, as per her notes: 'No chance. Too many games—54 already—and an extra game would be difficult. Also, don't want to mix men's with women's.'

'But this is the absolute clincher for me,' Reid says, explaining that another journalist asked Havelange if it was likely we'd see women's football admitted to the Olympic Games. 'Havelange said, "Can't be too greedy and want too many things at the same time."'

The tournament technical report was attitudinally indicative, too. It placed the United States and Norway in what it termed the 'Ambassador' class; Sweden, China, Italy and Denmark made up the quizzically titled 'Medium But Rare'; and the outright offensive 'Learning the Hard Way' included Brazil and Chinese Taipei. The report also deemed there not to be any need for sex-determining tests, because it was purportedly doable and necessary to determine sex just from looking at the players. Seeing these words typed plainly is disconcerting. Their innocuous typesetting belies their damaging nature. Even after all these years, Reid is able to quickly locate the report in the football ephemera she's collected throughout her career and can almost recite by heart the most troubling passages.[1]

Reid next draws attention to how the report hints at the writers' surprise that the players were fit, capable and not incapacitated by either exhaustion or dysmenorrhea (period pain). 'They proved the ball was in play more frequently at the Women's World Cup than at any other tournament, meaning it wasn't kicked out as much,' she says. So the women demonstrated skill and control. 'And that meant they also played a lot more.' So they were *extremely* fit and capable.

★ ★ ★

The opening ceremony was similarly informative, poking holes in the adage 'Sport and politics don't mix'. It featured Ling Ling, a giant illuminated golden phoenix mascot who was meant to symbolise women's football's rebirth after decades of dying a slow death through lack of funding and opportunity, and through outright bans.[2] (In addition to women being banned from playing football in Brazil, women in England, for example, had been banned from playing for fifty years.)

It was a remarkably political, statement-making mascot. (Reid, who was gifted a rather impractical 90-centimetre-tall stuffed Ling Ling toy she then had to wrangle into a bag to get home, terms it 'China really posturing to the world'. She recently gave the toy to the FIFA Museum in Zurich.) Ling Ling's agenda-advancing statement has possibly only been matched by the 2007 mascot, Hua Mulan, a woman who disguises herself as a man and achieves great accolades, surprising everyone when she reveals her sex. Interestingly, both mascots came from when China, a country better known for toeing the conservative political party line, hosted the tournament. Other tournaments in other countries veered towards more generic, cartoony characters. There was Fiffi, a friendly looking, helmet-adorned Viking, for Sweden in 1995; Nutmeg the fox for 1999 in the United States; Karla Kick, a cat, for Germany in 2011; and Sheume, an owl, for Canada in 2015. In 2019 the mascot was Ettie the chicken, the daughter of 1998 Men's World Cup France mascot Footix.

The players weren't necessarily aware of all this political and cultural intrigue. If they were, the attitudes were so ubiquitous as to be mere background noise. As with the 1988 iteration, teams largely entered the tournament with little preparation and even less understanding of their opponents. All the associations were operating on bare bones, so team cohesion was just as much a focus as their opponents given there had been limited or no training camps.

Wendi Henderson appeared for New Zealand in this Women's World Cup and would go on to appear for the team again in 2007, the next time New Zealand would qualify. This double effort makes her the first player, woman or man, to represent New Zealand at two World Cups. To be part of the 1991 tournament was, she says, 'absolutely amazing. Not only to be at a World Cup for women's football, but to be part of history by attending the first ever [Women's] World Cup ... We weren't just focused on the football, we were consumed in the massive occasion it all was.' As she notes, 'I just couldn't believe this was all for us and for women's football.'

The tournament was a resounding success. Former US player turned coach, instructor and administrator April Heinrichs termed 1991 a 'silent trigger' that sent women's football to another level.[3] That included both players and officials, specifically referees. Cláudia Vasconcelos Guedes and her assistants, New Zealand's Linda Black and China's Zuo Xiudi, became the first all-woman team to officiate a FIFA finals match. Overseeing the third-place-determining match was an auspicious honour but one burdened by expectation and judgement: just before the team headed out to the tunnel, a FIFA Referees Committee delegate told Guedes the future of women's football refereeing hinged on her performance.[4] She and her team performed admirably.

At the tournament's final press conference, David Will talked about the women referees' extraordinarily high standard. 'He said something about when the women officials went out to do the game and started the game, people didn't see female referees, they just saw referees,' Reid says. 'So I thought, right, I'll be cheeky and ask the question: Do you think we will see women refereeing at the Men's World Cup in '94?' Havelange's non-committal response, according to Reid's notes, was 'If they're that good, but it's too early to tell, and we have fitness levels [they'd need to meet] and that sort of thing.'

Regardless, the referees had proved themselves and sparked further women referee development and inclusion through FIFA policies that facilitated future Women's World Cups to feature pre-dominantly women and then all-women refereeing teams.

★ ★ ★

On 28 November 1991, two days before the tournament's end, Reid and some other women's football administrators and advocates gathered in the Dongfeng Hotel—in room 2519, to be precise. Perhaps aware that the meeting was auspicious, or perhaps ever the diligent secretary-meets-sports-administrator, Reid minuted it in her notebook. What she documented was attendees formulating a plan for women's football's inclusion as an Olympic sport.

It might seem an unusual focus given the group was at the Women's World Cup, but the plan was deliberate. The Women's World Cup was in a fledgling state; the Olympic Games were at that time much more esteemed and, crucially, received more media coverage and money. 'For a lot of countries, Olympic status is important because of government funding,' Reid explains. (Australia experienced that firsthand with the 2000 Olympic Games. 'Hosting the Olympic Games in 2000 was huge because we got a full-time Australian Institute of Sport [AIS] program in the lead-up as part of the gold-medal plan,' Reid says. 'That full-time residential program meant players could just focus on being players, with all the bells and whistles—sports science and nutrition and all the things that went with them.')

'It's also important because when people watch the Olympic Games and the Paralympics, they're watching the Australians, they're watching their own nationality participate, and the gender stuff is diminished,' Reid continues. 'So they're not watching women—they're watching Australia participate in sport. Research into media coverage of sport clearly shows that during Olympics and Commonwealth Games, the coverage of women skyrockets because it's about watching Australia rather than watching women.' She's not wrong. Women's sports coverage increases during the Olympics in a more gender-blind or at least gender-neutral 'Olympic Games effect'.[5]

'We mobilised to put pressure on FIFA to have the competition added to the Olympics for 1996,' Reid says of the actions that emerged from that room 2519 meeting. FIFA had actually already requested that the International Olympic Committee (IOC) add women's football to the 1996 Olympic sport list, but IOC president Antonio Samaranch had regrettably informed FIFA the 1996 list was already set and the IOC would instead revisit the issue for the 2000 Olympics. That was the catalyst to start, or step up, lobbying. 'We all started writing letters to various people. But most importantly there was a bill from a congressman that went to the US Congress to make women's football a gold-medal game in Atlanta 1996,' Reid says. That bill did the trick. Suddenly, women's football was in the Olympics.

The Australians didn't qualify for the 1996 Olympics: there was no time for a separate qualification tournament, so the Olympic competition admitted the 1995 Women's World Cup quarter-finalists. Australia would achieve some impressive Women's World Cup results, but in 1995 it wasn't a quarter-finalist.

3

1995:
GREAT EXPECTATIONS

THE YEAR 1995 was when Pixar released *Toy Story* and Sony released the PlayStation. It was the year of the Sarin gas attack, the Oklahoma City bombing and the Srebrenica massacre. It was the year a jury found OJ Simpson not guilty of double murder. It was also the year Hillary Clinton, speaking at the United Nations' Fourth World Conference on Women in Beijing, gave an iconic women's rights speech.

Defying internal US State Department and external Chinese political pressure to soften her statement, First Lady Clinton declared that 'human rights are women's rights and women's rights are human rights'. Her thesis was that it was no longer acceptable to treat women's rights and human rights as mutually exclusive.[1]

It's unlikely Clinton was thinking about women footballers, given she was delivering a speech in a country with a contentious human-rights record. But she'd also likely acknowledge, were it put to her, that the entrenched, endemic nature of the issues she was discussing extended to women's football. It was 1995, recent in our history. But women were participating in only their second official truly world football tournament, and they were yet to be given the same media coverage or paid adequately, if at all, for their efforts preparing for or playing in it.

To make that tournament, the Matildas took the same Oceania qualification route as 1991: each Oceania team played each other twice in a round-robin tournament across a seven-day period. Except this time the tournament was held in Papua New Guinea and the outcome was in Australia's favour through a reversal of goal difference.

'I'm the coach who lost the last game to New Zealand, and I'm the coach who started the run that has seen Australia unbeaten against New Zealand since 1994,' Tom Sermanni says. It's a record encapsulating Australia's development acceleration, which put daylight between it and New Zealand—then a team against which results could go either way. 'The very first qualification game, it was us against New Zealand and we lost. New Zealand at that time were probably slight favourites to qualify for the World Cup,' Sermanni says. But after soundly defeating Papua New Guinea twice and then defeating New Zealand 1–0 the second time round, Australia qualified through goal difference.

Julie Murray scored the deciding goal, but it came about through defender Sonia Gegenhuber going against the grain. 'We went against the wind in the first half and I remember just getting pelted with balls,' Gegenhuber says. The ball was bouncing around waist height. 'I went, *Stuff it, I'm just going to have a shot on goal from the halfway line*. So I've kicked it and it's hit the 18-yard box, hit the crossbar, came back, and that's how Julie Murray scored.'

The wider Papua New Guinea challenges had been eye-opening for the Australians. 'The first thing that went wrong was our football strips, [which were] coming from Adidas in Melbourne and were sent up there but never actually arrived,' Sermanni explains. So they played their first game in the boys' AIS strips, which contained not a skerrick of Australian colours as they were red with touches of blue and white.

For safety reasons, the team had to stay in a compound surrounded by armed security guards, and the bus in which they travelled to and from training and the games had bars on the windows. 'Back in those days there were two Travelodges in Papua

New Guinea, one in the centre of town and one called The Islander. We actually stayed in The Islander, which in accommodation senses was probably the best place you could stay because it had some grounds so you weren't claustrophobic,' Sermanni explains. 'You couldn't go out of the hotel, particularly the players. They were in the hotel and in the grounds and just basically went to the games and back again.'

Former Football Fern Wendi Henderson describes the experience as 'challenging': 'I could write a book about all of the things that happened during th[at] tournament!' For starters, the New Zealanders were in the cloistered, less-premium accommodation. 'Years later we found out the New Zealand squad were stuck in a cheaper hotel and they couldn't go out either,' Sermanni says. 'We had an advantage in that sense, in that our conditions were actually much, much better than the Kiwis'.'

Gegenhuber recalls a time when 'one of the [bus] windows was open and these bloody guys grabbed in and tried to grab stuff off us and we were trying to close the window'. (One man succeeded in plundering a hat directly from a player's head.) Sermanni recalls that, too. 'I think we went sightseeing one day and people were literally sticking their hands through the bus window if it was open. You literally had to keep the players under guard because people were either stealing stuff or almost physically assaulting the players. It was the same at the grounds. You had to have your stuff almost under security-guard lock and key. If you left anything unguarded, it was gone in a heartbeat.'

The on-pitch conditions reflected the off-pitch ones. 'The field was terrible. It was rutted, not much grass on it, poorly looked after—conditions you probably wouldn't even play a local league game on these days,' Sermanni says. 'A significant wind blew right down the field. When you were shooting into it, it was tough. When you were shooting with it, it was a little bit easier.' It was against that wind that Gegenhuber and Murray combined to create that winning goal.

So it was challenging and confronting. 'The thing is, in those days, just going away with the national team was—treat isn't the right word, but it was a treat. The fact that things were happening was a bonus,'

Sermanni says. 'To my knowledge, none of the players complained about anything in the sense of being stuck in the hotel ... because we had come from a place of players previously having to pay to play for the national team to at least getting good preparation.'

Trying qualification circumstances aside, the result meant Australia had booked a berth at its first—and the tournament's second—official Women's World Cup. Their excitement at qualifying was undoubtedly tinged with relief at not repeating the 1991 campaign. 'It was the very first time we had qualified for a FIFA Women's World Cup, so we celebrated in style,' says former Matilda Alison Leigh Forman. 'I still remember the after-party.' (Sermanni remembers that the celebrations began with the Australian players jumping in the hotel pool.)

Having attended the inaugural Women's World Cup, it was distressing for New Zealand to miss out on the second. The New Zealanders didn't know it then, but they wouldn't return to the tournament until 2007. 'Once we had gone to the 1991 World Cup, we were really hungry to get to the next one,' Henderson says. Having 'lived and breathed [football] to make it', they were, she says, 'gutted and devastated'.

★ ★ ★

Still, qualifying was just the beginning, and the Matildas' World Cup experience didn't pan out as hoped. 'Unfortunately, we pooled Denmark, US, and China,' Sermanni says. As he puts it, 'We pooled a group I didn't particularly want to pool.' That's a wry understatement. 'I don't know if world rankings were out at that stage,' he continues, 'but the US were perceived as number one, China were I think number three, Denmark were about number six, and we were number no number.' (Speaking to the calibre of the opponents and the toughness of the group, Sermanni notes that the 1996 Olympic final played out between the United States and China.)

No one involved considers the Matildas' 1995 Women's World Cup tilt a success, but they may be being unduly harsh. The lessons Australia learned in 1995, many of the other teams had learned in 1991. Games had been few and far between in the years after the team failed to qualify for 1991, so 1995 was a litmus test applied to a team that had a compressed timeframe in which to prep.

'I think at that time you basically got letters sent to you saying, "This is your training for the week",' Gegenhuber says of the geographically dispersed, honesty-system-reliant training the players completed. Early-1990s strength and conditioning programs weren't as tailored as they are today. 'So you just had a training program you had to follow—there wasn't much of how much you were supposed to do. And then you had plyometric training, and you'd go up to the oval and do it and then couldn't bloody walk for a week because you'd go, *Oh, this is easy, I'll do a bit more.* Then, *Oh god, too much of this stuff.*' As she puts it, 'We were all just doing our own little thing in our own little states.'

'They were fitness programs with a bit of ball work,' Dodd says. 'It was all individual. This is where the system of men's football could have—*could have*—given us a much better environment, for example by providing some mixed-gender football ... Mariana Milanovic and I trained a lot with each other because we were the two in the national team. And Jill Latimer, at different times. But there'd be no more than two or three of you training.' Which was problematic given you needed eleven to make a team, and another eleven to provide an opponent.

'Imagine if we'd gone and trained with some under-18s [men] who were decent, or the under-16s or a youth state team or something like that,' says Dodd. 'If they'd let us join that environment, we would have become better players. We were already the best players in South Australia. How were we going to get better? We could become fitter and get physically better, so that's what we did. That's a no-brainer to do that. Get that done: tick. How do you become a better player up top? How do you get better game awareness or more pressure on you so you have to increase your ball speed if you want to keep the ball or get your pass away? How do you do that? One idea might have been to have us training with boys. But we didn't have access to that system.'

(Tangentially related, but noteworthy given that Professional Footballers Australia (PFA) is the union that advocates for players' rights and seeks to improve opportunities and conditions—the exact organisation that would have benefited the women's players and the women's game more widely—'We weren't allowed to join the PFA because we weren't professional,' Dodd says. The definition of professional at the time was that a player had to earn more than it cost them to play—a low bar but one still too high for unpaid women players who were self-funding their football careers. So 'I was never a PFA member. They didn't take women members at that time.')

Western Australia–based goalkeeper Tracey Wheeler faced equivalent challenges, both due to her west coast location and the fact that there were fewer goalkeepers to train with. 'My club and state teammates in WA helped me with extra training in Perth,' she says. 'Otherwise, I had very little support in terms of coaching. At one stage in 1998 [but applicable across her career], I was driving two hours from Perth to Bunbury and back once a week to get goalkeeper coaching. I was also working for myself five-and-a-half days a week.'

Realistically, Wheeler did well to be at the tournament at all. Her 1995 Women's World Cup experience would be sandwiched between rehabilitation for not one but two anterior cruciate ligament (ACL) reconstructions, in 1993 and 1996. It wasn't just the rehab that was tricky. 'Each time away from the squad coincided with a change in coach, meaning I had a job trying to re-establish myself in the squad and then trying to become the first-choice keeper,' she explains. She also injured her shoulder just eleven days before the team's opening match. It was an injury that would normally sideline a player for up to six weeks, but Wheeler was the first-choice keeper and the team needed her, so she played with her shoulder heavily strapped and local anaesthetic injected into the acromioclavicular (AC) joint just prior to the match.

Sacha Wainwright also did well to be there. She had had to contend with the fact she was both young—her first cap was in 1994 and she wasn't sure where she stood or what her chances were of making it onto the plane—and that she was racing the clock to rehabilitate an ACL. (She missed the qualification tournament after tearing her ACL in a tackle during a Cairns training camp. It was the first of three knee reconstructions she would undergo.)

'The team doctor or physio came on and went ee, ee, ee [mobilisation sound] like you do to test the ACL. "There goes your World Cup campaign" were his words,' Wainwright says. 'So that was quite a shock. But I don't know, something in me didn't want to accept that there goes the World Cup. And even though the support services weren't what they are now for the Matildas, our national team physio was also based in Canberra … He was, I still say now, one of the most influential people in my career. You know, the physio who gets you through injury. And we did some crazy things. You have this mapped-out rehab program of what you can do, and you can't run until eight weeks post-op. Do all the strengthening stuff, then at eight weeks you can do your first straight-line jog.' She was determined to follow the program precisely. 'On that morning we were meant to do the first run, a 100-metre job, it would have been as slow as a snail. And it was *pouring* with rain. We used to meet at 5.30 in the morning before he had to go to work. He was like, "It's pouring. Should we leave it?" I was like, "No, I'll see you there." So I turned up at the oval, spent three minutes jogging 100 metres, got soaked, went yep, tick, that one's done.'

For her part, Gegenhuber was not just working on fitness but teaching herself the techniques she needed to thrive. Players like Julie Murray may have played football since they were five or six, but Gegenhuber was a relative newcomer. She had wanted to play football with her brothers while growing up, but was steered towards 'girls' sport' netball instead. She hated netball. 'I remember my father was a football coach and every Friday afternoon he'd sit down at the table and I'd come and sit next to him and go, "Have you got enough today?" Every week. And then every time they played, I'd go to the game and say, "Got enough?" hoping, *hoping* they wouldn't have enough and I'd be able to play.' It wasn't until she was sixteen that she got her chance.

Gegenhuber had actually always known she wanted to represent Australia—she just didn't know in which sport. She even tried pole vault at one stage. 'Pole vault. I know. I tried it. I loved it. But back then there was nothing. I could go fairly high with it, but they had no women's competition.' So football was one of many sports she turned her hand to, once she was finally allowed, and she pursued it as far as she could. A natural and hardworking athlete, Gegenhuber received her representative football call-up in just her second season of playing. But it came with attendant challenges. Because she read the play and applied skills she'd developed in other sports, everyone assumed she knew what she was doing. She didn't. 'I'd always just go up and practise by myself because all these people could play and I hadn't even learned how to play this game. Like all of a sudden I'm in the state team going, "OK, how do I cross a ball?"'

Gegenhuber and her teammates were also doing all of this while trying to work and study. It was a tricky existence. 'You had to try to find a job where you only worked four days a week,' Gegenhuber explains. 'You had to find a job that finished before your training started ... You then worked out you were going away for tournaments for four weeks and would think, *Well, who's going to give me that time off?* So you're forever changing, going, *They're not going to give me time off, so I'll go and find another job.*' Former Matilda Angela Iannotta concurs: 'It was hard, because all I wanted to do was play, play, play. And it's hard because you have to think about working, studying and playing. Because it wasn't playing, studying and working. First you have to work, and then study, and then play.'

Many of the players were underemployed. 'Half the time you could only find part-time or casual work to fit around,' Gegenhuber explains. 'No one supported you. Even when I was an Australian player, I was a qualified teacher but I never got assistance. They didn't want to have you, because you were going to be away.' (A seven-word, rapid-fire Q&A answer Gegenhuber gave *Total Sports* magazine around this time hints at this and the awareness of the brevity and financial precarity of elite sporting careers. In answer to a question about which other sportsperson Gegenhuber would be if she could choose one, she nominated tennis player Martina Hingis: 'She's young, successful, and earns heaps.')

Tellingly, Gegenhuber still has a letter of support Sermanni wrote for her. Sermanni explains, 'Essentially, I thought it was important to keep employers in the loop. That way there was more likelihood they would support the player and feel they were part of the process ... It also showed the player that the program was supporting them. We were on the road for long periods of time during that period, and players were either working or studying. So we needed to rely on the goodwill of employers.'

Current Matildas are effectively told they need to gain as much international experience as possible: playing in top overseas leagues stands them in good stead for selection. But in and around 1995, there was little, if any, available footage of players playing internationally. Iannotta had travelled to Italy on holiday and trialled with an Italian team on a whim. She was offered a contract and has been in Italy pretty much ever since. But the geographic challenges and isolation players felt domestically were even greater for overseas-based players like her as they struggled to remain front of mind with selectors. Iannotta had to phone or fax home to stay in touch ahead of tournament call-ups: 'I'd always be knocking on the door saying, "Hey, look, I'm still around."' Fortunately she persevered and became the first Australian—woman or man—to score in a World Cup when in the 1995 tournament she intercepted and scored from a defender's poor pass in the team's group-stage game against China.

★ ★ ★

The team didn't have a lot of resources or tournament experience heading into the Women's World Cup itself. 'It's interesting to contrast, when you think back, how little you knew in regard to preparation ... It's like another world,' Sermanni says. 'I remember we brought at least a couple of eskies, a couple of ball bags, a couple of boxes. We were Adidas then. Although the women's federation and the men's federation were separate at that stage, the World Cup had to go through Soccer Australia because FIFA only recognised one national body. So we did that and played in Adidas shirts. In those days it was all men's cuts—there was no such thing as a female cut—so they were a bit roomy.' (Surprisingly, Wheeler notes, the 1995 goalkeeping uniform was a good fit. Lightning didn't strike twice, though: the 1999 uniform was so large she had to cut off the sleeves.)

SBS TV was teed up to broadcast highlights of the team's Women's World Cup campaign. (Team communications manager Janene Mar reported in the 9 May 1995 *Australian and British Soccer Weekly* that SBS could only show highlights as it had had to bid higher than anticipated to outspend pay-television for the broadcast rights—there wasn't enough remaining budget for a longer show.[2]) It might have been just as well there was reduced coverage. There's a dissatisfaction among the players interviewed about the 1995 Women's World Cup—they don't feel the team performed as well as it could have. (On paper, there was definite room for improvement: Australia scored 3 goals but conceded 13.) Yet the players are arguably doing themselves a disservice—their formally funded program had only just begun. 'I guess that's the elite professional athlete mentality coming out … and not making excuses,' Murray says. 'It sounds a bit odd to not have the resources to do something, but still fundamentally you're in this mindset of *Yeah, we can get through the next [game] … we can do this.*'

'You think back over some of the rationales of what you did,' Sermanni says. 'What happened is we had gone on a tour to Europe just after I'd got the job in about July '94, and that was probably critical in us qualifying, because it helped bring the team together and helped our preparation. By the end of the tour, the team was where we wanted it to be.'

That Europe tour included friendlies in Moscow—or, rather, 500 kilometres outside Moscow. It was, by all accounts, something else. 'I had literally just got the job, and the first thing we did was go on a mammoth tour of Europe,' Sermanni says. 'I forget how long it was, but it was at least three weeks. The first stop was Austria: Innsbruck. We based ourselves there because the AIS had accommodation there.' From there they bussed up to Munich where they played Bayern Munich, then headed on to Denmark for some friendlies against Fortuna Hjørring. Moscow was next. 'We basically got on a bus, then a ferry, then we went down to Frankfurt Airport and flew to Moscow,' Sermanni says. Cats fell through the ceiling above the Moscow airport baggage carousel, but that was just the beginning of their Russian adventure. First, the team was loaded onto a bus and driven around Moscow before arriving at an unexpected destination: a military airport. The bus drove up the runway, passing planes of various shapes, sizes and vintages, before disembarking the team at a ramp leading into a cargo plane for an unanticipated onward internal journey.

'We literally got our gear, went up this ramp into the back of the plane—propellers each side like a Fokker—lobbed all our gear into the middle, and there were wooden bench seats either side,' Sermanni says. Envision military movies with assemblies of para-troopers. 'And all our luggage, there was a net over it in the middle. Up the front of the plane there was a table with a map on it and four chairs—it was obviously a military map [and a place] where the commanders or whoever could sit during the flight—and the only two windows were up there. We didn't know where we were going. We flew east for about two-and-a-half or three hours to a place called Samara, near where they made the Lada cars.'

'I guess there wasn't the sophistication around organising friend-lies as there is now,' Wainwright says of her memories of that trip. 'We arrived in Moscow, then drove on this bus. The economy at the time was devastated. Buildings were dilapidated on the edge of the road. They took us to an airstrip and there was a cargo plane wait-ing. We weren't actually prepared. There were a few players in tears, I think [from the shock of it]. Apparently, it was safer than the local Aeroflot from the commercial airport. The people we were with didn't speak English. I think that was the difficulty. We were in the hands of these people and they were just throwing our bags into the back of this military aircraft. The back opened up and there were two bench seats and protective earmuffs and your feet were on your bags … but they couldn't really explain it.' (Teammate Karly Pumpa put it simply: 'We honestly thought we were dying that day.')

'I remember it took us about thirty hours from Denmark on buses, boats and aeroplanes to get to this place,' Sermanni says. 'And we got there in the evening and everybody was just a write-off. So we said, "We've got two games here. We need to get up and get into a routine." So breakfast, whatever it was, was at nine o'clock.' It turns out they'd travelled so far east they were in another time zone, so their timing was actually out by an hour. 'We never knew we'd been travelling east, to be perfectly honest,' Sermanni says. 'We got up and breakfast was just awful. They did their best, but they had boiled eggs that weren't boiled.' As a whole, he says, 'The food was not, shall we say, appealing.' Compounding this was the fact that the Australian staff, taking one for the team, had had to politely join the Russian hosts in day-drinking as vodka was served up as a mealtime staple. Still, Sermanni says, 'It was such a valuable tour in the sense that it became folklore—"Oh, you should have been on the Russian tour"—you know? It was one of those. It set the standard for everything that happened after that.'

Players echo this sentiment. 'We all got really sick from the food,' Pumpa says. 'Everyone got gastro. It came to game day and I got hit with it—I was one of the last ones—and I remember they left me in the hotel room with a guard outside the door … We got toilet paper delivered to our hotel room on a tray and the guard had a big gun with a knife out the end of it.'

'It was a great experience. We bonded as a team,' Wainwright says. She, too, nominates food as one of the more challenging aspects. 'We were unprepared, looking back, going to that type of country. We didn't pack enough back-up. Because the food was horrendous. We all lost significant weight. I remember fighting over packets of two-minute noodles. We were rationing a packet of two-minute noodles.'

The return trip—when they were looking homewards and forward to more edible food—yielded yet more memorable moments. Same plane, reverse direction, with the team loaded up shortly after breakfast and sitting on a tiny runway that appeared so little used that there was long grass growing through and around it. 'We were supposed to leave after breakfast, so about 10 a.m.' Sermanni says. 'They've come, they've dropped us there, waving to us, thank you, that sort of stuff. Then we're sitting there, waiting … There's nobody around except a couple of pilots, but they're just army guys. It gets to 11 o'clock, 12 o'clock, still not going anywhere.' Players passed the time playing cricket on the runway. Then the officials that had farewelled them returned and took the team for lunch. 'They said Moscow was fogged in or something like that, which was rubbish.'

They finally took off about 3 p.m. Sermanni and a few others had been scheduled to go on a mid-afternoon Moscow tour, which Sermanni had been looking forward to because Russia wasn't a country you got to travel to often and it was only a few years after the Iron Curtain had come down. By the time the team arrived in Moscow it was around 9 p.m., but Sermanni was committed. He grabbed some food and said, 'Let's go'. 'I remember we went for the tour, parked at Red Square, walked down Red Square, and it started raining and I thought, *This is a really appropriate end to this trip—sightseeing tour in the dark, you get out and walk down the road, whooshka, raining*,' he laughs. He wasn't alone in his disappointment. The late arrival also meant the team missed going to McDonald's, which the players had been craving for a week.

A less arduous version of such a team-bonding trip is what Sermanni and his peers aimed for in the weeks preceding the Women's World Cup. Though useful, it didn't inspire the cohesive effect the Russia trip had. 'When we went to the World Cup, we stopped in Canada, played a couple of games, we stopped in Scotland, played a couple of games, and then we went up to Scandinavia,' he says. Though glamorous-sounding, that was a lot of long-haul travel and time zones to span, and money and professional-standard facilities were scarce. 'In hindsight, by the time the three weeks were up the players were more in a mood to go home rather than go to a World Cup. So what you thought was good preparation, in hindsight some years later, you think, *We were away for too long*.'

Also, the group was tough and the start was rough. 'We had a horror draw,' Dodd says. 'In the first game, there was a very, very harsh red card a few minutes in.'

'The first game was against Denmark, and it was one of those games where what could go wrong did go wrong,' Sermanni says.

The lead-up had been fairly civil, with Forman set to face off against her Danish club teammates. 'I received a fax from Fortuna Hjørring in Denmark, wishing [me, my] teammates, and everyone all the best in the tournament,' she says. The Danes later gave the Australians soft-toy lambs.

Australian fans were invited to fax well wishes or congratulations to individual players or the team as a whole. The requisite 'Matilda-Fax' details, which included hotel addresses, fax numbers and the fact that Sweden is 'AEST less 8 hours' were compiled and published in a 6 June 1995 *Australian and British Soccer Weekly* article by Janene Mar.[3] The itinerary included tips from the team physio for limiting jet lag, including remaining hydrated, and team stretching sessions at every stopover.

But once the tournament commenced, things didn't go especially well for the Australians. 'I think they scored a couple of early goals, and then we got Sonia Gegenhuber sent off on what I thought was a poor send-off,' Sermanni says of a tangle Gegenhuber had with Danish striker Gitte Krogh. 'It was a rubbish decision.'

That rubbish decision saw Gegenhuber become the first Australian to receive a red card at a Women's World Cup, something that smarts even now as, by all accounts, it was unwarranted. '[Krogh] has linked arms with me, screamed out, fallen to the ground, I've fallen on top of her. The referee hasn't seen any of that, just turned around and [issued a straight red card],' Gegenhuber says. '[Our opposition] was always saying we were competitive but physical. I think the first game we played there was one red card and six or eight yellows, because every time you went in for a tackle they'd scream out. So you were on the back foot already, and they played on it. I guess now they've brought in VAR [video assistant referee] it's a bit fairer.'

'The red card cruelled our chances of getting something out of that game,' Dodd says. Compounding it was the fact that it occurred just twenty minutes in. 'We had to play for so long with ten. It was one of those things where you're chasing ...' Dodd's recollection is that the incident occurred near the halfway line. 'I mean, anything can happen between there and the goal. But it was just ... Sonia felt absolutely shattered by it, and we all did for her and for the team. It was the worst possible start to a tournament. She was one of the most committed players you could find.'

Gegenhuber still has a copy of the officials' post-match report on the red card, a slightly macabre souvenir. It's two pages affixed by a now-rusty paperclip. The cover note is addressed to the Scandic Västerås hotel, where the team was staying, and requests that the report be passed on to the Australian head of delegation. The second page contains two sentences of note: they state that the FIFA Disciplinary Committee has met about the red card and elected not to take any further action, and that Gegenhuber will be suspended for one game.

'So it wasn't the best of starts,' Sermanni continues. 'But in saying that, the team bounced back really well in the next two games. I think we lost 4–2 to China, but we actually came back to 3–2 and gave them a couple of scares. They scored a late goal. Then, of course, we were famously leading the US 1–0 for the first seventy minutes.' (Australia has only ever defeated the USWNT once, and that was in 2017.)

'The other thing in that World Cup is that they tested [coaching] timeouts—not heat, not weather, nothing to do with that,' Sermanni says. 'I think you might have been allowed two during the game. The upside is we took one as soon as we went down. The downside was the game went on for about ninety-nine minutes because they kept adding on time. I think we lost two goals in that extra time against the US. From a coaching perspective, there's stuff we really didn't know at the time in preparing the team or in relation to being in a major tournament.'

Really, though, other teams would have had the same experience in 1991. Sermanni agrees: 'Not only that, but those other teams had far more international experience than us. Our program basically started in July of that year, when [Australian] women's football became government-funded. That was the first time we had a full-time [paid] coach and the first time players didn't have to pay for everything.'

Two years prior, Sydney had been named 2000 Olympics host and football had been added to the 1996 Olympics. The Olympic inclusion injected funding to raise the AWSA's annual turnover from around A$100,000 to A$1 million and marked a new era where the Matildas didn't have to pay their travel costs to represent their country. It was, as former AWSA director Kerry Harris terms it, 'a significant milestone'.

Still, the organisation and program were far from flush and 'the funding had to be stretched to cover all aspects of supporting the team', Harris says. 'There was no apparel or equipment sponsorship, so the AWSA purchased unbranded team kit from apparel companies and the athletes purchased their own boots, shin guards and gloves.' (Players attest to that. Like her peers, Gegenhuber owned one pair of boots, which she had to nurse through as many seasons as possible. She never sought treatment from medical professionals such as physiotherapists because of the prohibitive cost. Iannotta doesn't have many images from her time playing, and none from the 1995 Women's World Cup. 'At the World Cup, they used to take photos and send them out to you and ask if you wanted to buy them,' she says. 'Because I didn't have a lot of money, I'd think, *Twenty dollars? No thanks. I can't spend $20 on a photo.*')

The team was approached by an apparel manufacturer with an offer to supply synthetic parachute-material tracksuits; they were likely highly flammable and wouldn't have been out of place in a *Kath & Kim* episode. 'The crazy thing is that we accepted the offer,' Harris says. 'I don't think the athletes were very happy. Around that time there was another apparel-maker wanting to make a women's football bodysuit, similar to the bodysuit worn by the Opals [Australian women's basketball team]. What this highlighted to me was how women's football was viewed at the time and how it was valued, which was as a novelty, an avenue to experiment with, a testing ground—not something to be taken seriously or to be consciously invested in.'

Regardless of the funding and tracksuit situation, the ability for the team to spend more time training and playing together is something all agree would have benefited them. 'We really had less than a year's experience of international football, trying to bring a program together and change the dynamics,' Sermanni says, 'whereas particularly the European teams, particularly China and obviously the US had far more significant international experience by that stage. I think that made a difference.'

Dodd makes a similar point: 'In Europe, they could get regular quality competition by driving a few hours to the next countries. Australia was so isolated, there was no support from the men's federation as far as I know, there was very limited support from government and sponsors, there was no television coverage, and the differences were enormous. For example, there were times when I felt New Zealand had better opportunities because at least they could get together more often and train as a team. Getting us together didn't happen more than once or twice a year, in a good year.'

★ ★ ★

Notably, two people were missing from the 1995 on-pitch team, and their experiences are emblematic of what it meant to be a woman pursuing a career in football. One was lost to football for decades; the other made it onto the plane, albeit temporarily, but not as a player.

'I went as an official, in weird circumstances,' Dodd says. 'I retired for a year in '94 because I had the chance to study an MBA at my employer's expense, which was a pretty huge opportunity. I was very torn about it, but in the end decided I didn't feel the team was progressing well at that point and this was an education that would be worth tens of thousands of dollars, even in that era. I'd been in the national team for years by that point and I thought, *I'm going to sit out for a year.*

'Then '95 was looming. We qualified and I thought, *OK, I'm going to put the MBA on pause and get my boots back on.* I did that. I actually trained like a maniac. Looking back, it was the classic ACL injury lead-up: being less fit for a while and then coming back and overloading yourself, and there goes your ACL. Actually, that year leading up to '95 was an absolute shocker. I recall that there were nine ACLs, and I was the ninth. So you just kept seeing this happening and thinking the grim reaper was coming and *Oh my god, who's next?* All these top athletes suddenly go down with an ACL and nobody understood why. There had at that point been very little research on it—there's still not enough research on it—but you were thinking, *Please, not me, not me.*'

Sermanni's feeling is that the lack of strength and conditioning contributed to the spate of ACL ruptures—or, as he terms it, 'going from doing not very much to an awful lot' in a short timeframe. 'My thoughts are that you basically went from the girls playing park football to suddenly you've put programs in place where they're training more, the international calendar, their camps just went through the roof. So they went from being park players to almost professional players in the sense of what the loading became.' He notes, too, that at the time players weren't being developed from the ages of fourteen to seventeen: the players they were selecting were twenty-one, twenty-two, sometimes older. That meant that 'All of a sudden, players who didn't have that background and lead-in were having this loading they'd never had before.'

Dodd ruptured her ACL in the classic non-contact fashion: changing direction while trying to close down a player. She was initially misdiagnosed. 'I flew home economy class with my knee in a bandage, and my calf blew up to about the size of my thigh.' Her physio had to break the news to her that it was an ACL, not a medial ligament. 'I went, "What?!" Of course, that meant I couldn't … That was the end of January and the World Cup was midyear, and there was no way I'd be back for that. It's a pretty sick feeling when you get told that by your physio, having been diagnosed with a much less serious injury.'

Dodd shelved her Women's World Cup selection aspirations, returned to work and re-enrolled in her MBA. She later received a phone call asking if she would be available to join the team as a supporting official. 'As I understand it—this is how small the entourages were at that time—FIFA had [traditionally] paid for four officials and the number had been increased to six. So there were two extra spots on the plane and apparently there had been a bit of an arm-wrestle about who was going to go. I believe I was a compromise candidate, and so I got a call out of the blue.'

The gig sounds glamorous, but it involved plenty of problem-solving and grunt work. 'Team official jobs included looking after all the passports, getting people on flights home when there was a strike on Scandinavian Airlines, and making sure the washing was done,' Dodd says. 'I mean, you just pitched in and did whatever needed doing.' That included listening to lots of hold music while waiting to rearrange flights. 'I was on the phone from the bench for most of our final game—I'd been waiting for ages and I didn't want to hang up! In the end, it wasn't possible to get us all on the same flight or even the same route. Some players flew out through London, others via the continent. These days FIFA Travel would just send new flights, but back then it fell to the team admins to listen to hold music and hang on the line for several hours.'

★ ★ ★

Karen Menzies' experience of missing this era was distressing and entirely avoidable. To understand it, it's necessary to understand the context.

The first time Menzies got to play football unhindered by perceptions that it was a game unsuitable for girls came just hours after she arrived at the Newcastle institution that was to be her home for the next five years. Weeks earlier, she had been removed from her foster family—at the time, the only family she had ever known. That traumatic forced removal and institutionalisation—the second in her life, but the one she remembers—marked a juncture that steered her towards the game she loved. Suddenly, Menzies was not only not discouraged from playing football, she was actively encouraged to do so. 'When I got to the institution at Newcastle when I was thirteen, I was at a soccer field 2–3 hours later that afternoon, attending training in a girls' team. I didn't even know that was possible.'

It was a confusing time, especially as Menzies had been moved to the institution despite having a loving Sydney-based foster family whom she variously describes as 'beautiful', 'gorgeous' and 'supportive'. Her foster parents had actually sought to adopt her, which the state had falsely led them to believe was possible. Menzies later discovered her biological mother had not voluntarily given her up, much less relinquished guardianship, which is why the adoption never materialised. 'It was never processed legally because it was legally impossible: my birth mother had never signed the consent form,' she explains.

On obtaining her file many years later, Menzies would discover her mother had regularly written letters begging first for her daughter's return and second for at least a photograph. She was offered a photograph just once, and it was proffered in exchange for signing the adoption papers to formally surrender custody. Although Menzies does not explicitly remember the moments herself, it's likely that around this same time she was subjected to initial institutional conditions that involved inadequate staffing levels of 10:1, which meant toddlers and babies were left crying in cots and to feed themselves despite lacking the gross motor skills to manage cutlery. This is supported by other Stolen Generations testimonies, historical records, and Menzies' responses and skills evident to her foster family. She remained non-verbal until she was almost three years old and exhibited challenging behaviours consistent with childhood trauma.

But Menzies knew none of this at the time. She knew her family was non-biological. She knew she was a ward of the state, but not why. Most pressing was that her foster status kept her on authorities' radar. This came sharply into play when she started testing limits in early adolescence by smoking cigarettes, wagging school and mixing with the 'wrong' crowd. 'The thing is, I had the welfare watching that,' she says. 'It wasn't just Mum and Dad.' The authorities stepped in and moved her to an institution.

Football and the freedom to pursue it provided Menzies refuge during the five years until her discharge as an eighteen-year-old. Without football, she says, she'd be a statistic. Including herself, she can count on one hand the number of people who emerged from that institution 'whole'. 'There was a very strong clinical aspect to them,' she says of the facilities there. 'If I hadn't had soccer to go and practise each day, to go to training with the rest of the team and play on weekends … It was a life force.'

Fast-forward a further three years and the prodigiously talented Menzies, then twenty-one, became the first Aboriginal woman to represent the Matildas. She didn't actually know she was Aboriginal until she was sixteen (nor did her foster family), and the information was delivered bluntly and with no thought of providing counselling as she grappled with news that upended her sense of self. (Menzies marvels at the fact that she would be accompanied by a welfare worker to see the dentist, but was suddenly entrusted to catch four planes unsupervised to meet her birth family in Queensland.) Off the back of the abruptly delivered news, the initial meeting with her birth mother and siblings, who were at the time complete strangers, unsurprisingly transpired very poorly. Menzies would later discover that her mother and grandmother had been removed from their families at a young age too, eliciting three generations of matrilineal intergenerational trauma.

'I had no idea. If you've seen a photo of me, I don't look like the pictures of what you're taught Aboriginal people are when you're in primary school. There was nothing in my sixteen years that made me question it, so it came as a complete and utter shock,' Menzies says. She's referring to the arbitrary appearance-based grounds on which authorities assigned her identity and guardianship under the assimilation policy. It was part of what she terms a welfare-system-led 'de-culturalising and re-culturalising' of Aboriginal children.

'The reality is that Aboriginal people during my schooling in the '70s were deemed to be undesirable, and I got caught up in that unconscious bias and subscribed to it. So here I'm being told: "This is you now." I didn't embrace that. And I was sixteen, so it was a very delicate time to try and navigate the fact that I'm not actually the culture I thought I was for sixteen years and I'm this other culture, which I hear very derogatory things about. It was tricky. It wasn't really until I was in my twenties that I started to unpack all of that and get comfortable in my skin.' (One perhaps unanticipated upside, if you can call it that, was that because neither she nor anyone else associated her with being Aboriginal, Menzies never experienced racism in her football career.)

Fast-forward again to 1995, when, after successive serious knee injuries, Menzies was no longer able to play. She pursued a coaching pathway and, having completed her Level 2 coaching licence with a view to completing her Level 3, was in contention for a national team assistant-coaching position. 'I'd come from playing, and realising I'd never play again was incredible grief and loss,' she explains. 'Then to find such enormous satisfaction coaching, which I didn't think was ever going to be possible, I thought, *Wow, I can go further. I can continue in this game that's shaped who I am from when I was a kid and meant so much to me.*'

That was until one of the coaches asked Menzies, who had always been open about being gay, whether she was worried about the allegations that could be made about her: 'I was shocked by the arrogance of the question and the inference that because I was gay and working with female athletes I would be unethical. That question, and its suggestion of a potential abuse of power, was and is just so removed from who I am.'

Not only was Menzies the first Aboriginal woman to play for the Matildas (she identifies as being of the Wonnarua people in the Hunter Valley), she was likely one of the team's first openly gay women. The year 1995 was early to be out; homosexuality was, for example, criminalised in Tasmania until 1997. But Menzies wasn't especially aware she was being progressive. From her perspective, it was so obvious she was gay that there was no point trying to pretend otherwise. Also, she notes, 'I had this parallel thing going about my Aboriginal identity. It was like, *Well shit, I can't have both going at the same time.*'

With a background in social work, Menzies worked in child protection concurrent with her playing and coaching careers. (She actually applied for and was appointed to her initial Department of Community Services (DOCS) job at the same time as her Matildas debut.) In addition to the inappropriate question put to her, Menzies says she was troubled by the homophobic language and behaviour she witnessed from some male coaches. 'My child protection work, my child protection brain, and the protection of vulnerable kids is 24/7. It's not a nine-to-five job. The homophobia that existed was just … it was rife, it was terrible.' So she spoke up. To no avail. 'I left the Australian Institute of Sport that day after raising the issue and it not being seen as a serious breach of ethics or a failure of duty of care … I just thought, *I can't be a part of this.* So that was the end of it. That's what made me leave football altogether, which for me was so, so difficult.'

It was an avoidable tragedy for Menzies personally given football's central, steadying presence in her life. (She was lost from the game for more than a decade. It took the launch of the W-League to begin to lure her back as a fan.) It was also a tragedy for the sport—there were and are few women coaches, and even fewer Aboriginal women player and coach role models. (It's well documented, for example, that current Matilda Kyah Simon's sporting inspiration was not an Aboriginal footballer but sprinter Cathy Freeman.)

In her brief coaching time, Menzies coached and mentored players who would go on to feature for the Matildas: Cheryl Salisbury, Sunni Hughes, Alison Leigh Forman and Bridgette Starr. (Starr is also an Aboriginal woman.) 'All four of them were exceptional,' Menzies says. 'I'd like to say I was a major contributor, but they were all incredibly talented and it was just about providing the right kind of guidance. They were always going to perform extremely well.' Yet it is definitely a case of rueing what might have been had Menzies been able to realise her coaching potential.

Menzies didn't let her premature departure from football stop her. In 1996, she was seconded to the Australian Human Rights Commission as a social worker for the Stolen Generations inquiry. So, she says, 'although I'd lost soccer, this new path opened that was life-changing and completely transformative for me professionally and personally'. Her work bearing witness, and her research into the Stolen Generations' ongoing individual, collective and historical trauma, will help ensure that such assimilation policies are better understood and never again enacted. ('Hearing the testimonies of adult men and women aged fifty to seventy, hearing what happened to them as children, that was harrowing … Even my team, even the Human Rights Commission, wasn't equipped [to deal with it],' she says. 'No one was aware of how devastating and horrible the testimonies would be.')

Menzies later completed first a Master of Social Work and then a PhD. (The latter advocates viewing the Australian Government's forcible separation and assimilation laws, policies and practices through a trauma framework as a way of more appropriately and

compassionately understanding the far-reaching, enduring consequences of such trauma for First Nations Australians.) Employing
such knowledge, she now helps to train the next generations of
social workers as a lecturer at the University of Newcastle. She has
recently returned to football in an official capacity as a member of
Football Australia's National Indigenous Advisory Group (NIAG).
Among the group's first tasks is helping to support First Nations
people to participate and stay in the game at all levels.

★ ★ ★

Menzies' experience notwithstanding, some positives came for the
team in and around 1995, even if the team didn't know it at the
time. 'Experience is never wasted,' Dodd says. She points to the fact
that players who were otherwise unknown or lacking opportunities
were able to demonstrate their talent. Lisa Casagrande, Dodd says,
was 'a revelation … There were players who went on to serve
Australia well. Just simply by being there, the team was able to
make a mark on a World Cup and show the next generation that
such a team existed and could be aspired to.'

Jane Oakley, too, lists a number of personal highlights: first,
'making the final XI (with such a formidable group of players)',
and second, playing against world champions the United States,
with Casagrande giving the Australians the early lead. 'I spent most
of the game trying to keep [USWNT star striker] Mia Hamm
quiet—near on impossible, but I did OK considering my technical
and physical capability fell well short of hers.'

The team's football horizons were also expanded in 1995. As
Gegenhuber says, 'It's all the experiences. We went to Sweden, we
didn't have to pay for it, we travelled to another country. FIFA put
everything on: you stayed in the accommodation, you're playing
against the best teams in the world and going "Wow, women's
football." You live in your own little Australia here, going "OK, we
all play." Then you go over there and think, *Look at these amazing
women, how good they are. How come we never knew about this?*'

There were highlights among those highlights. 'Playing against
the Americans was good, the Mia Hamms and Michelle Akers,'

Gegenhuber says. 'I remember Tom Sermanni going, "Right, you've got Michelle Akers." I thought, *Brilliant. Cool. Bring it on. I'm not going to let her score.* And she never did.' Also: 'We put Australia on the map. OK, we didn't do well, [but we] got there and we've been there ever since.' Gegenhuber is right: Australia has qualified for every Women's World Cup since 1995.

Cycle through the list of various countries' women's football team names—Japan's Nadeshiko, the US's USWNT, Nigeria's Super Falcons, Jamaica's Reggae Girlz, and the UK's Lionesses, for example—and Australia's Matildas holds its own. It's certainly an improvement on the 'Female Socceroos', 'Lady Socceroos' or 'Soccerettes', names the Australian team was variously known by in the years preceding the 1995 tournament. All three names were a diminishing and othering of the default male team's position befitting the Matilda Effect. (It's difficult to imagine now, but in 1995 the Matildas were a long way from having the household name and affectionate recognition they do now. Iannotta recalls how the conversation would always go: 'What sort of national team are you?' 'We're the Australian national women's soccer team.' 'Oh, have we got a national women's soccer team?') So the AWSA teamed up with SBS to run a poll to elevate the team and the game. 'I remember watching SBS and them announcing this competition to name the Australian women's football team,' Murray says. 'I was like, *Oh, OK, that's cool* and then *Actually, that's a bit odd. Why wouldn't we be called the Australian women's football team?* But later you go, *Ah, that's Australia—we have nicknames for all of our sporting teams.*'

The now-indelible 'Matildas' is a reference to the song 'Waltzing Matilda'. It was one of five shortlisted choices (also bandied around were 'Soccertoos', 'Blue Flyers', 'Waratahs' and 'Lorikeets'). To register their preference, fans had to dial 0055 phone numbers that cost more than the average local call. By the poll's close, the Matildas name proved by far the most popular (arguably because the other names were pretty ordinary). Sermanni was driving between Canberra and Sydney when SBS called to inform him that 'the Matildas' was the winning entry. In circumstances made for a cinematic retelling of such a historic moment, the weather was inclement. Sermanni, ensuring safety before sating his curiosity, pulled over to the shoulder of the road to take the call on his early era 'brick' mobile phone. Rain pelted his roof and the windscreen wipers struggled against the water volume, punctuating the conversation at timed, factory-set intervals as Sermanni sat roadside, straining to hear the SBS contact convey the poll results.

'I remember thinking it was a great initiative but I must admit I wasn't sure about the name,' Oakley recalls.

'I think it was like, "We're not having the Soccerettes … That would be the worst decision",' Murray says of the intra-team discussions and poll suspense. When 'Matildas' was announced, it was 'OK, let's take that on board.'

Oakley notes that the name has 'proved to be very successful putting Australia's women's football on the map [globally]. I absolutely love it now—it just took me a while to get used to it. I always knew women's football was worthy and with such talented players would only continue to evolve.'

Considering that it doesn't hint at football at all and yet is so widely known, you could say the moniker has definitely done its job of raising the women's team's profile. Although some of the players and Sermanni weren't initially enamoured of it, it would be impossible now to imagine a better name; it's undoubtedly one other teams would happily poach. 'It's an iconic name now,' Murray agrees. 'You can mention the Matildas and even non-football people go, "Is that the soccer team?"'

The newly named team was strategic in leveraging travel and friendlies to their full potential. 'I think generally the sense was we were a bit disappointed at the performance, but not too shocked,' administrator Maria Berry says of the 1995 tournament. But for her, compared with the 1991 non-qualification it was something they could work with. 'After the mediocre performance—not a disaster performance, just a mediocre performance—of '95, the AWSA started working on how to take the next step.'

Although the Matildas hadn't qualified for the 1996 Olympics, the USWNT invited them over to play two friendlies as part of its own Olympic prep. 'Traditionally the way it worked is if you got an invitation, you had to get yourself there. So you had to pay the airfares, basically, and they would pick up costs on the ground,' Berry explains. That meant the Matildas stayed at the luxurious Orlando Hilton and got to train at the United States team's premier Orlando football facilities. That alone would have been excellent, but the Matildas levelled up. In addition to playing the USWNT games, they arranged friendlies with China and Japan, another two teams on their way to the 1996 Olympics. On a budget, of course. 'When the US was paying, we had lunch at the Hilton. When we were doing it ourselves, we went out and bought bread and fillings and made sandwiches and ate those,' Berry says.

The team also shifted from the Hilton to motels and saw the upside of the more modest, cost-effective accommodation: 'They were good because we could do our own laundry and they were nice and spacious.' It didn't stop there. 'When the US was paying for us, we had the big coach and stayed at the Hilton, right? When the US wasn't paying for us anymore, we went out and hired minivans and filled them with people and gear. There wasn't really enough room, but we solved the problem of not enough seats by getting one of the coaches to lie across the luggage at the back.' Safety and legality aside, it worked. As Berry notes, 'It's different now, but it's what you had to do to get started.'

Sermanni recalls those vans well. 'We hired three transit vans,' he says. 'Two fifteen-seaters and one without seats for the gear.' They were, he says, 'piling in the vans, piling in the gear, and away we went.' He, physiotherapist Ed Hollis, and former Socceroos goal-keeper Jeff Olver were in one of the vans for a particularly long trek that saw them driving cross-country for a China game. Olver 'basically slept the whole journey on the equipment, on top of the bags at the back,' Sermanni says. 'That was his contribution: he slept most of the way.' That same drive was when the players requested, then reconsidered their request for, a mid-trip toilet stop. There were no available bathrooms; the best the staff could offer was to pull over so players could discreetly relieve themselves behind shrubbery. Sermanni sets the scene: 'There's all these canals, and in the canals you saw the eyes of alligators. There were three or four alligators in the bit of the canal where we just happened to pull up. I think a lot of the toilet stops were put on hold.'

Having traversed the country, the Matildas arrived at the ground in time only to change and then take to the pitch. They led the match 1–0 but conceded 2 goals in the last ten minutes. Overall, they achieved a win and a draw against China, a draw against Japan, and 1–0 losses to the US. (Berry is clear: 'These were no kick-and-giggle matches—they were fair dinkum matches.') The Matildas were then able to use those results to show that they were internationally competitive and worth investing in. That led to a full-time AIS program that enabled twenty players to prepare together in Canberra for the 2000 Sydney Olympics (and the 1999 Women's World Cup), and to leverage that into obtaining funding for the Women's National Soccer League (WNSL), a national competition to give them formative domestic preparation and experience.

'So then we had a set of matches, events where we'd bring different countries out and play them and provide more evidence that we were internationally competitive so they'd keep funding us, funding a national league, and getting us ready to be able to go to the '99 World Cup, which, as far as the funders were concerned, was the curtain-raiser to the Olympics,' Berry says. It worked like this: 'We get to the World Cup because we have money invested in the program. We get money to invest in the program because we've proven to the funders that they're not backing a dead horse. You have to see it strategically that way, in how all the bits link up. So we got more support when we went into '99 than we did in '95 because we were more of a proven product. And the evidence of that in the first instance was the performance of that tour in the US, which was done on a shoestring.' So credit must be given to the ingenuity of the team's coaches and administrators and to their motel-made sandwiches and overloaded hired minivans.

4

1999:
THERE'S SOMETHING TO THIS

DI ALAGICH DREAMED of being an Olympian when she was a child, but football wasn't yet an Olympic sport or, that she could see, one played by many girls. The first time she saw other girls playing was when she trialled for the under-16s South Australian state team, so her formative football development had come from playing backyard football with her brothers. 'The first time I really followed [the Women's World Cup] was in '95, when I realised we had a national team,' she says. Although not an on-paper success, that tournament showed Alagich there was an elite-level football tournament she could aspire to. She made her Women's World Cup debut in 1999, a time when the Y2K problem seemed to pose the greatest hurdle and September 11, the event that destabilised the modern world, hadn't yet occurred.

As World Cups go, '99 was a good one. The Matildas qualified by beating New Zealand 3–1 in the 1998 Oceania qualifiers; the goal New Zealand scored was the only goal Australia conceded throughout. That lone conceded goal was evidence of Australia beginning to edge ahead of New Zealand in women's football development, but the Australians didn't take qualification for granted. The Olympics were still higher profile, and the Australian players and funding bodies viewed the '99 tournament as a 2000 Sydney Olympics warm-up. Funding for those home Olympics meant there was money for the players to train and play out of the AIS for almost the entire pre-ceding year. It was the kind of concentrated football training and cohesion Matildas of previous years had dreamed of, and it made a difference both in terms of preparation and in encouraging women to stay in or return to the game. Also, Maria Berry notes, 'We would have qualified in '99, but we would have been so much less prepared if we hadn't been funded on the basis that we were next going to the big event, which was the Olympics.'

Shelley Youman is an example of a player for whom Olympic funding changed options. She had fallen away from the sport as the pay-to-play approach was 'hard yakka'. Youman recalls her mother constantly doing lamington drives and other fundraising to support her and her football aspirations. 'I just thought, *Why am I paying all this money to go and represent?*' Youman had married and had three children, but the Olympic inclusion and funding injection inspired her to put her boots back on. She was selected for the training squad and she and her family made their way to the AIS in Canberra.

'People would have thought we were privileged because we weren't paying for anything—everything was paid for—and we were given a small amount of money to be down there,' Youman says. 'So we were getting an allowance, and you could live in, so it's not going to cost you too much because food's there and stuff like that. I had a husband, so I was lucky, but people would have had to have a job for other things surrounding that.' Her husband worked two jobs to supplement the pay she received. That said, players who were not selected for the Olympics had to find their own way back to their respective states: their scholarship ceased and they were not provided with any relocation costs.

Youman narrowly missed out on World Cup and Olympic selection but, notwithstanding a few injuries hampering her, she was definitely in the mix. She was also likely one of the first Matildas to have returned to the sport post- or in the absence of formal maternity leave. In returning to the sport, she debuted at age twenty-seven, which, with the exception of Michelle Sawyers, who debuted around the same age in 1987 and after having two kids, may be one of the most mature Matildas debuts we've seen.

Karly Pumpa similarly benefited from the influx of Olympic program funding, albeit through it through an off-pitch gig. With ACL injuries curtailing her career (like Wainwright, she ended up undergoing three reconstructions), Pumpa started working full time with the team as an analyst, a role that enabled her to stay involved with the team and sport she loved. Pumpa was interested in the subject matter and its capacity to refine and elevate the team's performance, so it was a good fit when combined with her existing playing and game-reading experience, even though the specialist software the AWSA bought was a little temperamental. 'It had a million and one glitches in it. It was super time-consuming. The minute you had one tiny glitch, when you got to the end result to spit out the statistics, sometimes it didn't work,' Pumpa explains. They found they could achieve just as good analysis sans software. 'I was videoing games, sitting with [the coaches], stopping the video, cutting it and pasting it together. Then we'd do a full game analysis session with the team and replay scenarios and choices that [the players] made versus ones that maybe they should make.' Tech issues notwithstanding, that analyst role, which lasted as long as the Olympic funding did, allowed her to travel with the team on international tours and to the Women's World Cup.

The 1999 tournament preparation included a three-game tour of the Democratic People's Republic of Korea (North Korea), a country about to make its Women's World Cup debut, albeit a tour the Australian Government advised against. (Youman recalls the coverage around that trip, particularly given the media didn't normally pay the team much attention: 'They weren't really interested in the soccer. They were more interested in us not taking notice of the government.' She adds, 'Any publicity is good publicity, I guess.')

In travelling to North Korea, the Matildas became the first Australian sports team and first women's team of any country to tour there. (It was the first of three trips to date. 'They all kind of meld into one, because nothing ever really changed from when we got there, to be honest,' former Matilda Alicia Ferguson says. 'I always joke I'm a friend of North Korea, because I've been there three times.' That's three more than pretty much the entire world.)

To get to North Korea, the team had to fly to Beijing and purchase visas from the North Korean embassy. 'You had to do it in China, and you had to do it in US dollars in cash,' Berry says. With a guide from the embassy as its liaison, the group passed the visa-processing downtime visiting such sites as Tiananmen Square before catching an ancient Russian Air Koryo plane to Pyongyang. They stayed a full seven days because there was only one flight in and out per week.

Knowing they were largely on their own save for a Swedish embassy potentially able to offer emergency assistance, the Matildas took their own doctor and medical supplies. They also packed back-up food that included breakfast cereal and the Australian staple Vegemite. Still, it was a discombobulating experience, as Youman says: 'I was a young mum then. I had three small children. I think, *Why wasn't I worried about going to that country? Some people don't come out of that country.* You stepped off the plane and there was a lot of military around, and they weren't welcoming smiles that you walked into.'

'That was a black-and-white country, really. People were kind of petrified of us,' Pumpa agrees. 'I was really surprised back in the day that we were allowed to go.'

On all three trips, the Australians were not allowed to leave the hotel without an escort. Youman says this was ostensibly because they might be mistaken for Americans, whom North Korean people consider to be enemies. ('Every day we would go on a walk around the little town, and every day we would get followed by a car and guys. And every time you turned a corner, they were there again. You'd be like, *This is weird,*' Pumpa says.) Youman remembers their young chaperone who had grown up with the propaganda and was completely immersed in the North Korean tale. 'She would probably have been eighteen,' Youman estimates, 'but she talked about how they had beaten the Americans in war … Because they don't get any outside information, they don't know anything about the outside world. They think they've got the best country in the world.'

'They took us to the big statue of Kim Jong Un's father [Kim Il-sung],' Pumpa recalls. 'It was up the top of a big hill with lots of stairs, and it was a hot day. We just happened to sit down on the stairs to take in the view and a lady ran over to us and said, "You must not turn your back to the statue."' Youman continues, 'The food wasn't great and there wasn't an abundance of it. Even the chickens looked like they were pigeons,' noting that the situation was bleak but not unexpected. The power intermittently cut out, which made players wary of catching the lifts. Propaganda was broadcast on televisions that would turn on at predetermined times. There were unsettling noises given the absence of other guests; the players had an overwhelming sense that they were constantly being monitored, including through walls and bathroom mirrors and phones. Their calls home would end abruptly if they said anything negative about the country. Meanwhile, the method for maintaining the football-pitch grass length was a couple of goats tied together, or North Korean people hand-trimming the grass with scissors. The Matildas witnessed both incredible sights firsthand.

In all, the trip was unimaginably different. 'It was very isolating. You couldn't take in phones or radios or anything. It was just so repressive it was bizarre,' Berry says. While there, she penned a carefully worded article that was published in *The Age*: 'I faxed it from the hotel and had to be careful what I wrote!'

Some memorable moments occurred while the team was in North Korea. The country completed a missile test—a troubling development made more troubling by the fact that the first the team knew about it was when their concerned parents stumped up international phone-call fees to check they were safe. The team liaison told the Australians it was a satellite, not a missile. In another incident, the night before one of the games they were woken at 3 a.m. by the sound of thousands of people marching and chanting. It was purportedly a (very oddly) scheduled rehearsal for a national day of celebration—or, as Youman believes, a tactic to put the Matildas off their game.

In football terms, the three friendlies were unfriendly. 'It was tough. I mean, home refereeing was one thing, you expect that.

But there was no way we were going to get anything out of [those games],' Berry says. 'I remember being in the rooms after one of the matches saying, "Oh gee, it was a tough game—they were pulling your shirts the whole time" … They said, "Maria, they weren't pulling our shirts"' and lifted their jerseys to reveal torsos bruised from repeated pinching. Other intimidation tactics employed by the North Korean players included screaming right next to players' ears and jabbing fingers between their ribs. So it was unsporting, but Berry acknowledges this was understandable given that, for the North Koreans, winning or losing may well have been a case of life or death.

It's not quite North Korea, and Bathurst is normally a town associated with a car race, but that regional town and Melbourne also played host to the Matildas and the USWNT for pre–Women's World Cup friendlies in a continuation of the team's means of gaining valuable international experience and results to leverage into funding. 'Playing in country regions was always a good strategy,' Berry explains. Funding for regional tours was easier to come by, with state and local governments footing the bill, and the whole town would turn up to games. 'So you'd have a small stadium full of people who were really into this thing. It was very important to keep demonstrating women's football's potential and value.'

Proving such potential and value was central to the 1999 Women's World Cup. Compared with the boutique 1995 set-up Sweden had staged, with stadiums facilitating fewer than 20,000 fans, the United States opted to go big. That meant it had to sell enough tickets to fill the grander stadiums and cover costs while wearing all the risk. Reminiscent of how Julie Dolan and other players had letterbox-dropped flyers promoting the Australian team's first match, the USWNT's players actively promoted the tournament, including physically turning up to junior football camps and carnivals to hand out flyers.

Fans heeded the call. The police-escorted USWNT bus was engulfed by supportive fans in standstill traffic on the New Jersey Turnpike on the way to the team's opening game at Giants Stadium. That traffic was there, snookering and almost inadvertently making the team late, because almost 80,000 fans were travelling to watch the match. It set the tone for the crowd figures, optimism, enthusiasm and attention the tournament would bring.

Themed 'Watch Me Play'—perhaps a call both to buy tickets and attend matches, and to recognise women footballers' skills—the tournament gave the first hint that the world had fallen in love with women's football. Over a million people attended matches across the event. More than 2500 media reported on the tournament, with all matches shown live on television and 40 million Americans alone tuning in to watch the final. NSYNC played at the opening ceremony; Jennifer Lopez played at the final. Four jets flew past while Hanson performed the US national anthem, 'The Star-Spangled Banner'.[1]

A record 91,185 fans, including President Bill Clinton, filled the Rose Bowl in Pasadena to witness the USWNT win the Women's World Cup—a live women's football crowd figure that wasn't exceeded until 2022.[2] (The 2022 figure was 91,553, which came via the Barcelona v Real Madrid Champions League quarter-final. It was surpassed just a few weeks later when 91,648 fans turned up for the Barcelona v Wolfsburg FC Champions League semi-final. So many similarly record crowds and viewerships followed for other games and leagues in the latter half of 2022 that it's impossible to catalogue them all.) The feat in Pasadena was massive, especially given the United States is a country where football is not a primary or premier sport. The USWNT defeated China 5–4 on heart-in-mouth penalty kicks in front of the record crowd, and Brandi Chastain's iconic shirtless goalscoring celebration sparked initial furore and later respect. With those giant strides, the tournament set the Women's World Cup benchmark and signalled to administrators (and even the players themselves) that, like all ideas whose time has come, women's football was a thing.

'It was amazing because it was *so* American,' Berry says. 'Let me tell you, it took people by surprise. It took a lot of the Americans by surprise. It certainly took FIFA by surprise. Just the way it was done and also how it was promoted and the merch and the hoopla. It would stack up today against anything you want to put out there.'

It was quite the spectacle. 'The opening ceremony at Giants Stadium at New Jersey was [more than] 60,000, sold out,' Berry says, 'and not fake sold out, like *really* sold out.' It was the polar opposite of the 1995 trip: 'They've gone from being in a minivan with the maximum number of people, driving round, having sandwiches for lunch ... Now they're at the World Cup and it's hoopla.'

Berry and her partner Jacki not only attended that opening match but experienced it from the VIP section. 'Like, *the* VIP,' she explains. 'It's full. They have bloody Kofi Annan, the secretary-general of the UN, doing the opening thing. They have NSYNC with this guy, oh, Justin Timberlake. He wasn't quite as famous at the time as he is now, but NSYNC were pretty big. So NSYNC did the sing-y bit at the beginning. It's chock-a-block. There's merchandise, merchandise, merchandise ...' (That's significant because women-specific merchandise was, at the time and for decades to come, nigh on impossible to secure. Sponsors and governing bodies weren't convinced there was a market for it.)

Berry recalls, too, when she and her partner went to return to their seats after enjoying the half-time VIP canapés. Saying 'Pelé's coming', security held them and the nearby VIPs back from entering the lift. Brazilian football great Pelé and FIFA president Sepp Blatter—the 'VVIPs'—entered the lift together for an exclusive trip; Berry and the rest of the VIPs were allowed in the lift only once the pair had gone.

The USWNT won that opening match against Denmark, 'which means the script is being followed,' Berry says, 'and it's like, wow. Banners in the streets of New York. Yeah, it's a big deal.' As Berry puts it, 'If you went to Sweden and then you went to this, it was absolute chalk and cheese.'

'The '99 World Cup was always going to be infinitely better than '95,' Julie Murray says. 'It brought out everything you'd expect in a World Cup: the crowds, the stadiums, the atmosphere, the media, everything.' It garnered recognition that this was a sport to support.

'We'd played in front of some fairly big crowds in China or Europe, but nothing like this,' Alagich says. 'Like getting 20,000 to our first game, just to watch Australia play.'

It was, as Tracey Wheeler says, 'a step up from 1995 in terms of quality of the competition and organisation. The United States had also had the 1996 Olympics, including women's football, so they probably benefited from that.'

Opening match over, Berry and her partner flew to Boston for Australia's first match at Foxborough, the New England Patriots NFL team's home ground. To get from the team accommodation to Foxborough, some 30 kilometres away, they travelled in the official car with AWSA president Dennis O'Brien driving the unfamiliar vehicle on the unfamiliar side of the road, trailing in the wake of the police-escorted team bus. 'The police were in front, and the police were behind,' remembers Berry. 'Then they did the whole—not sirens, just lights, and they went at a gazillion miles an hour across Boston and onto this freeway and zooming along. And Dennis has to keep up in this car while the [traffic] lights were flashing. It was like we were important or something. But that's because they set the lights up so we could go through. It was all wow.'

American football (NFL) stadium configuration is different from that of football—the VIP seats are behind the end zones as opposed to on the halfway line. It was an extremely hot day as Berry and her partner sat in the open-air VIP bleachers, but they'd chosen their spot well. Seated not far from them happened to be Blatter and his daughter. 'So these FIFA flunkies come down and hand out FIFA baseball caps to keep the sun off and FIFA cushions for people to sit on,' Berry says. 'I've got a set of FIFA caps I kept from the event because they handed them out to everyone sitting near Sepp—we must be important because we're sitting near him.'

The tournament was challenging for the Australians. Alicia 'Eesh' Ferguson earned the fastest red card in Women's World Cup history through a second-minute dismissal in the game against China. It wasn't at all the way Ferguson had envisioned her tournament going. Just a teenager, she was homesick and hadn't slept well. She was both nervous and excited at being given a chance to prove herself and wanted to make an impact early in the game. 'It's all character-building,' she says. 'That red card made me realise I was putting too much emotion into my preparation, rather than just treating it as another game, which is why I was so inconsistent as a player as well. You have one good game—and that's what happens with a lot of young players—and then you get overawed by the occasion or you put a lot of pressure on, and you're already thinking about being a goalscorer or doing something exceptional and all the rest of it. Rather than thinking about the process, you're too busy thinking about the outcome. So it was a harsh lesson. But it was really a lesson to just treat each game as each game. Make sure you have a good first touch.'

Coach Greg Brown lost his cool during a half-time talk, but Ferguson wasn't around to hear it. She felt she'd let her team down and was in tears away from the change room, on her own, further down the tunnel. 'If the plan was to rev them up for the second half, it didn't work,' Berry says of Brown's speech. China were a powerhouse—they would progress all the way to the final—and the depleted Matildas were up against it. Their tournament ended at the group stage.

Decades on, the red card is something Ferguson and her teammates are able to laugh about, with plenty of ribbing about her leaving them with ten players for some eighty-eight minutes on what was a stinking-hot day. 'God, it was so hot. It was *so* hot,' Ferguson says. 'Apart from me feeling absolutely horrible about getting sent off, it was so hot in that game. Ten players against China. Sorry, girls. I owe you all beers when I'm old enough to buy them. I was only sixteen.'

Ferguson notes that the tackle was mistimed and there wasn't any malice in it. 'The thing was that I was a striker then, hence why my tackling technique was so bad. I was definitely more suited to being a holding midfielder. That was probably case in point, example A.' She recalls that a contributing factor to the straight-red decision was that it was also FIFA Fair Play Day.[3] 'It's one of those things. When something like that happens quite early in a game, it can go either way.' A different referee might have told her to settle down and issued a yellow (something there are ample examples of in the men's game), but referee Sandra Hunt opted for red. The rest is history, literally. 'It's a world record, so that's pretty cool. Also, people still want to ask me about it, so I maintain my relevance because I got sent off in '99. No one can forget. Actually, my little nephew found it randomly in his school library in the *Guinness Book of World Records*. He took a screenshot and sent it to me.'

There were positives, too. Murray performed so well that she was named in the FIFA All Stars team to play the USWNT in San Francisco. The pre-match press conference for that game illustrated just how US-centric the focus was and raised awareness that there were other skilled women footballers in the world. 'I remember being asked what I thought the score would be: 8–0, 10–0 to the US?' Murray says. She thought it an odd question and responded, 'I'm pretty sure we'll go close to winning.' 'They were like, "Oh, really?"' Murray and her peers left the press conference a little puzzled, and perhaps determined to prove the journalists wrong. 'We walked off and were like, "We're some of the best in our country, we're some of the best in the world, and they think we're going to get absolutely smashed."' The All Stars Team defeated the USWNT.

It wasn't just the journalists who learned about the talent and opportunity women's football entailed. 'The '99 World Cup opened my eyes to how to the rest of the world viewed football,' Alagich says, referring to the millions of girls and women who played football in the United States and other more established footballing nations at the time. 'It showed me what was possible. I even remember Sepp Blatter saying that the future of football is feminine.'

Heather Reid speaks similarly of that tournament. 'I watched '99 from afar and saw, in the space of ten years—when you think about China in '88, and this was '99—just how much the game had progressed.' She, too, recalls Blatter's statement. 'He meant that, I think,' Reid says. 'He was often clumsy with his words, Blatter, but I think he meant it in a genuine way. It was about marketing and bums on seats and how much FIFA could make if they really invested in the women's game.'

In many ways, the success of the 1999 Women's World Cup wasn't a surprise to the players, who intrinsically understood the potential of the women's game if it were properly funded and promoted. The US team's success was the catalyst for the first

US women's professional football league. But that league would only last three seasons and would be gone by the time the 2003 Women's World Cup was transplanted to the United States from scheduled host China due to the SARS pandemic—a sign that women's football couldn't succeed without proper investment and backing. (That harsh reality was never far away. Life after the 1999 tournament involved a fairly brutal return to reality. 'I came back from the '99 World Cup and didn't have anywhere to live,' Alagich says. 'I'd packed up everything before I left. I didn't have any money so I had to purchase a bus ticket back to [my hometown] Adelaide. That was my welcome-back. On a bus. But I wouldn't have had it any other way. It made us appreciate every moment.')

Perhaps the two most memorable such moments from in and around 1999 came not from the football but from the reactions to women footballers' actions. They were telling.

USWNT coach Tony DiCicco decided that Brandi Chastain would be the fifth penalty taker in the United States' penalty-kick win over China. He decided, too, that she would take the penalty with her non-preferred left foot to wrong-foot Chinese goalkeeper Gao Hong. Chastain followed the instruction to a tee despite being the final penalty taker in the most nerve-racking, pressure-cooker situation. The goalkeeper correctly anticipated the shot's direction, but Chastain put enough power on it to beat her. When the ball hit the back of the net, Chastain dropped to her knees and ripped off her shirt in celebration, both fists in the air and the jersey clutched in her right one.

The controversy subsequent to her celebration was both surprising and unsurprising—men had been ripping off their shirts in goalscoring celebrations so frequently and for so long that the regulation-making body, the International Football Association Board (IFAB), passed a rule that such a celebration would automatically earn a yellow card. But men's bodies aren't policed in the same way as women's. Chastain was engulfed by a furore about the purported gender-appropriateness or otherwise of her celebration. (She later wrote a book entitled *It's Not About the Bra*, a title that speaks volumes about the inanity and overanalysis of the unscripted moment.)

Time and distance have taken some of the steam out of the pique, and Chastain's celebration is now considered seminal. It was immortalised in a bronze statue unveiled on the twentieth anniversary, which coincided with the 2019 Women's World Cup. The body police might have wrung their hands about notions of femininity, but most young fans saw it for what it was: an impassioned celebration by a fit, talented athlete whose penalty had just won her team the World Cup.

Many players cite Chastain's tournament-winning penalty as inspiring them to become professional footballers, including Matildas great Kate Gill, now co-CEO of the PFA. Gill remembers how that moment made her feel and how it showed her there was a footballing pathway, and how the media coverage afterwards elevated women's football's profile. As she says, 'Brandi Chastain's image was all over *Inside Sport*' (and many other media outlets). Thea Slatyer, too, saw that goal and 'realised what the future could have in store and what the potential was if [women were] given the opportunity. A few years later I found myself lined up against Chastain in a stadium tunnel alongside the other stars of the game at the time, legends Mia Hamm and Kristine Lilly. It's a surreal experience when your sports idols become your opponents.'

It's interesting that Chastain's shirtless celebration attracted all the furore but another moment of joyful celebration was censored into invisibility. When US goalkeeper Briana Scurry ran to the stands to kiss her girlfriend, the camera immediately cut away. Former USWNT player, LGBTIQA+ person and human-rights advocate Joanna Lohman wrote two decades on that 'America was ready for women to compete in front of massive crowds, but it was not ready for a same-sex couple to kiss on national television'.[4] (Former Brisbane Roar media manager Michelle Gillett (née Tobin) recalls an equivalent scenario when USWNT player Abby Wambach kissed her then-wife Sarah Huffman at the 2015 Women's World Cup. Gillett noticed that the photo caption in an article she was reading said 'embraces friend'. Whether the tag deliberately camouflaged Wambach's same-sex relationship or signalled a lack of knowledge about who Wambach was seeking out, it aligns with the 'compulsory heterosexuality' that infuses so much media coverage.[5] But some improvement in this space was apparent by 2019, when USWNT defender Kelley O'Hara, who had never explicitly come out, kissed her girlfriend in the stands after winning the Women's World Cup. That kiss, reminiscent of Scurry's, fell into the more progressive and normalised category of 'casual acknowledgement' rather than 'scandalous coming-out'.[6]) Consequently, the controversy around controlling women and their bodies centred on, and engulfed, Chastain's shirtless goal celebration. It was excessive and unnecessary—and she wasn't even naked.

Shortly after returning from the 1999 Women's World Cup, twelve Matildas players participated in a nude photo shoot in the AIS auditorium for a calendar to be released ahead of the 2000 Olympics. Like the SBS team-name poll preceding it, the calendar was strategic. Featuring the tagline 'The New Fashion in Football', its primary purposes were to raise money for the players and raise the team's profile. An additional implicit purpose was proving that the players were 'real women'. (The unhealthy obsession with players' femininity and sexuality was—still is—a source of inappropriate speculation.) The players who participated hoped the calendar would achieve the trifecta.

Their aspirations were understandable. The 1999 tournament might have ignited women's football in the United States, but the spark hadn't extended to Australia. The team remained relatively unpaid and unknown, and it lacked vital sponsorship and media coverage. Nude calendars were then a popular fundraising tool. So while not to everyone's tastes, such a calendar may not have seemed entirely out of place, and not to players who were confident in their bodies and used to getting changed while others were around. (As Youman notes, 'Everybody was fit, and getting your gear off is not a big deal when you're looking good.' She initially put her hand up to be in the calendar. 'I didn't think anything of it. I just thought, *I'm going to do it.* My husband probably didn't want me to do it, but he didn't tell me I couldn't. He just said, "I think you should talk to the kids." I did that and my daughter, in particular, said, "Is Dad taking the photos?"' They weren't comfortable with a stranger taking the photos, so that was enough to rule out Youman's participation. Her son, who was entering Year 3, was later asked by his classmates if his mother was in the calendar, and Youman realised she'd spared him some teasing. 'I *can* say I wasn't going to be completely naked if I did it. I was going to put things in front of bits,' she says.)

Unfortunately, women's bodies are scrutinised and regulated in ways that are neither fair nor rational. The issue likely arises from the question of need, not want. If the players had been paid appropriately or even adequately to pursue their football careers, and if media had provided decent women's football coverage, the calendar could potentially have been viewed as one of empowerment. And there *was* an element of that—the players who were involved maintain that they are proud of the calendar and did not feel taken advantage of. But the nagging unspoken question 'Why did they need to do it?' gets to the heart of the matter.

For starters, money was still scarce. Even with the full-time AIS residential program, the players were being paid comparatively little. Most were supplementing that income with side gigs. Angela Iannotta, for example, worked as an AIS tour guide. 'And I was a minibus driver when they had congresses,' she says. 'I never drive. I haven't even got a car, and here I was driving a minibus around Canberra.'

Perhaps contributing was the fact that the Matildas' on-field results weren't what they are now and there was little else for media to write about. Consider, too, how truly empowered you can be when you're otherwise not being well-remunerated and, being in your teens and twenties, are not yet world-wise (or perhaps world-weary) enough to know that women's bodies are, for reasons not bound by logic and beyond your control, sites of contestation. Also, its current upward trajectory notwithstanding, women's sport has traditionally been given little airtime—the percentage of sports media coverage given to women's sport generally sits in single- or low-double-digit figures in any given year.[7] Is it really appropriate that the limited media coverage was excessively dedicated to an attention-grabbing nude calendar that was, in large part, necessitated by the lack of media coverage and pay the women received?

Just as Chastain's momentary shirtless goal celebration extended far, far beyond that moment, the Matildas' calendar and the attention it attracted overtook the intent and the team. Twelve players participated, but the calendar had ripple effects for the entire team for more than a decade. Tal Karp recalls, leading into the 2004 Athens Olympics, 'feeling pretty frustrated that the only coverage of the Matildas I saw in Athens was of the calendar five years earlier. I wanted our team to be recognised for our skill, strength and resilience on the field, not for how the players had looked without their gear on in 1999.'

Sacha Wainwright, who was a lawyer, declined to participate in the calendar. 'I blamed the legal profession, which is a little conservative, and gave it a miss,' she explains. *New Idea* ran with the slightly more sensationalist headline that she was 'The Girl Who Said No'. 'I think I was a bit more diplomatic than that in the interview, but underneath what I said were strong views that women's sport should not need to do this and one day it would be recognised for athletes' sporting abilities.'

The jury is still out as to whether the calendar was empowering or exploitative, profile-raising or reputation-damaging, money-making or another example of players giving up more than they were being paid. 'People have their opinions,' Ferguson says. 'I can understand why some think of it as exploitation, but we agreed to do it, we were happy to do it. It definitely had the desired effect, which was to do something really bold and make a statement and get people's attention. Whether it was negative attention or positive attention, it definitely got attention. But yeah, it's nice that we've moved on from that type of thing.'

One way to understand the calendar's implications is through what came after it: an innocuous-sounding Japanese toothpaste commercial. 'Players were flown to Western Australia and taken to a beach somewhere to do this ad, and they were asked to take their clothes off,' Reid explains. The nudity brief was sprung on them. (Wainwright recalls that she wasn't selected for the ad, which in retrospect was likely because the advertiser knew her response would be no.) It was an example of how there was an assumption that getting naked once meant the players would do so again and without notice.

'Some of them said, "No, that's not why we came here. We're not doing this,"' Reid says. That would have been incredibly difficult: the players were far from home and had travelled at the advertiser's expense. Those who did agree to participate were filmed chasing a football along the beach while topless and wearing only a beige G-string. 'It was very controversial,' Reid says. 'It caused a lot of fuss.' A senate inquiry into the ambush and purported potential financial anomalies relating to the calendar followed at the urging of Shadow Minister for Sport Senator Kate Lundy.[8]

Viewed through a contemporary lens, it's fair to say it's unfortunate that a nude calendar was the option players were presented with and felt necessary to pursue. It's unfortunate, too, that little else in the Matildas' history is so regularly resurrected or so front of mind for media and fans. It feels like baggage for players before, alongside and beyond that they can never quite discard.

More paramount, as Ferguson points out, is that the calendar will never need to be repeated. So perhaps it should be compartmentalised as a touchstone in the Matildas' history to appreciate just how far beyond it the team is now.

5

2003:
COULD HAVE BEEN
A CONTENDER

IF YOU HAD to summon one adjective to describe the 2003 Women's World Cup, it would be the simple four-letter 'lost'. Australia lost a bid to host the tournament. It lost the national association that had been driving women's football domestically, too. Scheduled host nation China lost the tournament at the last minute due to the SARS outbreak. Women's football lost momentum despite the success of '99 and despite the World Cup being held in the United States again. With little marketing and media coverage, it remains largely lost from women's football history. The 2003 tournament was, in short, marked by lost opportunity.

Australia had never won a game at a Women's World Cup at the time it bid to host the 2003 tournament (that win wouldn't come until 2007). But it was widely recognised as a sporting nation, in terms of on-field achievements and off-field fandom across many sports (not to mention offering a winning combination of sun, surf, sand and spectacular landscapes). The bid it submitted to host the 2003 tournament leveraged the country's sporty reputation, including noting that there were more than 60,000 registered women players in Australia at the time, a participation rate that would no doubt be boosted by the increased visibility, sponsorship, media coverage, inspiration and esteem that hosting a Women's World Cup would bring. (Netball and hockey, then the sports primarily competing against football for women's participation and registration fees, were likely watching the bid with interest, as they and sports such as the Australian Football League's women's competition (AFLW) no doubt are in 2023.) Also, with the bid submitted four years out, in 1999, the impending 2000 Sydney Olympics were generating additional hype.

AWSA CEO Warren Fisher compiled the bid documents and obtained commitments from state governments. 'And in the course of doing that, [everyone agreed that] yeah, we can do a Women's World Cup here,' Maria Berry says. Significantly, Women's World Cups were at that time relatively small, manageable events, much smaller in scale than the Olympics. 'We were thinking, *We can snare this*. It wasn't that glamorous. Sweden had done it. I didn't go to Sweden, but it sounded like it was pretty low key.'

The AWSA's glossy eight-page colour bid brochure demonstrated support from the highest government levels as Prime Minister John Howard contributed supporting words that included espousing Australia's capacity to provide food ranging from gourmet to the humble, quintessentially Australian barbecue. Accompanying the brochure was a professionally produced video designed to invoke awe and emotion. 'I remember goosebumps. You know, hairs on the back of your neck rising,' Heather Reid says of seeing the final cut. The backing track was Australian band Icehouse's song 'Great Southern Land', with the video panning to showcase Australia's diverse blonde-beach-meets-red-outback landscape and landmarks.

The AWSA submitted the bid, including the video and brochure, under Soccer Australia's auspices (FIFA has a rule of recognising only one official member federation per country, and the men's association was the one it recognised), but that was the extent of Soccer Australia's involvement. 'All we could manage to get them to say was "What? Yes, yes, of course we support it, yeah, sure,"' Berry says. 'They were not driving it.' As she puts it, 'It wasn't opposed, it just wasn't important. Some stupid fight between two Greek clubs was always more important.'

FIFA traditionally holds a women's football symposium just before the Women's World Cup final, and the 2003 Women's World Cup hosts were to be selected at the 1999 symposium. 'What happened was we go in and we're representing Australia, effectively,' Berry says. Brochure in hand, video at the ready, the Australians were primed to deliver their pitch. 'We were the only competitors for it. There were no other bidders. China wasn't a bidder. Understand that: China was *not* a bidder.'

Given Australia's sole bidder status, other delegates logically assumed it would be awarded the tournament and were preemptively issuing congratulations. 'People are saying. "It'll be really good, see you in Australia, it's going to be great in Australia, dah dah dah." Because we're the only bidder, remember. We've got the glossy, we're the people with the signed thing from the government saying, "Yeah, yeah, yeah, we'd love to have one of these, whatever it is."'

It's not that the Australians weren't nervous. The United States had set a new high-water mark for what the tournament could and should be. 'You know, we're thinking, *It's going to be so hard for us to meet this bar that the Americans have set, but we'll give it a red-hot go*,' Berry says. 'When we're over there with the brochure, we're thinking, *Oh shit, this is the new benchmark. We could do the Sweden benchmark and smash it. The new benchmark? OK, we're the only bidders. I guess we've got this. Right, fine.*'

Whether or not they could put on a tournament that would reach the United States' high standard turned out to be the least of their worries, because what transpired was characteristic of many women's football experiences: the men's game's political manoeuvrings overshadowed and intervened. 'The guys have all flown in and they've got their own meeting over to the side, where China are trying to get the World Youth Cup,' Berry says. As the Australian contingent nervously awaiting the Women's World Cup determination soon found out, China's Men's World Youth Cup bid didn't get up, and the Chinese delegates, rueing the loss, were politely but definitively miffed. To appease China, and in a move that simultaneously devalued the Women's World Cup and signalled that FIFA viewed it as a consolation prize, the association announced that

China would instead host the 2003 Women's World Cup. 'So they got it. That's it. It was a bizarre deal,' Berry says simply.

The Chinese delegates sheepishly apologised to the Australians—they weren't happy either, but their hands were tied. China knew that rejecting the offer would have accorded a black mark against its name and hampered it achieving its end game: hosting a senior Men's World Cup. Australia had to wrestle with the mental contortion that it was both the only contender and not a contender at all.

Neither Berry nor Reid considers missing out on 2003 a blessing in disguise that left the door open for a much better 2023, when Australia and the women's game would be more ready. 'If we'd had our act together twenty years ago—and maybe the Women's World Cup would have helped us have our act together twenty years ago—then we'd be reaping it,' Berry says. 'Would it have been as glamorous as 1999? Possibly not, but we would have been at least as good as France and Germany and China have been.' She qualifies and contextualises these statements pragmatically: 'I'm not saying we would have won a World Cup in 2003, but as far as a kick-along to the sport, it would have been absolutely massive. And if you're looking for whether we would rather have had a legacy twenty years earlier to help us fight off what other sports might be doing …' She references the AFLW, which began in 2016, as the main competitor; it appeals to first-choice players due to its apparent glamour, despite the fact that it's a domestic competition with no international opportunities. Comparison to the Matildas is incorrect: the AFLW equivalent is the A-League Women's.

'So I don't think missing out in 2003 was a blessing in disguise,' Berry continues. She fully recognises that Australia, with football in its formative state, might not have made the most of the tournament: 'It was a real missed opportunity that we might not have taken.' But that sliding-doors moment means we'll never know.

China didn't end up hosting the 2003 tournament. The SARS pandemic proved an insurmountable plot twist, so FIFA scrambled to find a last-minute replacement host. Despite the fact that Australia would have leapt at the opportunity—it could have been a contender, again—previous host the United States was deemed best placed to stage the tournament at short notice. So the United States reinvigorated the 1999 set-up and FIFA promised China a second consolation prize: it could host 2007 instead.

The United States had approximately 120 days to pull everything together. That it managed to do so was a feat in itself, but the short lead time meant that advertising and marketing campaigns were undercooked to the point of being almost non-existent. This was, in turn, reflected in the lacklustre ticket sales. Compounding the challenges, the US league, the Women's United Soccer Association (WUSA), folded just days before the tournament kicked off, even after top-tier players had taken a 30 per cent pay cut to try to prop it up. (That folding was especially tragic as the WUSA was the first women's league that paid all players as professionals. Its collapse lent credence to arguments that women's football wasn't a viable business.) So, just four years after the high highs of the '99 tournament and one year after the break-out success of feelgood movie *Bend It Like Beckham* had inspired legions of new women's football fans, the women's football momentum all but dissipated.

'You talk about overnight. It pretty much *was* organised overnight,' Tom Sermanni says. 'I was actually in the US at that stage and had planned to go to more games because I was coaching in the WUSA. But literally maybe a week before the World Cup started, the WUSA folded. The whole timing of it was incredibly bizarre.' Sermanni had planned to scout for players, but without a league to recruit them to, his plans were kyboshed. His wife, Alison, worked at the WUSA club as well, so both of them were out of a job. 'I had a bit of breathing space because of my contract situation, but there were other parts of life it impacted,' Sermanni says. 'We'd literally just signed a new lease on the house we were staying in on Long Island.' They had to sublet the place to extricate themselves.

'They did a great job for a last-minute change,' Berry says of the United States' efforts. And there were some significant highlights. Germany, for example, won its first Women's World Cup, making coach Tina Theune-Meyer the first woman coach to do so. (A few years before, the German team had implemented a policy of training and employing women coaches for its women's team—an enviable ongoing development and succession program.) Still, things were a little off-kilter. Matches were played at unusual times to accommodate the last-minute nature and contingencies. Funding and contracts and sponsorships weren't forthcoming as the tournament didn't kick the women's game on or generate serious commercial revenue. Indicative, too, of how far attitudes to women's football had yet to travel, FIFA president Sepp Blatter would later suggest that women could play in more 'feminine' clothes—for example, tighter shorts. (Ignoring the remark's sexism for a moment, it's worth noting that uniform choice was largely out of players' hands—sports brands didn't offer such shorts because they didn't consider there to be a market for women's cuts.)

In some ways the 2003 tournament mirrored the challenges women's (and men's) football was facing domestically. 'That whole period from '99 to 2003 was tumultuous for soccer generally,' Reid explains. 'You have to remember that [Soccer Australia] was in a mess in the late '90s … I often say we limped towards 2000 when we knew we had to put on a good show for the Olympics, but there was no excuse after that not to review the management and governance of the sport. The federal government and prime minister's intervention in 2001 with the initiation of the *Independent Sport Panel Report* [the Crawford Report] was critical for reform.'

It was a perfect storm of competing issues. The national women's association was for all intents and purposes about to be absorbed into the men's national association, Soccer Australia; this had been on the cards for a while. The men's association barely cared about or understood women's football. Even if it did, it was battling its own demons, much of which came to light in the Crawford Report. The women's association, starved of funding but with the board not made fully aware of the true state of affairs, went into unforeseen receivership. Soccer Australia entered similar territory soon after.

At the time, the Australian Sports Commission (ASC) was funding the AWSA via Soccer Australia. 'Now, can you see what's wrong with that?' Berry says. 'Apart from the principle, there's the practical. The fact is that the funding went into Soccer Australia's bank account. Did it come out of the bank account in the same way? No. So we've got ongoing cashflow problems because the Sports Commission [is giving the funding] to people who had nothing to do with the women's game. Soccer Australia has huge financial problems, so instead of giving money to us, they drip-feed it and make it really painful to access. But we're managing. Just.'

'The AWSA board had had a meeting with Warren Fisher on the weekend as a handover,' Reid says. 'He was leaving, and we asked him if there was anything we should know about. He ran through a few things but never mentioned that he'd allegedly managed, more than once, to hold off legal action against us for going into liquidation or receivership for bankruptcy. On the Monday after that meeting I got a phone call from Sacha Wainwright, who was in the national team and was a lawyer. She was at the ACT courts and had noticed that the AWSA had been listed to appear in court to defend wind-up charges.'

Wainwright's work periodically took her to the Supreme Court where, upon arrival, it is customary to check the list to see where your matter is being heard. Scanning the list, she spotted AWSA winding-up proceedings. 'I was like, *What? What is that about?* And I knew it was serious.'

Wainwright completed her own matter, but acknowledges that and the subsequent hours were a blur. 'I was completely distracted that day,' she says. 'I remember thinking, *Do I leave my matter and go and fight?*' Her recollection is that the AWSA matter was called and no one appeared, which was problematic because that generally means it is automatically processed. 'I wanted to jump up and appear, but I couldn't. It's not how it works,' Wainwright explains: you can only appear if you are the appointed legal representative. 'A different person probably would have said, "I'm here as a current player who's just heard of this matter" … I didn't. I just got on the phone as soon as I could, in a panic.' Her mind was racing: *This is bizarre. I'm an athlete, it's my association, I'm a Matilda in this organisation that is organising tours for us.* She recalls, 'I did my matter and then rang Heather Reid: "What's going on? The winding-up of the association is on the list."' It's just as well she did: Wainwright's call is what tipped the AWSA off.

It will never be possible to determine entirely what led to the winding-up. But contributing to, and compounding, the financial pressures were two elements you couldn't script. First, a law firm owned by former Socceroo Danny Moulis was chasing the AWSA for legal costs relating to advice about the calendar (that is, a former Socceroo was involved in legal action that contributed to the Matildas' administrative downfall). Second, the AWSA needed to acquit itself of monies claimed by former coach Ernie Merrick. Merrick had been appointed, but his tenure, it quickly became clear to all, would be untenable—Berry and Reid say he viewed the AIS, technically his employer, as the only authority he was responsible to, with no authority resting in the women's association, which ran the national teams and the national league. Suffice to say, it wasn't a workable situation. 'He's the only coach to have been appointed who never met the team or held a training session,' Reid says.

'That big fight with Ernie Merrick meant we had a certain level of payout, but because Soccer Australia wasn't giving us our money, we couldn't pay. It was essentially the thing that led to the liquidation,' Berry says. 'It was messy, messy, messy.'

Merrick never got his money. The AWSA domino fell and the men's association domino fell soon after. Westfield founder Frank Lowy stepped in and the Crawford Report, with more than sixty recommendations for cleaning up the plethora of problems with football in Australia, including mistrust and disharmony, was released just prior to the 2003 Women's World Cup.

Fortunately, the players were largely oblivious to the behind-the-scenes tumult at the national level. For them, playing in a Women's World Cup was the realisation of a long-held dream. Tal Karp, for example, had made her way through the formative football pathways as most alongside or before her had: as the only girl on the boys' team. She was initially denied entry to the game and was only admitted temporarily to make up the numbers when her brother's team was short. Having proved herself by scoring the winning goal, she was allowed to stay.

Karp's dream of playing in a World Cup had started when she was seven. While watching Men's World Cup reruns, she professed to her family that she, too, would play World Cup football: 'At that age, it didn't resonate with me that I was watching a men's competition and that my access to the beautiful game might be different from my brother's. I just saw these amazing athletes on TV and wanted to be like them. My folks still tease me about how excited I was in that moment.'

That gender-blindness and focus paid off when Karp was selected for the 2003 Women's World Cup. 'I remember receiving our team kit and holding my playing jersey and staring at it for a really long time,' she says. 'It felt pretty surreal. It meant I had achieved what I set my mind to as a seven-year-old. But it also meant being part of something far bigger than myself—a tradition of incredible athletes and administrators who had pioneered our game.'

Her parents and late grandparents were there to cheer her on. Karp references an image that became her favourite 'once I got over my embarrassment'. It depicts her mother and grandmother holding up homemade, heartfelt supporter signs. The signs were bright-yellow tea towels to which her grandmother had affixed 'AUSTRALIA GO TAL GO' in green fabric letters.

Family was central to Heather Garriock's tournament experience, too, with her mother, father and sister travelling to support her. Her brother, Nathan, had been killed a few months earlier at just seventeen while attending a house party for his best friend's eighteenth birthday.

The tournament must have been hazy for Garriock and her family. 'It was but it wasn't. It was what kept us going, I think,' she says. 'They had already committed to come to the World Cup. Mum and Dad and my sister tinkered with the idea of not going, but they always gained joy in seeing me represent Australia, and Nathan had been going to come. So it was tough, but again, it's a purpose. It kept my mind off things until after the event.' Garriock wore white boots in tribute to Nathan, who had worn white boots in his own games, and he was both her motivation and the person to whom she dedicated a crucial goal she scored to earn a 1–1 draw with football powerhouse China.

Thea Slatyer experienced the heartbreak of making the team and then missing the tournament through injury. She ruptured her ACL and injured her lateral meniscus and medial ligament during a physical friendly against South Korea in Japan. 'I was heartbroken and had to be replaced for the World Cup only four weeks out from competition,' Slatyer says. (Her roommate Pam Bignold, née Grant, well recalls the day Slatyer was injured. An earthquake hit hours later, and the shifting surfaces and structures posed a challenge for the injured Slatyer, whom Bignold helped hobble from her bed in the shaking room to the safer hallway.) But Slatyer found a way to participate in the 2003 tournament: 'I quickly had the surgery and got over the self-pity and bought a ticket to go over and surprise the girls. I arrived late to the first game versus Russia held in LA at the Staples Center ... And to see the girls' faces as they came over to the stands and recognised me standing there cheering them on was worth the trip alone.'

Bignold kept a journal throughout the 2003 tournament—a scrapbook that is colourfully marked up with different pen and pencil text and sketches. It gave her something with which to fill the downtime and likely filled an invaluable gap left by the lack of media coverage and images documenting the team's journey. 'You don't realise. It's different now—you've got phones, you can take photos.' Then, not so much. 'You had to sneak a camera onto the bench [and take a] stealth photo so you didn't get roused on or look like you weren't focused. Otherwise, you got nothing.' (Wainwright remembers that, too. 'It was hard to get photos of yourself in the line-up—you'd have to ask someone to do it.' This meant it was almost too hard to achieve at times, especially as it also required people to carry cameras and film rolls with them— a significantly different scenario from today, when everyone has a smartphone in their pocket.)

A talented sports all-rounder and primarily a hockey player, Bignold had only started playing football in 1998, aged sixteen, after she was scouted through a talent identification program. 'Before that,' she says, 'I had no idea about anything, even who the Matildas were.' That's particularly interesting given, Bignold notes, that 'it's the sport I've stuck with'. Given her recent uptake of the sport, she was stoked to make the team. 'I was so new to football that I didn't have the skill set of some of the other players at the time. I was just happy to be there. Any opportunity I got was great.' Still, it was tricky as she and her roommate at the time were vying for the same position, and her roommate was the one selected to play. The selection or non-selection experience knocked Bignold's confidence, which she documented in her journal. 'I'd written about one of the games because I didn't feel confident to play—I didn't feel like the coach had confidence in me.' Additionally challenging was that Bignold was battling injury throughout the tournament. 'I actually rolled my ankle about three days before the first game. It was ginormous. I would have been out for weeks, but I strapped it up. I didn't play in the first two games but I got a game against Ghana. [My ankle] was so sore and so swollen ... I just remember being in pain the whole World Cup.' But no complaints.

'In the lead-up, we'd be down in Canberra for a couple of weeks, then home for a few weeks. We wouldn't get paid,' Bignold says. 'I was fortunate—I still lived at home. But I had two part-time jobs and was studying at uni. I couldn't get permanent shifts [because my availability wasn't consistent]. When we were back home, I would pick up shifts wherever I could. So even when you were home and could earn money, you couldn't really.' Still, she says, 'That's just what you did. I'd get up in the morning at 5.30, go to the gym, from the gym I'd go straight to uni, from uni I'd go straight to work for a few hours, then I'd go to training, then get home at eight o'clock at night. Then I'd get up again ...'

Of the tournament details, Bignold's recollection is simple and telling, and speaks volumes of the amount of unpaid labour players were putting in: 'I remember thinking everything was organised. It was nice having things organised for you. You were so used to doing it all yourself, picking up everything.' They were still responsible for their washing, though—something seemingly small but actually prohibitively expensive as laundry costs wouldn't be included for a few more years. 'When we went away for that trip for six weeks, I think we got four shirts,' Bignold says. The players did a lot of handwashing, or stomping on the shirts and their underwear in the bath, before laying them out on hotel towels to dry. Of course, those four shirts were, as per the perennial theme, men's cuts. Bignold says, 'I've given half my kit to my husband because it doesn't fit me. He still wears the tracksuits.'

The players accessorised those kits with temporary Australian-flag tattoo transfers applied to various limbs. Referring to the tattoos as a 'power pack', Wainwright recalls using them as a kind of physical and mental talisman to help push through in the late stages of a match when heavily fatigued. She applied one to her quadriceps as those muscles were where she first and most felt fatigue set in. The team also had an inflatable kangaroo mascot; Melissa Barbieri was customarily the designated mascot caretaker.

While the tournament passed smoothly, returning to Australia post-tournament meant taking practical steps to tackle the things that had been on hold. Karp had to dive straight back into her university study, 'making up for lost time and preparing for exams'. She also had to address the not-insignificant issue of finding a new part-time job to support herself and somewhere to live. 'I could never afford to pay rent while I travelled overseas, so I would pack up all my gear, put it in a friend's garage and find somewhere new to live on my return to Canberra. I lived in seven different houses over a three-year period.'

Hers was not an isolated experience, but that doesn't change the fact that it was tough. 'Playing football could never be my only focus,' Karp says. 'I combined a significant training load with a double degree in Law and Arts at the ANU, and part-time work to keep me afloat, because there was no money in the game at that stage.' These disparate worlds weren't always compatible or accommodating. 'Some lecturers didn't understand why I would risk missing important classes or compromising my exams to play football. And finding time to study on international football trips was really tricky. I'm sure I was very much the team geek, carting around my tax-law textbooks.'

In some ways, this made Karp more determined to make it work: 'I felt I had to go against the grain and push back on each of my two worlds to create the time and space needed to do both. Although it was a really difficult balancing act, it was worth it. I found that study gave me an out and a bigger picture when I didn't feel great about myself on the football field. And the physical and mental release that sport provided helped me with my studies and taught me to be really effective at prioritising my time.'

Wainwright says similar. She even won two awards for achieving some semblance of equilibrium in that hectic work-study-train schedule. 'I can remember thinking, *It's really great to have that outlet from work or study, to go to training and run around*, and then vice versa—as sport became more serious there's a *Take your mind off that and go back into your work or study*.' She acknowledges that in some ways she thrived off the scheduling craziness: 'You know, going to the gym and then going into the law firm and then stripping in the car—clever tricks to get back into your gym uniform for lunch or whatever. My car was a wardrobe for a long time between football boots, shin guards and legal suits. I think I joked that I could only buy suits that were anti-crease, because they were going to be chucked on the floor of my car.'

Karp's sole Women's World Cup appearance turned out to be 2003. She retired from international football soon after to focus on a career she felt could set her up for the future. 'It was a different world back then. There weren't professional opportunities or salaries on the table. The clear message from the state of the game at the time was that it wasn't a career—it was something you did for fun while you were young, and at some stage you needed to get serious about your life and find a career that could support you.' So she hung up her international boots at the age of twenty-three and threw herself into study, an associateship with a High Court judge, and challenging legal roles. 'Law became my new football, and later, when I began appearing in courts and tribunals, the courtroom gave me some of the adrenaline, and perhaps some of the white-line fever, that I had found on the football field. Although I came back to be part of the commencement of the W-League [she captained Melbourne Victory Women in 2008], my need for a career that could pay my bills and provide a career path moving forward closed the door on a playing future.'

6

2007:
A TOURNAMENT OF FIRSTS

THERE IS A succession of sliding-doors moments in Australian women's football's history—moments when, through missed opportunities and realised ones, paths diverged and markedly altered women's football's trajectory. The derailed 2003 bid is one such moment, relegating women's football to more decades of eking out an existence around and in the shadow of men's football and its comparatively large take-up of spotlight and funding. The year 2007—and the move of the Women's World Cup to Asia two years prior—was the sliding-doors moment, though, when Australian women's football's arc became ascendant.

For if the 2003 tournament was themed 'lost', the 2007 one was themed 'firsts' and 'found'. It marked the first time Australia won a World Cup game and the first time it progressed to the quarter-finals. It was the first time New Zealand had made a Women's World Cup appearance in sixteen years. It was the first time SBS broadcast all the matches and a documentary crew captured the Matildas' behind-the-scenes experience, which meant it was the first time fans could comprehensively follow the team's campaign. In short, 2007 was 2003's polar opposite.

Like most Matildas from that era, Alicia Ferguson considers the 2006 Asian Cup and the 2007 Women's World Cup 'the halcyon days, the highlight' of her playing career. The team had, as she puts it, a 'good balance of experience, and youth who still had experience'. Coach Tom Sermanni effectively leveraged that squad depth to rotate players through and ensure that everyone felt they were a valuable contributor. That's a difficult evenness to achieve, Ferguson says. 'Previously, I think my experience had been Starting XI, three or four subs, then everyone else.'

Lauren Colthorpe, who would score one of the team's most game-changing and iconic goals of the tournament, echoes that sentiment, saying that the tournament was probably her favourite national team experience. She indicates that the team culture was a major contributing factor. 'I was one of the youngest players at the time and we had a great core group of senior players—not just great players and leaders, but great people to be around. There was no unhealthy competition within the team—everyone wanted to do well for each other.'

Sally Shipard, too, remembers this time fondly. She points to the fact that she was buoyed by good players and the beginnings of resources and funding. 'I think I played at the most ideal time for me. I transitioned into the team really young and felt really supported by these women, who are the real pioneers,' she says, nominating players like Cheryl Salisbury, who created the path she followed and mentored her and others along the way. (So great were Salisbury's contributions that she recently had a Sydney Harbour ferry named in her honour.) 'I'm not a pioneer,' Shipard continues. 'I was just in this really sweet period of transition from the Matildas being recognised for their calendar and being true-blue fighters to being athletes. The fact that we were getting more funding and more internationals meant it was inevitable we would improve.'

Qualifying through the more difficult and intimidating Asian route via the 2006 Asian Cup was a huge undertaking, but the Matildas managed to do it by finishing second. The Asian qualification route marked the first time for some years that the team had been 'truly tested', as Thea Slatyer puts it, in World Cup qualification. Kate McShea, too, says of that material step up, 'It was good going to Oceania, but we needed more.'

'Getting to a World Cup qualifying through Oceania, with all due respect to the teams in Oceania, wasn't as tough as qualifying through Asia. We didn't think we'd be able to do it the first time,' Ferguson explains, 'but actually, it gave us the belief that we could go and compete.'

Ferguson attributes the 2007 success to belief and momentum, but also good team dynamic, proficiency and cohesion. 'We were all towards the back end of our international careers, so we were all experienced and understood our strengths and weaknesses,' she explains. As did their coach: 'Tommy [Sermanni] was always very open and honest about our limitations against some of the better teams.' He and they approached the games pragmatically. If that meant recognising that they were unlikely to have much possession against the at the time technically and tactically superior Japan, they would defend patiently and resolutely, frustrate the Japanese attack and then counter quickly. That they did. It helped, too, that although Sermanni was serious about achieving results, his preternatural calmness took the pressure off and freed players up to perform.

The build to the 2007 peak had begun two years prior. The Matildas, newly admitted to the Asian confederation, had gone on a reconnaissance and benchmarking tour. They only won one game, but Sermanni deems that tour 'very, very significant' because it showed them what they needed to do to succeed in and beyond Asia. What followed was the Matildas' breakout 2007 campaign, when they bested previous results and bested them again. They began by winning their first-ever Women's World Cup game with a 4–1 routing of Ghana. They drew 1–1 with former Women's World Cup winners Norway after that. Then came the Canada game. Twice.

The final group-stage match was delayed by twenty-four hours because, although the weather was perfect where they were, a typhoon delayed play where the other game was scheduled. FIFA rules dictate that the final group-stage games must be played concurrently, so if one game is postponed, the other has to be too. The cancellation came very late. 'We were actually on the bus, ready to go and play what at the time was probably the most important game we'd played in our history, because it was the chance we had to qualify out of the group. That was a challenge,' Sermanni laughs, 'because players were really keyed up for the game and ready to go.'

'We were on the bus and Tommy came on and said, "It's been postponed." We were all like, "Nah, he's taking the piss,"' Ferguson says. The weather was fine; the team had gone through all its match preparation and was literally setting out for the stadium. 'So we're all focused, and then we're like, well …'

Few players or staff recall what they did with their afternoon once the game was cancelled. It must have been difficult to go back to the hotel and have a nap, for example. But as one former staff member guessed, 'I think they don't remember because it's uninteresting once you go, "OK, the game's off."'

'You get pretty routine in what you do,' McShea explains. 'We went back into game-preparation mode, which is probably a good thing. In Olympics and World Cups, you have such a short turnaround that in hindsight an extra day is probably good for you to recover.'

'It really goes back to mindset, because you can expend a lot of energy getting yourself mentally ready and prepped for a game,' former Matildas physiotherapist Kate Beerworth says. 'We had a relatively experienced group at the time.' Still, she says, 'I don't think it gave us a huge advantage. I don't think we were under the pump from a time point of view for any soft-tissue injuries or anything like that.'

Ferguson's recollection is that Sermanni sent the players out to have dinner with their parents to disperse the stress. 'He was like, "Don't worry about it, we're coming back tomorrow."' Still, she believes that the postponement is what contributed to the team's 'bit of a dodgy start' when it finally got to play. 'It's that emotional energy that takes its toll on you. You know, that nervous energy' and the restlessness and sleeplessness that entails. 'So you've had two days of that, and then you have to get yourself back up for it again. And Canada got themselves back up for it better than we did, to begin with. I did think early on, *Oh god, this is going to be one of those games*. But it all worked out in the end, so that's good. Nothing like a bit of stress.'

That 'dodgy start' involved going a goal behind early—first-five-minutes early. The Matildas levelled 1–1 just after half-time, but had their hearts in their mouths when Canadian great Christine Sinclair edged her team ahead in the 85th. (Sinclair would go on to score the most international goals of either gender, with 190 compared to Cristiano Ronaldo's 118 at the time of writing. Such figures have also recently become the focus of the Correct the Internet campaign, a Matilda Effect–equivalent approach redressing biases that privilege men's results over women's. Featuring a young girl standing in the middle of a major stadium's pitch and asking the empty stands such questions as who scored the most international football goals, the factually incorrect answer she receives from a computerised voice is that the record-holder is Cristiano Ronaldo. Puzzled, the young girl shakes her head and quietly says 'That's not right', a subtle reference both to the answer's inaccuracy and the wider inequity the campaign is pointing out. One of the founders of the initiative, which was launched at a Football Ferns friendly in early 2023, is Rebecca Sowden, former New Zealand Football Fern and owner of Team Heroine, an international women's sports marketing and sponsorship consultancy.) The Matildas needed at least a draw to progress. Fittingly, it was Matildas stalwart and captain Cheryl Salisbury who levelled the score in injury time. The ball fell to her after Lisa De Vanna wrong-footed defenders in the box but one defender managed to get a toe in and prevent her taking a shot. Salisbury's goal wasn't overly convincing and travelled at an anxiety-inducing low speed, but its speed mattered less than the fact that it was composed and passed into the back of the net, not overcooked, as so often happens in such moments.

Former Matildas manager Jo Fernandes was pitch-side on the bench for that goal, and it remains her all-time favourite Matildas moment. 'That dribbly little goal,' she recalls. 'It was bobbling away like in slow motion. I can still see it. The defenders went after Lisa, then the ball turns up and Cheryl kind of fumbles it off her foot and it goes into the goal.' It was enough.

De Vanna, who was having a blinder of a first World Cup and was a firm fan favourite, hadn't actually started that game. It had taken extra steps to get her on the pitch. 'She was so nervous that she was in the change room for most of the first half,' Ferguson recalls. 'Even a bit of the second half, I think.' Having decided to inject De Vanna into the game, Sermanni looked towards the bench and started to say, 'Lisa'. Ferguson had to inform him De Vanna was in the change room, too nervous to watch. 'Tommy was like, "Eesh, can you go and get her?" I was like, "Yeah, OK,"' Ferguson explains lightly. 'So she came on.'

That Salisbury, who is normally a centre back, was up front speaks volumes about how last-ditch the goalscoring moment was. 'It was late, late in the game and it was like, "Go on, Chez. Get up front. See what you can do. Let's lump it in,"' Ferguson says. 'I think I came on and I was something like right back, and when the goal was scored I was literally like, "EVERYONE GET BACK!"' Ferguson laughs, re-enacting her neck-vein-popping scream. The players were celebrating, but there were still minutes left to play. They needed to focus and defend. 'Oh god, it was so stressful!' Ferguson adds. 'But it was an incredible moment.'

'I do remember that I've probably never been as excited as when Cheryl slotted that goal in,' Beerworth says. 'It's probably one of my most exciting memories of football. It was an emotional rollercoaster, that game. We were going home, we were on the plane, next minute we weren't, then we were, then we weren't … It was exhausting.'

That 2–2 draw propelled the Matildas out of the group stage and to their first-ever Women's World Cup quarter-final. There they went toe to toe with adversaries Brazil, suffering a narrow defeat: 3–2. Just like the Canada game before it, the Brazil game couldn't have made for more thrilling viewing. It was as if the Matildas instinctively went 'You think the last game was exciting? Hold our beers.' With the team having gone 2–0 down, De Vanna clawed back an initial goal. Colthorpe's perfectly timed header to restore parity remains one of the most outstanding and game-changing the Matildas have ever scored. 'That goal was just the case of right place, right time, I guess, and I was able to take advantage of a beautiful ball from Heather Garriock,' Colthorpe says modestly. 'Joey Peters, Katie Gill and I had done a lot of work in the air and on set pieces with our state institute coach, and it paid off in that moment.'

It took the individual and collective efforts of Brazil's three super-stars to extinguish the Matildas' hopes: Formiga would later become the only player, woman or man, to play in seven World Cups and seven Olympic Games; she's also the only contemporary player to have been born during Brazil's women's football ban. Cristiane's tournament goalscoring efforts were only surpassed by her team-mate Marta, who has been named FIFA Player of the Year six times. Five of those times were consecutive: 2006 to 2010 inclusive.

The Matildas' tournament might have ended with that loss—they were soon on the plane Beerworth spoke of—but their new era and legacy were really only beginning. Just as the 1999 tour-nament had inspired the next generation of players, watching the Matildas take on and hold their own against players of such high calibre in the 2007 tournament cemented dreams for the next generation of Australian girls watching the team's heroics in their lounge rooms in their pyjamas.

'People talk about tactics and structure and things like that, but one of the great things about that team was they were so comfort-able and confident with each other. I think that came through in that tournament,' Sermanni says. 'If you look at it, in most of the games we actually had to come from behind against higher-ranked teams to win. There was just a real confidence and belief about that squad.' Or, as one former staff member says simply, the Matildas' quarter-final berth and lasting impression 'felt like it wasn't luck—it felt like it was deserved at the level they were at'.

'I think all our hard work was starting to pay off and we were getting results,' McShea says. 'We got our first win at a World Cup in 2007 and it was kind of a relief because we weren't making up the numbers anymore, if that makes sense. We were there and we were competing.' (New Zealand, by contrast, was making up the numbers. Its return to the tournament after its post-1991 absence started with a 5–0 loss to Brazil and saw the team not progress past the group. It was also crunched financially, 'because all of a sudden New Zealand went from not qualifying for anything, really, to qualifying for everything as soon as Australia walked out of Oceania,' Sermanni explains. 'The reality is that the only team that struggled to qualify was the men's national team, and that was the only team that [brought] in any revenue—all the other teams cost money. Back in those days, there was no money in the Women's World Cup, so [New Zealand Football and the Football Ferns] had real challenges as a result of being successful in qualifying.')

Sermanni agrees about the Matildas' elevated competitiveness: 'I think what that tournament did was to set the tone for what the Matildas were and are about. You know, the documentary was called *Never Say Die* … From that tournament on, you always felt that no matter who you were playing, you could win the game.' It's evidence, too, of the team's grit, talent and graft. 'When we had nothing, we still made those quarter-finals and made it out of the group,' Melissa Barbieri says. And it encapsulates the team's efforts off the pitch, not least the way the players diligently continued working to improve their skills and standing to show that the team was a product worth investing in.

Testament to, and dovetailing with, the team's improving results, media coverage noticeably increased. This may have been aided by the fact that SBS was showing all the games and that the Asia-based tournament and its game times largely coincided with Australian prime time. Still, in an unprecedented move for women's football media coverage, one of Sydney's largest newspapers held the back page and its print deadline to report the result from the team's penultimate or ultimate game. The Matildas printed out and pinned up media clippings alongside the messages of support they received. 'I remember when we made it to the finals the hallway walls were filled with messages and newspaper articles,' Garriock says. 'We actually couldn't believe it.'

The media coverage still had a way to go. Former Matilda Julie Murray and her co-commentator, David Basheer, didn't travel to China to cover the tournament and worked with what they had in Australia. 'We couldn't get there for some reason, maybe budget,' Murray says. 'I just remember being in this little booth with a couple of TV screens and thinking, *I have to provide technical, tactical commentary here, and I can only see one line of players*. Because the camera didn't pan out.'

She clearly did well enough, because that media coverage and the more difficult qualification path aided attitudinal change. 'I think because we had qualified through Asia, the narrative was that we had proved we were serious players,' Ferguson says. 'I remember one of my brother's mates actually said when we got back, "Look, I don't want this to sound offensive, but I actually watched the game and you girls are really good."' Ferguson was fine with that. From her perspective, changing perceptions was imperative.

But that media coverage was relatively short-lived and didn't translate to commercial revenue. Former team manager Jo Fernandes remembers it well: 'Media attention back then was few and far between. We were getting a lot of media attention for that tournament, which was great, and then of course they made the quarter-finals. Basically, all the staff were like, "This is it, we've turned the corner."' Fernandes believes they probably had, at least for a few months. 'Then it just kind of rumbled back to what it was before the tournament. So for me the 2007 tournament was a big missed opportunity to build and keep going. Like it is now. Each time things happen, it builds on what has happened before. Back then, it kind of built a bit and fell away again, unfortunately.'

Still, 2007 elevated the team's and the players' profiles. It was, as Slatyer terms it, 'the moment when the general Australian public started taking notice. We broke some boundaries and became the first Australian football team to play in the finals, as I understand. So we had emails from the PM and politicians, ex-athletes and former Matildas all wishing us luck. It was very humbling and you really felt honoured to put on the jersey.' She notes that 'From that tournament on we were regarded as semi-famous, and seeing people's reactions when they realised you were a Matilda was something we had to get used to.'

Joseph Mayers was at the tournament as a lone photographer following the team. 'No one else was interested in them,' he explains when asked why he started photographing the Matildas.

He was friends with Slatyer and would take his annual leave from his IT job to travel and support her. He had noticed that the most media coverage the team received was a few words stating it had played. 'I remember saying to [media officer] Pete Smith in 2006, "How come there's no photos of the Matildas at the games? [The media] hardly mention it."' Smith explained that the Matildas (and women's sport more broadly) struggled to attract attention; if the team had a photo, he would provide it to the media to use. 'I was like, "I'm at all the games. Why don't I take photos?"' Mayers says. 'He said, "All right, you get better and we can make that happen." So I bought my first professional camera in 2006. I had no idea what I was doing but I got better and better, and by the time 2007 came around, Pete put in my accreditation as the Football Federation Australia photographer at the World Cup.'

Then Smith, Mayers and the Matildas made the most of it. At World Cups, media are generally allowed in for the first fifteen minutes of a training session and then the remainder of the session continues unobserved. Mayers recalls Smith's savvy way of ensuring that he and the other couple of Australian media had the access they required. 'Pete would tell us, "After fifteen minutes, go and hide in our dressing rooms and when all the media goes, come back out." So we'd go and hide in the dressing rooms and then they'd all leave and we'd come back out again and stay for the whole training session,' Mayers laughs. Smith's reasoning was that it seemed non-sensical to kick out the few media there for the Australians given the team was fine with them being around. Mayers' images of the relaxed, relatable team remain treasured historical artefacts, as does the groundbreaking documentary shot alongside them.

★ ★ ★

Documentary maker Helen Barrow is, by her own admission, not especially a sports fan. That perhaps made her the perfect person to produce a cut-through women's football documentary. *Never Say Die* follows the Matildas' 2007 Women's World Cup preparation and campaign, identifying and illustrating universal themes that transcend sport. The Matildas were used to having their training sessions filmed, so a documentary crew filming them wasn't that out of left field. Still, few could have imagined what a feel-good hit the documentary would become, what substantial history it would chronicle, or how it would endear the team to the general public. 'I don't think at the time we realised how much of an insight it would give of the team,' McShea says.

'I think the thing about working for the women's team is that it's almost a community sense within the group and, I guess, women's football is a bit more egoless,' a former staff member told me of the team then and more generally. 'It's football from back in the day, and I mean that in the best possible way.' Another noted that with the women's team, instead of the media officer being a 'media *prevention* officer', as is often the case in men's football, they can garner coverage that makes a difference to the team and its profile. Handily, the Matildas' thrilling 2007 results were a good-news story that lent itself to a great documentary.

Formulating her pitch and plan, Barrow had realised that the Matildas were better-performing than most male teams at that time (and still are), but that they plied their trade fairly anonymously: 'I don't play football myself, but what I really like as a storyteller and as a documentary maker are stories about people who push the envelope and who, through pushing the envelope, achieve great things. I definitely saw that in the stories of the Matildas and the research.' Barrow also wanted to create the documentary to inspire her daughter, who was aged six at the time. 'So it was a very personal motivation.'

Barrow recognised, too, the dearth of women's sports coverage and sought to help redress the imbalance that sees men's sports coverage dominate. Around that time, women's sport was generally only broadcast at inconvenient off-peak times such as 3 p.m., was largely unadvertised, and was invariably on a secondary, difficult-to-find channel. SBS's Women's World Cup broadcast went part-way to rectifying that, but men's sports were still privileged as a whole by the rest of the major media. 'They were all my motivations, really,' Barrow says. 'Let's get to know these women, what they've historically put into getting to the pinnacle of their sport, and in doing so hopefully bring a bigger audience to their game in the future. And I do think their profiles have changed since then. It's not because of the documentary—it's because of who they are as characters. The documentary helped to profile them and women in sport, I suppose.'

A World Cup is a pressure-cooker environment where teams don't always want media around, but to be successful, the documentary had to put viewers at the centre of the action. 'The camera has to be there seeing it,' Barrow says. 'We have to be behind the scenes while you're waiting to go on with that big crowd out there. We have to feel the nerves, which requires me being in the dressing room, in rehearsals, in your homes, talking to your parents.'

Building the requisite trust to achieve all that was vital. 'I spent weekends just filming them starting off on the field, then, over a period of time, sitting down and talking with them. And then [establishing] trust with the coach was very important, because if he trusted me, he would let me in the [hotel] lift,' Barrow explains of gaining access to the team's inner sanctum. 'Often I would spend time with them where I would film but not talk to anybody. So, after a period of time, I started to slightly disappear. I promised them absolutely that behind the scenes on the night of the matches in China I wouldn't talk to anybody, I wouldn't ask any questions. I'd just watch them with the camera rolling.'

That fly-on-the-wall approach enabled her to capture some goosebump-inducing moments. 'I don't know if you remember— there's this one shot, and I still get tingles when I think about it, but they're all getting ready, it's their final match, and they're coming out two by two. I placed myself right in the middle of them and walked out with them and the stadium's just going off with cheers. I'd never seen such crowds, and the camera was experiencing what those women and that crowd were experiencing.'

'I had a couple of interesting conversations with Football Federation Australia at that stage, because the organisation was comfortable with the documentary but wanted to put a lot of restrictions on it. You know—you can only be in the lobby of the hotel, you can only be here,' Sermanni says. 'I basically said, "Look, if we're having this, I want to control it. I want to be in charge of it. If we're going to do it, we either do it properly or not at all." I think if you bring people into the environment, you're more likely to get a better outcome than if you put restrictions on things, because they become part of the team. So from my perspective, it was important for the documentary team to feel they were actually part of the team, and I think that's what happened.'

Barrow confirms as much: 'I don't remember them ever closing the door on me and saying, "No, you can't come in." They're the times when you really want to film because those are the moments where you really understand what goes down and what's at stake. [They] are important to share with people.'

'There's got to be a story,' Sermanni says of the logic behind the access. 'The more you restrict things, the more the story can become about a thirty-second segment or a particularly controversial moment because they don't have enough footage or they have to make a story. I think they had such good access that they had too many stories in the documentary in the end. When I spoke to Helen [Barrow], she said it was a real challenge to knock the documentary down to the required time. I think that's what made it authentic and successful.'

The human element was key. 'The game is exhilarating to watch, but a game is a short-lived moment and the players have to go through a hell of a lot more to get on the field. So everything that comes before is as important as their performance on the night,' Barrow explains. She wanted the audience to understand that and the compounding complexities relating to such obstacles as the lack of income. But she also wanted the audience to understand the community that supported the players, 'whether it was their bosses who gave them time off work, or their colleagues who helped raise funds for them, or their family members who supported them financially and of course emotionally so they could put football, i.e. their training, in front of other things to keep achieving at the level they did. But they still had to go to work, so they were putting in longer hours than any male team members at the time, and they were earning far less money. And it hasn't really changed.'

One of the most memorable documentary moments is when Melissa Barbieri and her husband, Geoff, are folding a fitted sheet in their Melbourne home. 'He cops a lot of shit for it,' Barbieri tells me, 'because he had never folded sheets in his life. It was just something I needed to get done and the camera crew said, "Can you involve him?" I said he could probably hold the other end.' Although amusing, the moment is nonetheless illustrative of the never-ending juggle for Barbieri and her teammates having to fit their poorly paid elite-athlete commitments in and around their unpaid domestic-labour commitments. Laundry waits for no one and nothing.

The levity offsets a more serious take-home message. Barbieri overcame being banned from playing with boys from ages nine to fourteen, and a later misdiagnosed career-ending back injury, to reinvent herself as a goalkeeper. She had to fight to play in the men's state league in the absence of serious domestic women's competition so she could keep her skills up ahead of the 2007 Women's World Cup. Some of the most uncomfortable moments of the documentary are when it chronicles Geoff's, and by proxy our, experience watching Barbieri in those men's league matches and enduring other spectators' snide remarks. Another telling moment involves Barbieri explaining to the off-camera interviewer what a difference it made to her to be invited to train with the men on the 'good pitch' with the 'good lights'. It's an experience unlikely to register with men because that's what they get to do by default. Barbieri has had the last laugh, though: she not only succeeded as a goalkeeper but captained the Matildas and in her early forties continues to play professionally, for Melbourne City in the A-League Women's competition. As part of that she's playing on better pitches with better lights as conditions and support structures continue to improve.

Contrasted with Barbieri's story in *Never Say Die* is Shipard's. Sixteen-year-olds are commonplace in the Matildas squad these days, but Shipard was one of the first to make her senior debut at that age and one of the first to grow up in the team. (It was a family decision that she move to Sydney from Wagga Wagga when she was fifteen after it became clear she was a prodigious talent.) Having spent such formative years in that football environment, Shipard still considers Sermanni a kind of father figure whom she can pick up the phone to call any time. 'He heavily influenced me,' she says. 'I would spend more time with Tom in a year than my own dad.'

Shipard tells me she has been watching snippets of the documentary on YouTube to prompt her memory ahead of our interview. In recent times, she has moved from an all-consuming football world to a completely non-football world in which she is learning and applying impressive skills in, among other things, marriage celebrancy and carpentry. Seeing herself in the documentary, she says, 'feels like such a world away'. Shipard is nineteen in *Never Say Die*, her age and her impressive mullet forever preserved on screen. (Think short front and sides swept forward and mullet length extending below her shoulders. Think frosted tips.) 'Oh my god, isn't it hilarious?' she says. 'Everyone is into mullets now, but I was into them in 2007.'

Like Pam Bignold and other players before and alongside her, Shipard documented and likely processed her experience in a handwritten diary. 'What we did before Instagram,' she quips in a text message accompanying a picture of a cloth-bound diary she and her mother put together. Its fabric cover reads 'China 2007' next to strips of Chinese characters. 'I'm not sure whose writing it is, but there was a funny little match report after we beat Ghana,' she says. That match was memorable both because it was the Matildas' first-ever Women's World Cup win and because they didn't just win—they scored 4 goals. (De Vanna scored 2; Garriock and Walsh each scored 1.) 'I bruised my toe. There's reference to that. It was quite fun to read that.'

Bruised is an understatement. She injured her toe early in the game, but didn't remove her boot until after the match: her big toe and the surrounding area, spanning halfway up her foot, were startlingly black. We witness her sighting the extent of her injury in real time. 'I think in the moment I was a bit scared because I was shocked at the state of it,' Shipard says. She thinks the bruising probably made it look worse than it was. Still, the toe was so bruised that in retrospect she says, 'I don't know how I played on it.'

★ ★ ★

More than a decade on from when she shot *Never Say Die*, Barrow has been pleased to see the perennial pay-parity issue finally starting to gain traction. 'How many times does one have to fight for those things?' she asks rhetorically, then references a radio-news headline she recently heard that said that parity wouldn't be reached until after 2030. 'I did wonder, and you know you have to tread carefully, you have to highlight things. My role as documentary maker is not to go in and point fingers at people, that's for sure.' But through *Never Say Die*'s masterful storytelling, we gain insight into how much the players were sacrificing to pursue their relatively unpaid football careers.

Money pressure remained a spectre throughout the 2007 tournament, and not just for the players. The Matildas had managed to negotiate Football Federation Australia (FFA) footing their laundry costs, but, like just about everything in women's football, it was hard-fought. Garriock was part of a player group that worked with the PFA's CEO, Brendan Schwab, and the FFA's John Boultbee to negotiate some minimum standards that included having internet and laundry costs covered. 'It started to cause angst,' she explains: players worried it was too difficult an ask. Garriock held firm and was prepared to go it alone. 'I remember saying in a meeting with Brendan Schwab and [FFA CEO] Ben Buckley and Boults, "These are the minimum standards we want. We don't want to keep washing our undies in the sink, for chrissake. We don't want to buy internet. We're not getting paid a lot of money." We were getting paid a daily allowance at that time.'

The FFA did eventually foot the laundry and internet bills, but budget remained tight. Fernandes recalls the cost-saving measures the team took. 'There were some tours I went on where if we didn't have enough laundry allocation, we had to wash our undies and everything in the sink. That actually went on for quite some time. If it costs $5 to wash a pair of undies and we didn't have the budget, we'd be like, "OK, everyone do your own undies and bras and we'll do everything else", for example.'

'We certainly didn't get laundry at the hotel,' Beerworth confirms of the prohibitive laundry expense. 'The kit person, which was Sonia [Gegenhuber] at the time, would often go outside and source it so it was relatively cheap. There was still a fair bit of hand-washing at that point.'

'We were always looking for ways to meet budgets so that we could do more,' Fernandes continues. 'Way back then we didn't have much to spend, but we eked everything we could out of every dollar we had.'

There was actually an issue with one of their kits when it returned from an externally sourced laundry: the laundry must have used water that was too hot, because the numbers on the backs of the kits were melted together. Both Beerworth and Sermanni recall that many were, as a result, 'unplayable'. ('They obviously folded them when they were still hot, so all the plastic numbers were melted and the strips all stuck together,' Sermanni explains.) Buckley, who was travelling over, had to bring another kit. 'We were joking that the CEO was the extra kit man,' Beerworth laughs. As in: highest-paid kit person ever.

This was in stark contrast to the players' income. Around this time, they were receiving nominal payment, so casual first and second jobs combined with familial support and/or Centrelink provided stop-gaps. 'That's basically why I retired,' McShea says. 'I had a mortgage with my sister. It was when they started to bring in contracts. The amount of time we were going to be away and what we were paid, I just couldn't afford to do it anymore.' (Worth noting is that although the amount of money the players received was not enough to sustain a career, the shift from daily allowances to contracts represented great gain as players could prove gainful employment and stability when applying for such things as home loans. 'I remember thinking, *Oh wow, we're employed by Football Federation Australia,*' Garriock says. '*How cool is this?*' Of course, what was missing was the ample salary needed to service a mortgage. Still, it was progress.)

Slatyer perhaps had the most creative off-pitch jobs, and they were a bit more out of the box than waiting tables or retail work. In addition to being a DJ and a pilot, at various times she worked as an abseiler on such structures as the Sydney Opera House, ships and oil rigs. It was not unusual for her to be working while overhanging shark-populated waters. With a martial arts black belt and a firearm licence, she also worked as protective detail for such celebrities as Elle Macpherson, Russell Crowe, Nicole Kidman and Megan Gale, and transported millions of dollars' worth of diamonds and jewellery to and from movie sets and photo shoots. 'It was a bit exhilarating carrying a casual sports bag full of $4 million worth of diamonds on my first job,' Slatyer recalls, 'with guys planted on the street and a discreet look here and a nod there. As a 23-year-old it was exciting speeding away in an armoured vehicle, checking for vehicle tampering as you would work around organised crime syndicates.'

Another time, she was approached on the street by a man wearing a hat and sunglasses. 'I realised I was hearing the Gladiator's voice but it didn't click until he asked how the team was doing,' Slatyer says. 'It was Russell Crowe, just casually recognising me in the street instead of the other way around. He still has one of my Matildas jerseys framed and hanging up in his museum, I believe.' It was a sign, too, of how much the Matildas' profile had increased.

Although fascinating, and reminiscent of a James Bond film (literally, she prevented a known stalker from reaching former Bond actor Daniel Craig at the *Casino Royale* Sydney premiere), Slatyer's non-footballing career is a reminder of the necessity for players to find innovative ways to make money, including by working high-risk shift-work jobs they could fit around football. As Slatyer herself acknowledges, burnout and fatigue were things she had to grapple with, even if protecting diamonds and celebrities was a surreal and irreplaceable experience.

Money challenges aside, Barrow was heartened by how the staff looked out for players' mental health: 'I could see that that was paramount in their minds, that the mental health of the girls was just as important as their physical health, and that the balancing of those two would [enable] them [to be] good players on the field. I thought that was very innovative and progressive in those days.'

Of that care, Sermanni says it was both deliberate and not deliberate:'I think you're more than just a football coach, particularly with an international team. Part of that is you're actually together 24/7, so it's not like a club team where you do a couple of hours of training and everybody goes home and lives their life. With the national team, and particularly in the beginning, the amount of time we were together was phenomenal. We were together more than we were individually at home. I think it's also partly that if you become a coach, you have a duty of care to the players. It can't be just about football.'

He notes that elite sport is high-pressure and as coach you're invariably 'making really difficult decisions' about players: 'You're leaving players out of World Cups, for example, players out of squads. In a roundabout way you're having to retire players. For me, unless you have an environment where you care about those players, you're not going to be able to do that.' He was aware, too, of striking a balance between asking professional commitment of players to achieve excellent results and knowing that, without the accompanying pay, those players were juggling a lot. 'If you're paying somebody £100,000 a week, for example, you can kind of dictate what they're doing. If you're not paying them anything, you have to be more conscious of the things in their life. I had to be conscious of whether players had studies or exams or work commitments they had to adhere to.' (Sermanni famously gave up his business-class seat and sat in Shipard's cattle-class seat on one tour so she could complete her HSC maths exam. 'Every now and again [assistant coach Robbie Hooker] would come up and check on me with this big grin on his face,' Shipard recalls.)

'The other part of it that's important is that the families are part of it as well. The families are often the ones picking up some of the slack, particularly some of the financial slack, to allow the players to do what they do,' Sermanni continues. 'So for me as a coach, it's important that the families are involved in the process.'

Those families were central to the Matildas' tournament experience. Although the team's profile was starting to rise back home, the touring supporters were largely confined to their families. The Polkinghornes, for example, are a fixture on the Women's World Cup supporter circuit now, but 2007 was their first Women's World Cup. Even then, it was only father Tony who travelled. Tony Polkinghorne passed away in 2019, but in a serendipitous twist you can see him on screen in the opening moments of the *Never Say Die* documentary, when the camera cuts to the crowd after Salisbury scores against Canada. 'If you look to the left of the video, it's Dad there throwing an inflatable kangaroo around,' Tom Polkinghorne says, explaining that that kangaroo has been to every Women's World Cup since. 'I think we had issues with it in Canada in 2015 because they wouldn't let us take it in to the stadium; in one of the games it had a trip to the cloakroom.'

McShea was fortunate that her parents came to pretty much all of the tournaments she played in, including 2007. 'I don't think they missed any. Obviously they were quite proud parents, and it sort of made up for all those nights Dad and Mum spent eating their dinner in the car watching me train.' She recalls that the 2007 trip itself was really well planned and executed, balancing tournament focus with grounding downtime: 'They even organised team dinners where we went to a Mexican restaurant with our families to have some normality, to hang out with the people who are important to you and share that experience with them.'

Bizarrely, some of the Matildas' travelling supporters had to watch the rescheduled Canada match from afar. 'A lot of our parents and our supporters' group who had come from Australia ended up missing that game because they timed it to pretty much leave straight after,' McShea says. The 24-hour delay and inability to rejig travel plans meant they had already left town. Still, that was an anomaly. And when they were there, they got to experience fun, if slightly random, recreational activities.

McShea recalls a trip to Chengdu's panda research and rehabilitation centre: 'It was hilarious, because we had an armed guard. We were all just shaking our heads at this guy with a semi-automatic gun walking through a panda park, escorting us like we were celebrities. It was one of those funny moments where you're like, "We're meant to be enjoying the wildlife and this guy's got a gun."'

Ferguson smiles at the recollection. 'We went there and we had our bloody security guards with their big guns,' she says. She even got photos with the guards. 'Pandas are great, but oh my god, the height of laziness.' She remembers one in particular, reclining on its back, sleepily 'chewing bamboo in this nice little air-conditioned palace' and defecating where it lay. 'Pandas have the life. Pandas have got life fucking nailed.'

The panda park wasn't the only time the team had escorts. 'They would literally stop the traffic and there'd be police cars escorting us to the stadium,' McShea says. She acknowledges that they probably didn't need the escorts but says it was nice of the organisers and made the team feel special. 'Obviously the Chinese people wanted to put on a good show, and show they were really looking after us. I remember Bubs [Melissa Barbieri] had her wallet pickpocketed out of her backpack. We went back and reported it, and I think within three hours they had the wallet back, which was just crazy.'

'My wallet being stolen was a big one,' Barbieri agrees, 'because I felt like it was a national incident.' She had gone on the team walk with her bum bag slung around her shoulder. Mid-walk, she'd had an eerie feeling someone was behind her. 'Obviously it was true, because when I swung the bum bag around the zip was open. They are the best-of-the-best pickpocketers, because there's people everywhere.' Barbieri told the hotel staff what had happened and was quickly taken to a boardroom with an interpreter where she was asked so many questions it felt like an interrogation. Then she went back to her room and cancelled all her cards. She was called back to the boardroom within a few hours. 'This time there were about forty police officers,' she says. And they presented her with her wallet. The money was gone, but she was stunned they'd managed to recover it, and so incredibly quickly. 'All good?' they asked. 'Happy?' Barbieri asked how they'd found the wallet so speedily. They said, 'We have CCTV everywhere.'

Team walks aside, and in addition to seeking out the best coffee, players used to seek out pirate DVDs, which were selling for the equivalent of $1. 'That used to be the big mission. We'd go to a new town and wander round and be like, "DVD, DVD,"' McShea says. 'We'd be back in our rooms checking them and if the quality wasn't good enough, we'd march back out and swap them. Some trips, you'd come home with, like, 300 of the latest DVDs.' She recalls a time when they ventured down a labyrinth of back streets and walked through someone's kitchen in single-minded DVD pursuit. 'When we look back at it, we think, *Oh gee, that could have ended badly. They could have taken us away or something*",' McShea says.

Another day there was a note at the hotel that said, 'If there's air raid alarm at 2 p.m., don't be concerned'—which is precisely the kind of note that would make you concerned. The whole thing did, as one person termed it, 'seem very Cold War', but it added to the tournament experience. Likewise the different hotel set-up at the quarter-final stage. 'We checked into the hotel and it just happened to be that little bit better than the one we'd been staying in, and there was extra security around the US team, so there was X-ray security to get in,' Beerworth says. The lower profile Australians didn't really need the security. What they did need were baths full of ice to complete their recovery. Such ice quantities and application were foreign concepts to that hotel, which supplied the team with exorbitantly priced ice adequate to fill a cup, not a bath.

The 2007 tournament proved game-changing for more than just players and fans. Kate Jacewicz is now a central figure of the modern Australian refereeing era, but she first became aware of the potential of representing her country as a referee at a Women's World Cup when she heard that Tammy Ogston, for whom she had previously been an assistant, had been appointed to whistle the final. Through that, Ogston became the first Australian referee, woman or man, to officiate a World Cup final. (She had actually told her husband not to travel over as she didn't believe there was any chance that she, a referee from footballing minnow Australia, would be awarded the coveted gig.) Jacewicz knew she had to find a way to watch the match and was pleasantly surprised to find SBS broadcasting it. Seeing Ogston in action made the possibility of refereeing at the highest level seem not only possible but achievable. That achievable possibility became reality when Jacewicz was selected as a 2019 Women's World Cup referee.

Tuning in to the Women's World Cup for the first time, too, was Danielle Warby, who would go on to become a leading women's sports advocate. 'I still get chills when I think about Cheryl Salisbury's goal against Canada,' she says. 'It wasn't pretty and Lisa De Vanna most certainly did not pass the ball! But it meant so much, getting us out of the group stage for the first time.' Warby created her own website, *Sporting Sheilas*, in an effort to provide media coverage of sportswomen otherwise overlooked by media. 'Alt[ernative] media wasn't really a thing, so getting anything from the sports was almost impossible. Not just because they were probably like, "Who is this upstart?", but because they didn't know what was happening on the women's side of the game.'

Indeed, women's football was so poorly documented, or what was documented was fragmented, that Warby and peers such as Ann Odong provided crucial coverage for more than a decade in the absence of major media networks showing significant interest. Their work demonstrated that women's football stories were worth telling and that there was an audience for them. Still, it was a tricky space to operate in. 'This one is quite complicated, and I've changed my views over the years,' Warby says. 'I've come to realise that doing all the work we did for free just perpetuated the culture of free labour around women's sports media.' But no regrets, she says. (To give credit where credit's due, there were few other options at the time to fill the void when paid major media wasn't at the time interested in doing so. Without Warby's and Odong's work, women's football would have had scant to no media coverage at all. Their contributions are utterly invaluable.)

That experience and her recently completed Master's degree researching women in sports leadership inform Warby's current work. 'The dial has not shifted at all around the percentage of media coverage. Yes, there's more women's sport, but there's more of everything,' she says. 'Essentially my goal now is not to create more content/media—it's to change the systems.' That systemic change includes co-founding women's sport collective *Siren*, which recently partnered with the ABC to help increase women's sports media coverage and also provide development pathways and support to emerging women and non-binary sportswriters. In a paid capacity, of course. (While *Siren* does publish some work on its site, *Siren* co-founder Dr Kasey Symons likens the collective to being 'the wing defence [netball position] of women's sport. We're on the court, we're here if you need, but we're not where the ball should end up.' That is, *Siren* can and will pay to publish the work under its umbrella, but it'll primarily endeavour to help sportswriters to secure publication with paying major media platforms that boast significant audiences and reach. Under that innovative approach, *Siren* doesn't so much compete with major media as leverage platforms and networks to support and advance emerging sports content producers' careers. In doing so, it helps drive the aforementioned systemic change.) The ABC is aiming for 50:50 contribution and representation of women's and men's sports.

Warby is right about there being plenty more work to be done to move the lever of women's sports coverage. A three-decade-long study of women's sports media coverage found that media organisations generally adopt a 'one and done' approach: a token, relatively generic, single women's sports story to tick the box and then a succession of apparently more interesting, more in-depth men's sports stories.[1] (As US sociology professor Michael Messner termed it, 'men's sports are the appetizer, the main course and the dessert'; women's sports are framed as 'eat your vegetables'.[2])

In Australia, women's sport receives barely double-digit percentages of the media coverage men's sport does. Around the time the Matildas became the country's most successful football team, they received 20 per cent of the coverage the Socceroos did, and female horses famously received more write-ups than female humans did.[3] Worldwide, women primarily receive single-digit coverage. In New Zealand, that figure grew from 11 per cent in 2011 to 15 per cent in 2021, a still-too-low figure that actually makes New Zealand one of the best performers in the world in this area. It's not just the stories written about women that need an increase, but also the stories written by women, with just 20 per cent of New Zealand by-lines going to women—a figure comparable to what is occurring worldwide.[4]

Consideration needs to be given, too, to who is quoted in articles. Women in Leadership Australia (WILA) research found that women were quoted in 31 per cent of articles overall, broken down to being in 50 per cent of articles written by women and 37 per cent in articles written by men. That same research identified that almost 90 per cent of articles written about sport were written by men.[5] Perhaps related to this is that most football fans are presumed to be men (specifically, cisgendered heterosexual white men); most football researchers and writers actually *are* men.[6] The corollary is that there's a lived experience and a diversity of storytelling we're not yet seeing; nor have we figured out how to establish a wholly inclusive environment to facilitate such diversity.[7] The upside to these too-low figures is that we now have baseline data and it's being scrutinised. The pressure is on media outlets to improve.

★ ★ ★

In *Never Say Die*, Sermanni presciently tells the documentary makers—and by proxy, the audience—that what we should be focusing on is that women's football is a growth sport in the country by a large margin; that if resourced properly, women's football can make enormous strides. Those strides began and began to be recognised around 2007: Sermanni was named Asian Football Confederation (AFC) Coach of the Year, Ogston was named AFC Women's Referee of the Year, and Collette McCallum finished second runner-up for AFC Player of the Year and her teammates Cheryl Salisbury and Heather Garriock were longlisted. 'From an individual point of view, I was just happy when the team went well,' Garriock says of the longlisting. 'We spent a lot of time losing in the early 2000s. To be able to win games, and major games on the world stage, that was important to me.'

After Barrow had managed to edit the documentary footage down to a too-short fifty-two minutes, the Matildas and their families attended *Never Say Die*'s opening night. It was a 'jam-packed' event, Barrow says, 'and it was just incredible, because they could see that themselves being up there on the silver screen was going to have an impact for the future'.

That impact and future were realised with the establishment of a domestic league that acts as a training ground and launching pad for future Matildas' careers. Former Matilda and at the time recently appointed FFA board member Moya Dodd had attended the 2007 tournament as an Australian official, 'sitting between Austria and Aruba'. Alongside Sermanni and other women's football administrators, she advocated for leveraging the team's success and increased profile to shore up Australia's development foundations. 'You know, we've reached the last eight in the world, everyone else is going to accelerate, we have to progress here, we have to put the pedal to the metal and retain or improve on where we are,' Dodd says of the arguments they made. 'We don't want to look back and say, "This is the high-water mark of Australian women's football, making the last eight." We made the last eight in 1988. That cannot be good enough. That cannot be our goal.'

Their advocacy was persuasive: the W-League kicked off in 2008, the establishment of which Dodd believes is what enabled the Matildas to become the first Australian team, women or men, to win the Asian Cup just two years later.

7

2011:
THE GOLDEN GENERATION

T HE PREVIOUS TIME Australia and Brazil had met in a Women's
World Cup, Australia had fielded a mature, experienced team
with a number of players giving the sudden-death quarter-final
match their all before transitioning to retirement. One goal had
been the only separation between the two nations in that 5-goal
thriller. Four years on, the same teams were meeting, this time for
their first group-stage game of the 2011 Women's World Cup. One
team comprised primarily the same intimidating names: Formiga,
Cristiane, Marta. The other team was considerably less recognisable,
less experienced and a lot more youthful. In fact, it turned out to
be the tournament's youngest team on average.

The player specifically tasked with marking Marta was a relatively unknown, untested sixteen-year-old so oblivious to who
Marta was that she was neither awestruck nor intimidated. The
match was the mood-setter of the tournament and would dictate
the Matildas' subsequent games' strategies. Had the Marta match-
up gone wrong, it could have been disastrous. But the ever-steady
Tom Sermanni, who became the first coach to take the same team
to a World Cup three times (1995, 2007 and 2011), knew Caitlin

Foord would be fine when she shrugged at his instructions. To Foord, Marta was just another player she had to disrupt.

'Foordy came into the tournament as probably the most hyped youngster in the team,' former Matildas media officer Mark Jensen explains. 'I think everyone was a little surprised when she was given the job on Marta, but Tom and the coaching staff had full belief in her. From the whistle, Caitlin looked like she had a laser on Marta's back. She chased her everywhere and gave her absolutely nothing—a couple of times her ball-winning and -running created our most exciting attacking moments. Caitlin was immense that day ... In 2011 Marta was at the peak of her powers and feared in the football world. Foordy had no fear, probably helped by her age and limited exposure to world football at that stage.'

The Matildas lost that match 1–0; a single goal was again the only separation between the teams. With more time on the clock or on another day, the Matildas might have walked away victors. Perhaps having made selectors sit up with her nonchalant, fearless Marta containment, Foord was later named the Young Player of the Tournament. Her teammate Elise Kellond-Knight was named in the All Stars team. (That said, Kellond-Knight was pretty humble about being named in the team. 'It was so low key I didn't even know it existed. I didn't know much about anything at that point,' she says. 'I think someone else ended up telling me that it was announced and I still didn't really understand what it was. I mean, the women's game didn't really have the recognition that it does now, so I didn't really make a big deal of it. I still don't.')

That era and its Asian Cup lead-up marked the emergence of what we now call the 'golden generation'—a group of players whose advent was precipitated by the development programs and the greater experience gained from Australia joining the Asian confederation. While not yet able to train full time, they were, courtesy of improved funding and opportunity, able to spend more time than their predecessors enhancing their skills and gaining essential international experience. It showed. Foord and Kellond-Knight, along with teammates including Sam Kerr, Emily van Egmond,

Alanna Kennedy and Tameka Yallop (née Butt), were the 'youth with experience' Alicia Ferguson referred to. In some ways, they also hastened her retirement.

'I remember being in a training session and Tameka Butt and Elise Kellond-Knight had come in and we were doing two-v-two with me and Shorty [Kate McShea]. And these two were only fourteen or fifteen and they were running rings around us,' says Ferguson. 'I remember stopping and going to Shorty, "I think I'm done. I think I'm done. You see that next generation? I've had a really good run, but these youngsters are the future and it's time for me to walk away."' She elected to retire shortly afterwards.

Ferguson might have ended her playing career, but she commentated the 2011 Women's World Cup. That era was the beginning of women entering punditry and forging paid post-playing media-production careers. The latter is a lesser-known pathway that Ferguson is keen to showcase and help other former players pursue. She has former Matildas teammate Julie Murray to thank for her start.

Sports broadcaster ESPN was setting up a mobile studio to follow the USWNT around Germany and was looking for international talent to co-commentate with the American legends. The producer approached Murray as they knew her from her WUSA days, but she was already booked for FIFA gigs. She suggested Ferguson.

Ferguson was working at Queensland Health at the time and doing W-League co-commentary on weekends for ABC-TV. With Joseph Mayers' help, she collated some clips and uploaded them to YouTube. The ESPN producer called her at work and offered her the job the very next day. 'I was like, "Sweet, that sounds cool, I'll do that,"' Ferguson says. 'So they flew me over to Bristol, Connecticut, to the ESPN campus for a one-day seminar.' She found herself in a room with such legends as former German player Viola Odebrecht and former USWNT superstars Mia Hamm, Bri Scurry and Julie Foudy. 'I mean, I was sitting between [USWNT greats] Kate Markgraf and Brandi Chastain, I think. I might have been like, *How have I got here?* But the best part of the story is all these highlights.' The ESPN team projected promotional teasers showing highlights of each commentator's playing career, with a hyperbolic voiceover saying things like 'This is our talent. This is our talent roster. This is what's happening.' Ferguson says, 'The clip of me was basically me getting sent off, and then there was a second, really quick clip … and the second clip wasn't even of me. It was of a teammate, April Mann. I was like, "That's so funny. It's not even me. Brilliant."' (As Ferguson notes, the team wouldn't have been able to find much footage of her, both because she played the workhorse holding-midfielder role—which isn't the kind of position that sees a player scoring goals and turning up in highlight reels—and because there isn't much footage of Australia from that time in general.)

The Germany experience was what Ferguson terms 'a dream job', and it kickstarted her next career. She also met her husband on that trip, but it's not the romantic tale you'd expect. He was the ESPN UK executive producer. 'They asked him to look after the mobile studio around Germany and he was really cranky because it meant he didn't have a summer off, he wouldn't have any holidays,' Ferguson says. Obviously, he eventually got over it.

★ ★ ★

'I think 2011 was the first time, in media circles and football circles anyway, that we realised the Matildas could really do something and go far in the World Cup,' SBS journalist turned academic Vitor Sobral says. 'I know 2007 was the first time we got through— I remember that famous celebration for Cheryl Salisbury—but that was kind of unexpected. In 2011 it was "Hang on, we've got this really good young generation coming through. This team could do something."'

It certainly seemed so. The first hint came a year before the tour-nament, when the Matildas' Women's World Cup qualification again hinged on performing well in the Women's Asian Cup. They didn't just make the Asian Cup final this time round, though—they won it 5–4 on penalties during a match with rain so unrelentingly heavy and a pitch so waterlogged and muddy it's a wonder they were able to see straight or extract their sunken boots to kick the ball. That win, which saw them surpass their 2006 result, made them the first Australian team, women's or men's, to win the Asian Cup. Off the back of that performance, Kate Gill became the first Australian player to be named Asian Women's Player of the Year.

Recognising such accomplishments and potential, but nonetheless in a big move for the time, *FourFourTwo Australia* magazine featured Matildas Thea Slatyer, Melissa Barbieri, Sam Kerr, Kyah Simon and Sarah Walsh on its cover and in a twelve-page article previewing the team and the tournament. It was the first of the seventeen *FourFourTwo* franchises to feature a national women's team on the cover.

'We'd been speaking to *FourFourTwo* journalist Aidan Ormond about doing a cover for the World Cup,' Jensen recalls. 'I think he caught up with Sarah Walsh for it, too (she just missed the tournament due to injury), and it happened pretty organically. It was done long before the team was selected, and unfortunately Thea [Slatyer] and Walshy didn't go to Germany. We wanted to cover the group from a legacy to the rising stars.'

'The global cover story for that month was focused on young emerging male talent, which I didn't think was particularly strong for Australia,' publisher Andy Jackson explains. 'So we hatched the idea to run a split cover—where the content within the magazine is exactly the same but you create two covers to appeal to different audiences … In the end, we relegated the global cover story to around 20 per cent of the issues printed, so the overwhelming majority of magazines on the newsstands in Australia that month had the Matildas loud and proud on the cover, and we devoted more pages to the Matildas inside the mag than any other feature.'

For Ormond, working with the Matildas was a 'refreshing change' from the men's game and the more guarded professional male footballers. 'I thought, *One day, Australia will love these players,*' Ormond says. 'The shoot itself was like most I'd watched with *FourFourTwo* and other outlets: different poses, various angles, with the ball, without, while the player stands on a pristine-white cyclorama in their newly pressed kit … What I remember the most was how I felt. Twelve years earlier my publisher had aggressively yelled and screamed at me for arranging a modest photo shoot of a female footballer—the legendary Julie Murray, at the time an absolute star in Australia and

1988 pilot Women's World Cup team (courtesy Moya Dodd)

1991 Oceania Women's World Cup qualification tournament team (courtesy Sonia Gegenhuber)

1991 New Zealand Women's World Cup team bus and motorcycle escort (Wendy Henderson)

1991 New Zealand team about to take the pitch (Wendy Henderson)

In Russia on the 1995 pre–Women's World Cup European tour—the bus and plane on the runway where the players passed time playing cricket (Sacha Wainwright)

The players seated on bench seats either side of their luggage—the only windows were at the front of the plane (Sacha Wainwright)

Alison Leigh Forman and Jane Oakley in team tracksuits, 1995 (Alison Leigh Forman)

On tour in the team tracksuits, 1995 (Alison Leigh Forman)

The Matildas receive and autograph
fans' supporter materials, including a
'Save WUSA' sign, 2003
(Joseph Mayers)

The Australian and Chinese starting teams during the pre-match anthems, 2003 (Joseph Mayers)

Lisa DeVanna celebrates scoring a goal at the 2007 Women's World Cup while Collette McCallum runs up to congratulate her, 2007 (Joseph Mayers)

Clare Polkinghorne and Sarah Walsh contest the ball in the Ghana game, 2007 (Joseph Mayers)

Starting XI team photo before the quarter final against Brazil, 2007 (Joseph Mayers)

Heather Garriock, Lauren Colthorpe and Thea Slatyer in action in the Norway game, 2007 (Joseph Mayers)

Matildas Di Alagich, Danielle Small, Clare Polkinghorne, Collette McCallum and Joey Peters celebrate pitchside, 2007 (Joseph Mayers)

Matildas players celebrate on the sidelines, 2011 (Joseph Mayers)

Family, friends and fans support the team with Australian colours, flags, inflatable and soft toy kangaroos and homemade signs, 2011 (Joseph Mayers)

FourFourTwo Australia, July 2011 (courtesy *FourFourTwo Australia*)

Australian fans line the street to show their support for the Matildas, 2015 (Joseph Mayers)

Striker Lisa De Vanna in a foot race against Swedish player Elin Rubensson, 2015
(Joseph Mayers)

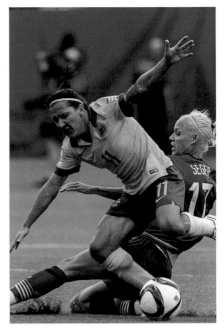

Striker Kyah Simon celebrates scoring, 2015 (Joseph Mayers)

Striker Lisa DeVanna is tackled by Sweden's Caroline Seger, 2015 (Joseph Mayers)

The Matildas celebrate after defeating Brazil to advance to the quarter finals against Japan, 2015 (Joseph Mayers)

Matildas 2019 Women's World Cup team (Rachel Bach/By The White Line)

Football fan and agent Fatima Flores wearing her Matildas 'Spew 2.0' jersey and showcasing her 'Suck on that one' shirt, 2019 (Rachel Bach/By The White Line)

Sam Kerr and Steph Catley celebrate at the final whistle after the Matildas completed their 'Miracle at Montpellier' comeback against Brazil, 2019 (Rachel Bach/By The White Line)

Matildas Emily Gielnik (foreground) and Steph Catley and Alanna Kennedy (background, left to right) celebrate scoring against Norway, 2019 (Rachel Bach/By The White Line)

The Croissants and their crocodile inside the stadium, 2019 (The Croissants)

The Croissants in their Statue of Liberty US supporter costumes, 2019 (The Croissants)

The Croissants in their 'pay me in pasta' Italy supporter costumes, 2019 (The Croissants)

Matilda Chloe Logarzo is comforted by her mother after the Matildas exit the tournament, 2019 (Rachel Bach/By The White Line)

Rebekah Stott, Steph Catley, Ellie Carpenter and Kyah Simon participate in the 2023 bid promotion (Ann Odong/Football Australia)

Player bid ambassadors Football Fern Rebekah Stott and Matilda Steph Catley (Ann Odong/Football Australia)

Sam Kerr's backflip goalscoring celebration projected on the Sydney Opera House (Ann Odong/Football Australia)

The moment Australia and New Zealand were announced as the 2023 Women's World Cup hosts. Jumping vertically are bid organiser Jane Fernandez and Matilda Alanna Kennedy (Ann Odong/Football Australia)

Matilda Steph Catley embraces fellow Matildas Lydia Williams and Alanna Kennedy in celebration. To the right: Football Fern Rebekah Stott (Ann Odong/Football Australia) rightly described as the female Harry Kewell—on the back cover of a weekly soccer newspaper I edited. It wasn't a pleasant experience getting the "hairdryer" treatment [a verbal tirade akin to having a hairdryer blowing in your face] from a gentleman clearly from a different era to me.' (Such a publisher was reminiscent of those who were in the media when players like Sacha Wainwright were seeking out women's football stories—the market Ormond instinctively knew existed. The main publication Wainwright read at that time was *Australian and British Soccer Weekly*. She says, 'I used to walk from the law firm to the local newsagency each week and open it up, and there'd be one page of women's football.')

But Ormond had persevered in trying to profile the women's game. 'And here I was, ten years later, working with another publisher, who partnered with Nike to bring this iconic cover to life, and he was actually telling us, "This is our next front cover." I felt proud of how far our female footballers—let's just call them footballers—had come, and the new era of football publishers.'

'Putting them on the cover was important, but I felt that the coverline was also hugely important and significant,' Jackson says. 'I didn't want it to appear tokenistic or patronising in any way, and so very quickly I had the idea that the coverline should be "Meet Australia's Best Football Team". It was both factual in terms of FIFA rankings [and the Matildas' 2010 Asian Cup win] and subtly provocative, and the decision to add World Cup interviews without reference to "Women's" was also deliberate. So we put a women's team on the cover for the first time, but not in an apologetic way, and the word "women" is absent from the cover, which was important to us too.

'The response was fantastic from all quarters, and it's one of those few times in your professional life where you can point to something you're not only proud of but that was also an important moment in time. It would be a further eight years and two World Cups before the UK edition put the Lionesses on the front cover, ahead of the 2019 World Cup.'

While the *FourFourTwo Australia* cover was an enormous stride forward, as with most things in women's football at that time it was completed with a modest budget. As well as being the talent, the players were their own stylists, requiring, as Slatyer jokes, 'a group of Matildas etiquette-class dropouts to do our own and each other's make-up'. One of her abiding memories from the day is doing Sam Kerr's mascara.

Slatyer also recalls, 'Bubs, myself and Aivi Luik did another shoot for *Alpha* magazine and we were given Nike sports bras and shorts to wear. They didn't brief us that we would be shirtless, leaving me and Bubs to complain that we didn't have enough time to prepare our stomach muscles for shooting. A gallant and oozing-with-confidence Aivi removed her shirt to reveal a ripped and perfect sixpack that was greeted with awe by the group of female stylists and make-up artists. "How many sit-ups do you do a day?" they eagerly asked her. Aivi very modestly shrugged it off and a defiant Bubs announced, "Don't expect the rest of us to look like that!"'

'There were a lot of magazine opportunities at the time,' Jensen recalls. 'I think the *Women's Health* feature was the best in terms of getting the players mainstream attention. Felicity Harley [editor at the time] was really supportive of the concept and we shot it in Western Sydney at a grassroots field with black-oil sidelines and square goalposts. *Women's Health* went all-out with the shoot and decided to juxtapose the football side with a bit more style, going for a "little black dress" football edition ... At the time we were trying to get the players as much exposure as possible in what was still a thriving magazine/media landscape. With the advent of digital advertising this quickly changed, but with *Women's Health*, *Alpha*, *FourFourTwo*, *New Idea* and others, there was a solid lead-up to the tournament back when the Matildas weren't a household name like they are today.'

★ ★ ★

Germany embraced the 2011 tournament and 'ran it like a real World Cup', Sermanni says. He's pointing to the professionalism and esteem with which players and teams were treated, and the thoroughness with which all aspects of the tournament were planned and executed. The Matildas left Australia kitted out in classy formal outfits courtesy of designer Carla Zampatti, and the German hosts provided an equally mature and polished tournament experience. Former Brisbane Roar player Rebecca Price, who is now an academic, had an equivalent fan experience: 'It was really moving. You saw everything coming together, whereas you normally heard that women's sport was a liability, it was philanthropy [to support it].' Instead, she witnessed the German fans getting behind the teams, even if it was clear they were diehard football fans but perhaps not entirely familiar with women's football. 'The Germans in the crowd really appreciated skill. Any time a player took on another player, they would applaud that.' She also learned a thing or two about German football etiquette. 'For example, make sure you're seated [when] the teams walk out ... I remember sitting down late and they were not happy about it.'

Sobral recalls the Matildas travelling to the group-stage game in Bochum. The hotel was right next to the stadium, but the team still had to get the bus. It was illustrative of the pomp and ceremony not normally seen around such an egoless team. The self-sufficient Matildas would carry not just their own luggage but also gear bags; they would physically pick up and move goalposts as required during training sessions; and of course they would work hours in physically demanding casual jobs, topping and tailing paid work with training. Here they were being driven a matter of metres—they could have walked to the stadium quicker and more directly than catching the bus. It signalled the step up a professionally run World Cup brings, even if it was slightly ridiculous—especially as the people primarily waiting around the hotel to wish them well and witnessing that bus trip were family and friends and a smattering of Australian media whom the team knew well. Sobral recalls, 'It was hilarious. That was one of the greatest moments of the World Cup.'

Former Matildas manager Jo Fernandes remembers that moment and understands the machinations behind it. 'The hotel had to be outside the security boundary of the stadium. You couldn't just have everyone hop off and walk through, because that's where the spectators were coming as well. So it's all to do with security and accreditation control.' In short, there needed to be clear delineation and no mingling. But she agrees it was brilliant: 'The hotel was here but the bus had to go up the road a bit, go round a roundabout and come back. So it had to drive *away* and then come back,' she laughs. 'It actually made the journey about 100 metres, I think.'

Dual international Ellyse Perry, who has represented Australia in both cricket and football World Cups, doesn't remember the bus moment specifically, but she recognises the kind of moment it was and the contrast with women's sports' usual pragmatism and self-reliance. 'Things happen in World Cups that add grandeur to the event. You feel like this weirdly protected species, when you're definitely not. Behind the closed doors, you're still doing everything for yourself.'

Staff noticed the difference, too. Physiotherapist Lauren Hanna (née Cramer) contrasts having been on lots of trips in countries where hotels were hit and miss and the team was travelling in relative anonymity, to suddenly going to a tournament where they were travelling on a bus with World Cup and country-specific branding and everyone not only knew who you were but wanted your autograph. 'It's that next level. It's the sort of stuff you see with the really elite and professional teams, but you hadn't really experienced that full gamut until you went to a World Cup or an Olympics or a big tournament like that. Even as a staff member, you felt this was palpable, this was different. Yes, it's the same stuff day to day, but it felt like it meant a lot more.'

That 'more' ranged from big things like more fan interest because there was more media about the tournament as a whole, to little things that gave it a personal touch. Not unlike the 1991 tournament, where players received M&M's packets on their pillows, the teams received different souvenirs from each hotel they stayed in. As Hanna relates, 'Some of them were pens, some of them things you could hook on your backpack, and one of them was a little music box that played Mozart.'

★ ★ ★

Kate Gill missed the 2011 tournament with an ACL injury. She travelled to the tournament in an ambassadorial role, but that would have done little to temper the disappointment of being Asia's best footballer and missing the chance to test herself against the rest of the world's best. A knee injury again prevented Thea Slatyer from participating in a World Cup on the eve of the tournament itself. In addition to battling burnout and anaemia bouts, she had to have a troublesome 10-millimetre piece of floating cartilage surgically removed from her knee just weeks before final selections. She rushed back to full competition, but the staff were wary of risking her, so Slatyer missed the second of three Women's World Cups for which she was in contention. She returned for the Olympic qualifiers a few months later, but the tight tournament scheduling and the wear-and-tear that entailed were brutal. Soon after, Slatyer elected to retire.

Laura Brock (née Alleway) hadn't expected to be at the tournament, but she was stoked about her surprise inclusion. Brock's is another tale of perseverance. She went from non-state selection and spending not insignificant time warming the W-League bench to Women's World Cup inclusion after Sermanni spotted her and elevated her to the national team. 'I think that taught me resilience, and that failing isn't necessarily a bad thing if you let it fuel your fire to work harder,' she says. 'The other thing it taught me was that not all coaches are going to appreciate what you bring to the table. You learn to put the team first and accept that your qualities might not be what the team needs at the time.'

The 2011 team illustrated tenacity not just by players but also by parents. Foord's mother, Simone, had for years driven back and forth between Wollongong and Sydney to facilitate her daughter's football dream. This was despite others' urging that it was perhaps a bit much and she should let it go. It was equivalent to the road-tripping cusp player Ash Sykes' family was doing from Dubbo and Ellie Carpenter's family would later do back and forth from their Cowra base. 'Yes, lots of travelling for our parents,' Sykes agrees of that parental sacrifice. 'Once, we [Sykes and twin sister Nicole] got identified through the system there were training camps most weekends or every second weekend in either Sydney or Canberra, which was five hours away. There was a season we played for

Bathurst in the Sydney NPL and we travelled two-and-a-half hours one way for training or home games, and five hours for the away games in Sydney. We could only manage that for one season as it was a lot!'

She recalls, 'Being from a regional area came with lots of challenges. Often there are some very talented players out there, but it's difficult to identify them and then provide a supportive training environment so that they develop at the same rate as other players their age. Most people end up making the move to Sydney to do this, but we decided to finish school at home. I think I was really lucky to have Nicole around to push each other forward and someone to train with. We were always super competitive with each other no matter what sport it was and this was an easy motivator in any situation to push yourself harder. We're obviously very close and getting to share many opportunities together in football just strengthened that bond.'

Sykes also notes that her community chipped in to supplement all the driving her parents were doing: 'Regional communities have a great way of bonding together to help each other out. We had a group of girls to train with a couple of times a week and carpool to state camps, etc. when we were younger, as well as a men's team, the Dubbo Bulls, who provided a valuable training environment for us while we were at home during the week or in between Young Matildas/Matildas camps. [The latter is the kind of training opportunity Moya Dodd mentioned she wished she'd had.] I'll always be proud of where I came from and grateful to those who helped that part of the journey.'

Foord's and the other young players' composed debuts remain some of former Matildas physiotherapist Kate Beerworth's standout tournament moments: 'That tournament we had those four sixteen-year-olds and that first game when Caitlin Foord didn't even know who Marta was and absolutely had her measure. You look back now and that was extraordinary. She just went out there without fear, which I think was such an excellent quality to have.' Of all the young guns, she says, 'They were impressive. I think back to myself as a sixteen-year-old, and wow.'

The players' collectedness is perhaps even more surprising given how much was unfolding on and off the pitch. Controversy that alluded to wider cultural issues began in the Matildas group even before the tournament began. FIFA suspended Equatorial Guinea striker Jade Boho because she had represented Spain in the preceding five years (FIFA has strict rules around switching representative allegiances—in short, it discourages it); three other Equatorial Guinea players were accused of being men. While the headline arguably framed this as the 61st-ranked country trying to field male players to gain an unfair advantage, the incident raised uncomfortable questions around gender, 'femininity' and homophobia.

The Equatorial Guinea game ultimately proved contentious, but not because of the players' purported gender. 'The other interesting thing was the handball,' Beerworth says. 'It was quite extraordinary. I don't think anyone could believe it. We were all on the bench thinking, *Did we actually just see that?*' She's referring to the puzzling moment when an Equatorial Guinea defender didn't just accidentally have hand contact with the ball in the box, she actually caught it, held it for a second or two, then dropped it. It should have been a penalty, but the referee and assistant referee completely missed it. 'Well. I don't think anyone could quite believe it. It was clear as day,' Jensen concurs. 'Everyone was just in a bit of shock—[striker] Leena [Khamis] especially, [and] Sam [Kerr] just standing with her mouth open, perplexed, pointing at what had happened.'

All round, the game was tough and could easily have derailed the Matildas' progression prospects had they not managed to score 3 goals to Equatorial Guinea's 2. Both Sermanni and Jensen agree that VAR, which wouldn't be introduced until 2019, would have been useful. 'So bizarre,' Jensen says. 'It would have been a lot worse had we not gotten the three points, however. Football, eh?'

'It was a physical game. I think it's the nature of football that there are such different playing styles around the world, but that was a very, very physical game,' Beerworth says. 'We were certainly, from a medical and a coaching point of view, pleased to get out of that one relatively unscathed.' For her part, Sally Shipard recalls, 'I had a feral cork in my thigh.'

The Equatorial Guinea game wasn't the tournament's weirdest moment. Five of the North Korean players failed drug tests partway through the group stage. North Korean officials' explanations included that the team had accidentally ingested steroids as part of traditional Chinese medicine incorporating musk-deer glands, a remedy purportedly designed to aid players who had been struck by lightning at a pre-tournament training camp. North Korea were disqualified, fined and banned from the 2014 Asian Cup and the 2015 Women's World Cup.

The North Korean explanation drew incredulity, but simultaneously sat—sits—uncomfortably. 'You don't know how the players are getting treated or if they have any rights about what they put into their bodies. So I do feel for them,' Hanna says. 'I think what was difficult for our players was that it always comes down to what's fair. Whether the Korean players knew it or not, if it's systematic doping then it's not fair for the people you're competing against.'

The Matildas felt the injustice even more keenly at the Olympic qualifiers less than two months later. Astoundingly, there was no drug testing at that tournament and Australia narrowly missed out on qualifying for the Olympics on goal difference. North Korea, despite the recent failed drug tests and bans, attended the Olympics instead.

★ ★ ★

No matter the tournament, drug testing falls into the category of something to be endured. And it's an aspect of tournaments that is largely invisible to fans. After each game, two or even three players are tested. The drug testers have to accompany them at all times to ensure the players don't substitute their own urine with someone else's. 'They have to be with them until they produce a specimen,' Hanna says. 'Which is really difficult. I remember many times when the players were so dehydrated it might take them an hour or two to go to the toilet.' For games that finish at 10 p.m., that makes for returns well after midnight.

Drug tests can mess with the media's best-laid plans, too, as they did after the Matildas' group-stage win over Norway. In that match,

Kyah Simon became the first Aboriginal Australian, woman or man, to score in a World Cup. Twice. Understandably, the documentary crew following her and First Nations teammate Lydia Williams was keen to gauge her post-match thoughts.

'When Kyah scored those two goals, we waited and waited and waited because she was so dehydrated that she couldn't pee,' *No Apologies* documentary maker Ashley Morrison says. (It's a cruel irony that standout performances also invariably earn players drug-testing attention as authorities seek to determine that the players' efforts were due to talent and training.) 'We were waiting to film because here she was, the first Aboriginal woman to score in a World Cup, and it was not only one goal, it was two goals. We waited and waited. Chris, the cameraman, said, "She's never going to come out." We waited over an hour for that interview.'

Adding to the complexity of telling the tale was that the documentary crew wasn't allowed to film inside the stadiums. 'It was like, "Bloody hell, we need some footage from the games,"' Morrison explains. 'So I went to FIFA and said, "Can we have about three minutes of footage, just the goals Australia scored, especially the ones Kyah got? For three minutes, they wanted US$15,000. I was like, "You're kidding." Then it was a lot of back and forth, back and forth, and I think in the end we had to pay $5000 for three minutes.'

FIFA perhaps wasn't aware of or concerned about how lean the documentary production was. 'I remember when the editor put it together, I said, "We cannot go over the three minutes or they'll probably bloody sue me,"' Morrison recalls. 'When we watched it back, we had a stopwatch and it was actually something like 2:58. I think we had two seconds to spare.'

★ ★ ★

From drug tests to gear transport and set-ups, the logistics of a tournament are, frankly, fascinating. 'The crazy thing about World Cups is that you turn up with all those gear bags and everything and you have to quickly set up your whole medical room,' Hanna says. 'The massage tables, the first-aid kits, the bags, the gear, you're blowing up the physio balls—and you're literally there for just three days.'

At the 2011 tournament, physiotherapists Hanna and Beerworth didn't have a specific packing plan, at least not that Hanna recalls, but they did have an informal rhythm and familiarity developed from working closely. 'I was probably the person who took on that stuff and making sure everything was in its place so when you got to the next place, if someone said, "I need a bandaid", we could say, "Right, that bag, that first-aid kit, that's where it is." As long as one of us was on top of it, it worked out pretty well. I don't think we misplaced anything major, which is always good.'

That said, Hanna knows that kit management is not for her: 'Hats off to the kit people. There's no way I could do that job.' She explains that she's not great at folding clothes, and a kit person prerequisite is having perfect folding technique. Folding is the least of her concerns, though: the physios have their hands full managing the 'pee jars' they have to carry with them, as in the single-use jars players use to provide urine samples to the team doctor so the doctor can check hydration levels. (The doctor carries out the tests, but as Hanna herself acknowledges, 'You can pretty clearly see: if it's burnt orange you're in a bit of trouble, and if it's fairly opaque you're OK.')

'It's annoying for us as the physios because the pee jars are in our kits and they're this big,' Hanna says, showing a size that's between a thumb and bent forefinger about half a handspan apart, 'but when you're carrying hundreds of them, they take up so much space and they're so annoying. Every time you pack the kits, you're like: "The bloody pee jars. Where are we going to fit these?"' The single-use jars don't stack well because they have to have sealed lids to maintain sterility—you can't disassemble them and stack their like components separately. 'You'll be rummaging through kits, and pee jars will go everywhere. They don't weigh much, but they're so big and annoying. In every kit bag you're always finding different pee jars in every pocket and every corner.'

★ ★ ★

The Matildas let off steam in small moments that offset the serious task of performing at a World Cup. Perhaps the most standout off-pitch moment came from their encounter with rapper Snoop Dogg. They spotted three luxe black buses with tinted windows occupying most of the hotel's drop-off zone. Given the Australians were moving twenty-three players plus staff and gear around Germany on a single bus during the biggest women's football tournament in the world, they figured that whoever warranted having such premium and large transport must be a big deal.

Shipard and Heather Garriock solved the mystery when they stumbled across Snoop Dogg and his entourage in a lift. 'He was in there with his posse and they were all eating Maccas,' Shipard says. She and Garriock looked at each other, looked at Snoop Dogg and his entourage and did the only logical thing: they stepped into the fast-food-scented lift and nonchalantly rode to their floor. 'He just gave us this mad nod,' Shipard says.

Word spread quickly within the team and players set up camp in the hotel lobby, determined to get a photo with Snoop Dogg on his way to his gig. The preternaturally cool Snoop Dogg was the kind of upper-echelon celebrity every team member wanted be photographed with, no matter how tangential their knowledge of his oeuvre. Teigen Allen, who was a massive fan and arguably the one who should have been in such a photo, was particularly torn when he hadn't yet appeared and she was due to go upstairs for a physiotherapy treatment. The fear of missing out on the photo wasn't entirely misplaced, as it was unlikely they'd see Snoop Dogg in Australia anytime soon: just a few months prior, the government had denied him a visa to enter Australia for the MTV Video Music Awards on character grounds, citing his criminal convictions.

When he finally made his way through the lobby, his security tried to clear his path but were no match for Garriock, her slight 165-centimetre frame inversely proportional to her determination and audacity. 'Heather bailed them up!' photographer Joseph Mayers laughs. 'The security were like, "Excuse me, ma'am. You have to move." Heather was like, "No way! We've been waiting for five hours!"' It was probably more like two, but anyway it was a long time and she wasn't having it. ('In life, you don't ask, you don't get,' Garriock says of her modus operandi.)

Snoop Dogg had no idea who the women were and probably thought them fangirls rather than accomplished stars in their own right. Either way, he read the room and consented to a single photo. The Matildas had only one chance to get the shot and the lobby lighting wasn't great. Mayers instructed the players to tuck in so he could fit everyone in frame. They wrapped themselves around Snoop Dogg, their smiles camera-ready.

One shot, a bunch of people to fit in, with poor lighting and only seconds to frame, focus and shoot while being watched by impatient burly security tapping their watches sounds like a pressure moment for a photographer. 'It could have been,' Mayers agrees. 'But I was sitting there drinking and then I think every half an hour I'd snap a picture just to check the light. I was ready to go.' That said, when he saw the photo in his viewfinder, 'I was like, *Good, that turned out.*' So phew. That moment and photo, Garriock and everyone agrees, remains 'one of the highlights of the trip'. Players quickly posted the photo to their social media accounts.

★ ★ ★

It's worth noting that the 2011 tournament played out against a background of fast-growing social media channels. Instagram had been released in 2010, and the already-established Facebook surpassed 1 billion users in 2012. With women and girls overlapping Venn-diagram-like as prolific social media users and the primary Women's World Cup audience, social media was well placed to engage the target audience and amplify the event[1]—even if its use hadn't quite reached maturity, and depictions and perceptions of players remained bound by notions of and rhetoric around femininity and heteronormativity,[2] and even if FIFA and football federations hadn't yet fully grasped the concept or its implications.

If 2007 represented the start of external major media coverage, 2011 marked the start of a new, self-reliant standard operating procedure that saw players and fans begin to engage with and build audiences directly, and ultimately control the narrative—be it to promote the game, raise awareness of issues[3] or share behind-the-scenes images featuring Snoop Dogg. And they needed to. In a disappointing regression from 2007, most of the 2011 games weren't broadcast in Australia. (Just because something has been implemented once in women's football doesn't mean it's subsequently guaranteed.) Major media wouldn't realise it yet, and it would be in greater force and provide greater examples in the 2015 and 2019 Women's World Cups, but the emergence of such social media and the sophistication with which this generation of players would come to use it signalled a fork in the media-coverage and narrative-controlling road.

Although beginning to wrap their heads around telling their own stories, players and staff remained open, accessible and helpful for major media covering the tournament. Sobral recalls a story for which Sally Shipard gave them a tour of the team bus. Leading the camera down the aisle, they explained that the staff sat up the front, including Sermanni with his famous daily newspaper cross-word puzzle, while the cool-kid players sat down the back. For a joke, they put Sobral in the bathroom as if it were occupied. When they started to open the door, he said, 'Privacy, please.' The video ended with a visual gag of opening the under-bus luggage hold and Sam Kerr and Caitlin Foord popping out to surprise them. 'Could you imagine this? We put two of the biggest superstars of women's football today in the luggage hold of the team bus and did a story where Sally was taking us through the bus,' Sobral laughs. 'And they wanted to do it.' They were, indeed, keen to be part of it. It's hard to imagine men's-team players being so unaffected and adventurous.

That adventurousness definitely stemmed from the top. Sermanni himself was an active participant in an April Fool's joke to tell the team he had resigned and wouldn't be taking them to the World Cup. Sarah Walsh, one of the primary instigators of the joke, is hands-to-mouth at the recollection of it. 'It backfired bad,' she says. Players took the joke literally, possibly in part because Sermanni went full method and brought the gravitas-adding head of the AIS along for the prank. Some players were in tears. 'I do recall catching up with Tommy afterwards and saying, "We did that too well,"' Walsh says, shaking her head in disbelief.

The levity also served the coaching staff and team well tactically. Sermanni and his assistant and goalkeeping coaches Spencer

Prior and Paul Jones played games such as 'football golf' (a.k.a. 'foot golf') on the pitch prior to kick-off. Sermanni explains: 'The worst part of game day is that period at the ground before the warm-up, because there's nothing much you can do. You're sort of in limbo. So to relieve the boredom and stress we used to play football bowls or golf.' It was through one of them nearly slipping over while taking a kick during one such game that they realised how soft and slippery the just-watered pitch was. They hurried to the change room to advise the players to put on their studded boots, which provided better grip in the wet.

The takeaway of such approaches is that the Matildas had a coach who ensured they were equipped with downtime to decompress but also the tools and backing they needed to perform. 'Tommy played an integral role in the Matildas' rise, and he did that because he knew how to manage each individual player and wanted to keep players happy, but happy within reason,' Garriock says. 'I would say I was probably one of the most high-maintenance players in the team, because I had high expectations. But I knew what I wanted, and I think that was important.' She cites the example of Sermanni ensuring she had the boots she felt most able to excel in by covering the costs of her preferred, non-sponsor brand. 'I'd worn Adidas boots my whole career. When we came on board with Nike, I tinkered with the idea [of wearing Nike] but didn't feel they allowed me to perform like I knew I could. He said, "Because we got several pairs of Nike boots [free as part of the sponsorship], here's some money—go and choose your own online."' She and Collette McCallum did just that.

Speaking of managing players, Sermanni had had to send Lisa De Vanna home from a training camp in the 2011 tournament lead-up. 'I don't think it's a secret. Every coach who's managed Lisa, particularly in her younger years, had some challenges,' he says. 'But the challenges came from her intent to do the best she could and the pressure she put on herself.' Sermanni, like many others, describes De Vanna as a little like a pressure cooker, but reiterates that her releases are never directed at the team.

The 2011 situation came about because De Vanna returned from playing overseas to an almost unrecognisable squad. 'She turned up at camp and the whole dynamic of the team had changed quite significantly, because all of a sudden there were ten or eleven young players she really didn't know much about, didn't have a relationship with, didn't know how good they were,' Sermanni explains. 'So her first thought was *What's going to happen to this team?* It wasn't a case of wanting to come in and be deliberately disruptive. It was a case of "I've come into something I didn't expect to come into".' Having had some time to cool off, she returned to the squad for the tournament itself. The Australians weren't to know it then, but the implosion the team later had at the tournament would have nothing to do with De Vanna.

After Australia had made the quarter-finals—both just the second and second consecutive time—the anticipation, media coverage and fan support were there. But after an intrepid group-stage lead-up that would have made the public fall more deeply in love with them, the Matildas had a horror quarter-final match not befitting their true skill. The issue wasn't just that they lost a game they likely could have won: Sweden was an ageing team and its coaches had admitted to Sermanni the previous day that they were nervy about facing the fearless young Australians. Nor was it that the Matildas lost a game. It was that instead of showcasing their talent and leveraging their success in the tournament to further women's football domestically, they didn't demonstrate their capabilities. The media coverage and potential increased funding, which had been imaginable and even glimpsed, dissipated like steam.

Ellyse Perry scored Australia's lone goal in the match. As goals go, it was remarkable. Periodically popping up in 'best goals' reels, its trajectory to the top-left corner is as sweet as any player could hope for. But Perry sees it a little differently: 'I don't know. I probably have a bit of an odd view of it because we lost the game and I feel like I was directly responsible for a few of the goals Sweden scored.' So, she says, while 'it's good for a highlight reel', it 'pulled out an individual moment that maybe wasn't the whole picture' and isn't really illustrative of what transpired in the game. 'When it went into the back of the net, I just went, OK, we've got two more to get. It didn't feel that great.'

'I feel like we came off a pretty big high from 2010. Following 2010, we really began making a mark,' Shipard says. 'That's what stands out. I guess there were different expectations for us to perform.' That's perhaps, too, what made the Sweden game so painful. 'I remember being incredibly upset following that game. In hindsight, they were a much better team, and a much better team on the day. We still had so much growing to do.'

The Matildas' departure was a case of so close and yet so far. There was a sense that at least until that Sweden loss, they were on the cusp of levelling up, that the FFA and the Australian general public were starting to pay attention.

'The lost opportunities really multiplied, didn't they?' Maria Berry says. 'That would have been a good time to have broken through.' Morrison expresses an equivalent sentiment: 'That Sweden game is tragic on a whole heap of levels and it's what killed them for the next ten years, basically. They just needed to go one more game and the FFA and everyone would have sat up a bit.' So the team's Women's World Cup departure, compounded by its narrow failure to qualify for the 2012 London Olympics six weeks later, meant that Australian women's football, which had been so close to a tipping point, plateaued for a few years. 'Because if you miss out on the Olympics, the cycle is broken and the calendar back then just stopped,' Jensen explains. '[The AFC Asian Cup in] 2010 was the awakening, 2011 was close to something special, 2012 it all went quiet until the cycle started again.' Shipard sums it up succinctly: 'From a personal perspective, 2011 wasn't my fondest memory. And then failing to qualify for the Olympics really stirred us up.'

Lauren Colthorpe's recollections aren't dissimilar, especially contrasted with the 2007 tournament's highs. She terms 2011 'quite a difference experience for me. I was carrying a knee injury that ended up being career-ending, so it was a pretty stressful and tumultuous time personally.' She's not exaggerating: she literally rode an exercise bike at half-time in games to keep her knee moving. 'The beginning of the warm-up was super painful knee-wise. After twenty minutes or so the pain would start to go but it would return as soon as I cooled, so I had to keep moving at half-time to keep it at bay. Doesn't seem healthy at all, looking back at it now. The damage that was present in my knee hadn't shown up on scans prior to the World Cup, so I thought it was just a case of pushing through the pain and that I wouldn't be doing any more damage to my knee, and I wasn't honest with the medical staff about how much pain I was experiencing.' A post–World Cup scan showed otherwise. 'I didn't know at the time that it would be my last World Cup, or that I'd play my last game there. I was only twenty-five but was considering retirement during the tournament just because it had been so long since I had enjoyed my football, so in a way I was relieved when I found out I might not play again. I realise now that I just needed a break. There's so much about football I miss now, but those were my honest thoughts at the time.'

Tournament challenges aside, Shipard was also grappling with disordered eating throughout this period. 'Being an elite athlete, you're restricted to a confined timeline and those four-year cycles,' she says. The eating disorder evolved from a belief that being thin would help make her a better footballer, and from trying to manage her emotions and regain some control in an environment where she had very little. It didn't affect her performance, she says, but it 'took up a lot of my mental and physical energy'. Shipard later spoke out about her experience, which was a relatively ground-breaking thing to do at the time. As she notes, 'I was ahead in both mullets and mental health.'

★ ★ ★

Significantly—and perhaps compounding the grief after the Sweden defeat—key pillars disappear almost as soon as a team's tournament ends, which is both mentally and physically tough. Hanna explains: 'You're knocked out and then you're packing up that room for how-ever many hours it takes depending on what time the game was … You go to a game thinking, *We might have another three days here or we might be going home tomorrow.* The unknown of it can be hard.'

'It's difficult,' Beerworth agrees. 'The way FIFA do it is that within twenty-four hours of losing you're basically logistically out of the tournament, and accommodation stops. So that 24-hour period, particularly for the team manager, is unbelievably difficult.' She cites a 2016 Olympics example comparable to Women's World Cup ones: 'We played at 10 p.m. in Belo Horizonte, went to extra time and went to pens [penalties], so we were still on the pitch at 2 a.m., and then all of a sudden the next day we were on an 8 a.m. flight to Rio. Then it's about trying to get a team of eighteen players plus twelve staff out of there. The logistics of that is really difficult.'

Having spent thirteen years as the Matildas' team manager, Jo Fernandes experienced a lot of those last nights. 'That last night.' She shakes her head. 'The last night is always crazy.' Although the team makes post-tournament plans, it's an odd exercise to undergo when you're mentally focused on staying in the competition. 'When you're eliminated, you have an idea and a list of potential flights and where people are going, but once it actually happens, you have to put it all into place,' Fernandes explains.

The last night of the 2007 tournament was particularly memorable. 'I could hear everyone down in the foyer having a nice social gathering,' Fernandes says. 'I'd be running down occasionally, saying, "Is this flight OK? Because this is what's happening." I think I got less than an hour's sleep because I had to get up and get everyone to the airport and pack my own stuff, too. Eventually, when it was 6 a.m. and light out[side], I got a bit of sleep.' Then she got everyone to the airport, saw them safely onto their planes, and turned around to repeat the process because the Young Matildas, a team she also managed, were arriving in China in the next two days.

Beerworth acknowledges, too, that the hurried disbanding 'doesn't give you an opportunity to debrief appropriately and see where it went wrong. It's hard to have all that process in place in terms of a post-game review and make sure that everyone's OK and medical exits and that kind of important debrief. Certainly as time went on you'd forecast that and put strategies in place to mitigate it, but it's still challenging.'

'It's the worst. It's really the worst,' says Sarah Gregorius, a former Football Fern who is now FIFPRO Director of Global Policy and Strategic Relations for Women's Football, of the swift exits. 'You have to make really snap decisions. Do you stay? Do you go back to your club? Do you take the opportunity to take some time off? And you're dealing with probably the most heartbreaking moment of your career up to that point and having to make all these ridiculously difficult decisions and check out of the hotel at eight in the morning in order to be on the bus. They're horrible, those moments. I actually think it's a little bit inhumane. There's no reason for it … Fun fact: it's not the rule for the Men's World Cup—it's only at the Women's World Cup. Yeah, fun fact: you get it if you're a man.'

What Gregorius is saying is that the men get two nights' accommodation after their last game compared with the women's one. So no matter how late it is, the women have to combine dealing with leaving the tournament with recovery and logistical decision-making and packing and early check-out. The men get the night of the game and then another night to recover, debrief and regroup before having to depart.

★ ★ ★

That juncture and its attendant challenges are perhaps front of mind for New Zealand players generally, and Gregorius specifically, given it's something they've had to think about a lot. New Zealand's and Gregorius's ability to get in the Women's World Cup door and stay inside it has been a challenge for some time. Gregorius now spends her workdays examining and seeking to improve conditions and their knock-on effects.

Gregorius made her Women's World Cup debut in 2011 despite years of being told she was too small to play football at an elite level. 'I'm not very big. I know that,' she says. 'It was never really a problem until I started to knock on the door of the national team and things started to get serious. I was told, "It's pretty tough, you have to be quite a robust athlete, and the game's pretty physical", and things like that. I was told it directly and indirectly for quite a while, particularly coming out of youth football and trying to come into senior women's stuff.' Rupturing her ACL just before she was due to make her senior debut didn't help. But the setbacks pushed her to play smarter and be tactically sharper. 'I had already figured out that I was relatively quick—quicker than most defenders. So it's like, all right, you can't squash me if you can't catch me.'

Still, her debut was a reasonably overwhelming, tough experience, perhaps partly because, as she acknowledges, New Zealand is right now a minnow in the footballing world. With Australia's departure, New Zealand is a big fish in the small Oceania pond until it enters the much bigger Women's World Cup pond. Gregorius is far from the only interviewee who touched on this.

New Zealand haven't ever won a Women's World Cup game, but they have a habit of giving teams a run for their money in the group stage and those teams go on to finish tournament winners or runners-up. That was the case in 2011, when New Zealand made Japan work for their win. Japan beat the Football Ferns 2–1 in the opening match; it wasn't an entirely convincing victory, but it got the job done. On New Zealand's part, such a loss to the eventual champions was, in retrospect, a solid result. The pattern of challenging but not defeating eventual finalists would repeat for Canada and the Netherlands in 2015 and 2019. Still, 2011 represented progress compared with their 2007 tournament, which included a 5–0 pummelling by Brazil. It was there that New Zealand picked up their first-ever group-stage point courtesy of a 2–2 draw with Mexico.

'I think World Cups for New Zealand are interesting, because for a lot of reasons we probably shouldn't be as competitive as we are. But we're also not competitive enough in some respects,' Gregorius says. 'I think we've let ourselves down on a couple of occasions. They're not the tournaments you want to go into hoping for a bit of luck. You need to be good enough to create your own luck.' That's where greater investment (and the recent addition of a New Zealand feeder team to the A-League Women's) to enable the geographically dispersed team to train together more frequently could help them improve on the one-percenters—to achieve game-changing results.

While New Zealand's on-pitch results aren't what the team is after, the off-pitch ones are pretty great. 'The best part is easily the family and friends stuff,' Gregorius says. 'For my family, in particular, my parents aren't exactly sporting prodigies—they are confused,

I think, at the fact that I became a professional sportsperson. Like really confused, regularly … They love when their kids are happy, but they weren't helicopter football parents who were like, "You need to open out on your left foot a bit more." They had no idea. Half the time they wouldn't even know the score. For me, that was the best because around these tournaments my parents were all in.'

She remembers a moment after the gutting 2011 Japan game defeat: 'All the friends and families had been put in the one section, and we were walking around the stadium clapping the crowd. When we got to where the Kiwi supporters were I looked up, and my dad, who is this pasty white guy, is in the crowd with his shirt off, swinging it round like one of those classic football supporters. And we'd lost the game! I don't know what he was doing … I caught up with him later and he was like, "I was just really caught up in the moment." So it's those little things that I think are the best.'

★ ★ ★

The 2011 tournament ended for the Australian team, and the New Zealand team before them, but it continued for Australian referee Jacqui Hurford (née Melksham). Following in Tammy Ogston's big-game footsteps, Hurford officiated both the opening match between Germany and Canada, and perhaps one of the most memorable quarter-finals in Women's World Cup history, between the USWNT and Brazil.

'You're guaranteed one game when you go there, and anything after that is a bonus,' Hurford says. 'Referee that one well and you have a high potential of being appointed to another game.' It's high stakes, as Hurford acknowledges: 'If you don't perform well in your first match and you affect the outcome, that's pretty much your tournament gone.'

It was a lot of work for a single game—a three-year candidature cycle completed in and around other work commitments in the absence of proper pay. 'It was also a financial investment in yourself to pay for your sprint coaches, nutritionists and all that sort of stuff. That came out of our own pocket,' Hurford explains. (The 2011 tournament pre-dated the training retainers that referees are now starting to receive, but even what they're receiving now is nominal.) Factor in, too, how your country is faring. The deeper the team goes into the tournament, the fewer the opportunities for its counterpart referee. The quicker the team exits, the more chance the referee, who can then be awarded any game, has to progress. The two's tournament prospects are inversely proportional.

Hurford's guaranteed first game was also the tournament's first. It was reigning champions and host nation Germany v Canada. 'For the opening-ceremony match, it was the first time women's football had actually been allowed at the Olympic stadium, so that was a big moment in itself,' she says. And despite spending three years preparing for the moment, Hurford encountered a few curveballs. First, the ceremony entrance point was far, far away, encroaching five or ten minutes into her team's carefully planned schedule. 'It ate into our timings, which I'd never been that much affected by prior,' Hurford says. 'Also, we had twenty-five balls that had to be pumped up and there was no electric pump, so we had to manually pump them up.' It's moments like that where you're reminded that it's really important for referees to carry handy things like pumps— they might be needed even somewhere as seemingly well-resourced as a World Cup. 'Then our warm-up got pushed back by fifteen minutes,' Hurford says. 'Normally we warm up for at least twenty to thirty minutes, but I think we got ten minutes because of that. I never really, leading up to walking out, had a moment to myself in that game. We were just constantly rushed, and hence I was like a cat on a hot tin roof until …' Until she fell over. 'I thought the ball was going to go in front of me, and then all of a sudden the player's just stopped, and I'm right in that channel,' Hurford explains. 'And she's kicked it straight at my head.'

Hurford reflexively hit the deck. 'After that moment, I'm just laughing. I'm like, *If I can fall on my arse and that's televised live around the world in front of, what, 84,000 people … If that's the worst thing that happens today, it's going to be a good day*,' Hurford says. Assistant referee Sarah Ho was laughing, too. Fellow assistant referee Allyson Flynn, whose task required her focus not to be on Hurford at the moment she hit the ground, asked, 'What have I missed?' Hurford, still laughing, told her, 'Nothing.' To this day, Hurford doesn't know why the player chose to play back when there was a solid attacking option available. Regardless, as she recalls now, 'My reaction time getting up was pretty good.'

Hurford's second, bonus match between the USWNT and Brazil had absolutely everything. Think all the possible combinations of things that might pop up in a training scenario crammed in: own goal, red card, penalty (saved), penalty (retaken), time-wasting antics, extra time, and the latest-ever goal scored in extra time to push the match to penalties when Megan Rapinoe crossed a perfectly placed, perfectly weighted ball to Abby Wambach, who completed with a header—at 120 minutes and 21 seconds, to be precise. Brazil thought it had the match in the bag and had been running down the clock near the corner flag, but the USWNT went on to prevail 5–3 on penalties, and the match changed women's football and people's appreciation of it forever.

'I can still feel my heart rate,' Hurford says at mention of that match. 'It's taken me a long time to be able to sit down and digest that game. I'm still very emotionally tied to it, if that makes sense.' With good reason. Not only was it a career-defining match, but it also turned out to be her last international one: she had back surgery a few months later from which she wasn't able to successfully return. 'So yeah, I feel my heart rate and I know what I was thinking at the time.'

That quarter-final was Hurford's first time refereeing Brazil, but the USWNT was a team she'd refereed regularly. Brazil made its intent to hassle Wambach out of the game abundantly clear. 'Abby was targeted right from the first whistle. And they were just small, shitty little fouls against her, which riled her up.' It was tricky to handle. Stop the game and Wambach and the USWNT would be frustrated because the team retained possession and had attacking advantage. Don't stop the game and Wambach would become so frustrated by the cheap shots and that the referee wasn't protecting her safety that she would combust. In the end, at an opportune moment, Hurford cautioned Brazil for the persistent fouls.

Brazil had their own moments, though, including when Hurford ordered a saved penalty to be retaken on the grounds of encroachment. 'It was so loud,' she recalls. The USWNT and its fans were celebrating wildly after Hope Solo blocked the shot, so it took a few moments for the do-over message to make it through. 'You have nightmares as a referee that your whistle isn't heard—like, you're blowing it and no noise is coming out. I felt like that at that moment. I was blowing my whistle and it just didn't feel like it was being heard.' Brazil switched penalty takers and five-time world's best Marta assuredly buried the retake.

'Probably the proudest moment was when that Brazilian went down like she'd been shot.' Hurford is referencing the moment when Erika dropped to the ground and rolled about as if she were gravely injured. The melodramatic incident, milked for every available second, was so spectacular that she was stretchered from the pitch. 'I've got Abby in my ear going, "She's fucking faking it! She's fucking faking it!" And I'm just like, "I'm not a doctor. I'll get her off and add the time on,"' Hurford explains. 'Then I ended up cautioning Erika when she came back on, because she jumped straight off the stretcher.' It was an astonishing recovery. Hurford was wise to it, though: 'I brought her back on and cautioned her for unsporting behaviour. But the time it took was the additional time in which the United States scored because of her.' Ah, karma.

So the USWNT equalised and the match went to additional time. 'I mean, that's another record,' Hurford says. 'I've never done a final that's ended in ninety minutes. I've always gone to minimum additional time. Most of them have gone to penalties. So I was always prepared for 120 minutes, and so was my team.' It made for a long day. 'It was an insane time, because we were in Dresden and it was really, really late by the time we'd done all our paperwork. We were actually staying in the same hotel as Brazil and the USA.' On her return from the pitch, she found herself entering a lift that contained USWNT coach Pia Sundhage. 'There are coaches who, no matter what shit's going down, are cool, calm and collected— but underneath they might be paddling like a duck,' Hurford says.

Sundhage is one such coach. She politely acknowledged Hurford and they rode quietly to their respective floors.

The next morning, Hurford and her team flew from Dresden to the referee headquarters in Frankfurt. 'Obviously not much sleep has happened. Obviously there's all these reports coming in, especially about the send-off,' Hurford explains. Making it additionally difficult was that the available camera footage didn't reflect what Hurford had seen. 'Then we had to do our recovery, which ended up being a 25-kilometre bike ride out and around. We got back and I went straight into debrief, where I got pumped, absolutely pumped,' Hurford continues. 'The room was divided on the red card [issued to USWNT defender Rachel Buehler for a tackle on Marta]. It was probably the first time I felt attacked by my peers in that regard. I don't know whether I was just so emotionally fatigued or what.'

Regardless, it was tournament over. 'We knew we were going home. We'd done the two biggest matches of our lives, so we knew we weren't going to be sticking around. Normally there's a small party for those who are heading home, and then I was on a plane back home and straight back to work. There was no downtime or anything.' Referees have the same experience as the players of being ejected from the tournament. It's a brutal finish. And there was more brutality to come.

'I thought I had my social media locked down pretty tight, but Facebook posts or comments came up saying things like "Jacqui Melksham likes to suck Brazilian black cock" and I had over 200 death threats if I ever came to the USA,' Hurford says. Given the early days of social media, you could say she was at the vanguard of the online abuse we now know all too well. There was no regard for her mental health. 'It was really crazy. I'd been assaulted in men's football back here in Australia. I'd been spat on, had my car damaged and that sort of stuff. But I'd never been threatened with having my throat slit or being blown up.' Uncaptured and unhampered by non-existent spam or abuse filters, the messages arrived in her inbox unscreened. 'It was horrible, because they went straight into your message bank.' Peculiarly, most of the abuse stemmed from USWNT fans. 'I'm like, *You won!*' Hurford shakes her head.

'I understand that you're invested in the game, but you don't think about all the hours I've done training and investing, and all the family sacrifices I've made to get to this one moment ... and you think you have a right to say that I should die?'

While this was playing out for Hurford, the USWNT went on to meet Japan, a team not especially considered a contender, in the final. Japan had experienced an earthquake-induced tsunami just a few months prior in which almost 20,000 people died, and the Japanese players carried the weight of that tragedy and wanted to give their country something to celebrate. They had never previously made it to a semi-final, and they slingshot to win both the semi and the final. The team received messages from fans at home thanking it for its efforts and congratulating it on lifting Japanese people's spirits. The players had won hearts beyond Japan, too. They had received so many well wishes that they unfurled a banner after the game thanking their 'friends around the world' for the support.

More than 13 million people tuned in to watch the USWNT–Japan final, a match so tense and exciting that the USWNT received a heroes' welcome back in the United States afterwards, despite ultimately losing the game. In a glimpse of what could have been possible domestically, Australia admired from a distance the elevated profile and support the USWNT team received.

★ ★ ★

An off-pitch whole-of-women's-football gain began around this time, too. It stemmed from the notion that came onto Moya Dodd's and others' radar of the safety or otherwise of playing in hijab. Dodd had just become the Asian Football Confederation (AFC) Women's Football Committee's chair. 'It was on the meeting agenda and it was like, "What's happened here?"' she says. What had happened was an Olympic qualifying match between Jordan and Iran where the referee had ruled that no player in a hijab (headscarf) could take part. (The ruling was made under FIFA's Law Four, which stipulated that players could not wear anything that might endanger themselves or made a political or religious statement.[4]) That decision ruled out the entire Iranian team, for whom playing in hijab was mandatory, and some of the Jordanian players, too. 'So this thing came across our desk,' Dodd says. 'For me, it was quite a foreign issue. I'd obviously never worn a hijab.' She also didn't know and hadn't worked closely with many women who did. 'I thought, *OK, I need to learn about this and understand it a bit more.*'

The year 2011 marked a new AFC election cycle, and one of the new executive committee members was Jordan's Prince Ali bin Hussein, who'd been elected as FIFA's vice president of Asia. 'Obviously it was his team that had played and beaten the Iranians on forfeit. So he was very concerned about the issue and the signal it sent and the basic question of fairness,' Dodd says. FIFA President Sepp Blatter tasked Prince Ali with resolving the hijab issue, and Prince Ali called a roundtable meeting in Jordan and invited referees, coaches, players and administrators to hear from experts, assess the evidence and formulate a plan. 'I was invited to speak about some of the legal aspects of it, bearing in mind that there was a code of ethics around discrimination,' Dodd says. Her speech targeted key decision-makers—the FIFA administrators and medical committee—with good reason: medical concerns and safety were the primary purported reasons behind the hijab ban.

'We were told that the objection to changing the rules was for safety reasons, because if you wore a hijab, somebody might grab it and do you an injury, like a neck injury or getting strangled or something like that,' Dodd says. 'I found that curious, because it would be an infringement to grab somebody's hijab, just like grabbing somebody's shirt is an infringement, and the referee would stop it happening. And if you were worried about people causing you a neck injury by grabbing something, then there were some very good examples of people's ponytails being pulled that I found on YouTube—I showed these during the session—where people were flattened, brought to the ground by someone yanking really hard on their ponytail.' (Around this time, video of University of New Mexico player Elizabeth Lambert violently yanking an opposing player backwards by her ponytail had gone viral.) 'So it seemed to me that if it was dangerous to wear a hijab, then it was dangerous to have a ponytail. And no one had ever objected to either female or male players having ponytails.'

Former Football Fern, football administrator, academic and writer Michele Cox was an integral part of the roundtable. 'Yeah, I'm really proud of that,' she says of the group's work to resolve the immediate problem but open the door for many more women to play, 'because it [facilitated] access to the game for so many women. And it was so ridiculous, the whole issue.'

In 2011 Cox and two colleagues were brought in to help a local team establish the Asian Football Development Project, which was Prince Ali's Jordan-based foundation designed to promote social development through football. The hijab issue was one of the first things the team had to address; it was so vast it consumed three-quarters of Cox's role in that first year.

'The first thing we identified was that we didn't really under-stand the issue—cultural, laws of the game, medical perspectives, for example,' Cox explains. 'Legal issues were part of that. So when we decided to run a roundtable with experts in these fields from all over the world, we invited Moya [Dodd] to present the legal issues.'

Cox, who has a PhD in physical activity and health promotion, also applied those research and analytical skills to the flawed medi-cal arguments being used. She sought out experts at the Cleveland Institute and obtained a letter that dismissed the medical claims and accused FIFA of medical neglect. The letter and related research were critical in making FIFA back down. 'The outcome of this roundtable was sensational (including Moya's advice), and we were able to formulate a strategy that IFAB and FIFA couldn't counter,' Cox says.

Barbara Cox, too, has completed a PhD, and her research focused on the repression of women's sports in the early 1900s. Michele notes that more than a hundred years on from the very repression Barbara researched, the equivalent themes were still playing out.

'For me, it was interesting how the medical profession had played a role in repressing women's sport, saying, "You won't be able to have children if you play certain sports." And then 100 years later, the same thing was happening in football when they used the

FIFA medical office to say, "If you play in hijab you are at risk of strangulation"—or carotid sinus irritation, more specifically, which is ridiculous because it's a very rare condition and [generally] affects men over fifty.' Nor was FIFA's research entirely rigorous, Cox explains: it involved a Western woman donning a headscarf and committee members taking turns pulling it to see if it would come off. 'That was the testing.'

The hijab furore played out against wider context of Islamophobia—including hijabophobia[5]—thinly veiled as discussions about immigration safety and security. Just a few months before, France had become the first European country to ban the burqa, an outer garment that covers a woman's full body. FIFA was wary of upsetting its French constituents, so it sat on the fence. 'The problem was that when they did that, all the referees were left to their own devices because it wasn't clear. So some people were allowed to play and some weren't,' Michele Cox says. 'That was when it blew up, because Jordan and Iran had an Olympic qualification match and the players were told by a referee to take their headscarves off. Of course they're not going to, so they forfeited the match—whereas there were other teams playing in other countries where they *could* [keep them on through referees' discretion], so it was really unfair.' As Cox later outlined in a journal article she authored (with input on structure from Barbara and Geoff Dickson), most players and administrators who were consulted considered it a non-issue. One professional male footballer told Cox, 'They can run around and wear their undies on their head for all I care.'[6]

'The hijab was frustrating because there were deep objections to it that we just couldn't address. We couldn't get to the middle of the thing,' Dodd explains. But Dodd and her peers were eventually able to nullify those objections and the attitudinal and rule change did happen. 'It gave me some faith that you can work through institutions from the inside and achieve that sort of change.' The breakthrough came via a prototype 'safety hijab' affixed with velcro. 'If you pulled that hijab, it would just come apart and nobody would get strangled. I felt it was the trump card to the only real argument that had been put forward against permitting the hijab,' Dodd says. 'It had to be taken back to FIFA and digested. We felt that on that day we had convinced the FIFA medical chair that there was no significant medical issue. I had searched the internet high and low for anyone who had sustained a neck injury from wearing a hijab, in any sport. The only one I found from anywhere was in go-karting, and we were not go-karting.'

'It was that same issue of powerful medical people having [control] over women's bodies,' Barbara Cox says. Dodd concurs: 'Women's bodies are policed in every way possible. That is deeply embedded in, certainly, Western cultures and possibly others as well. The argument that bikinis are appropriate but burkinis are not— can you get your head around that? There is no logic to the way in which women's bodies are policed about what we can wear and how we can be seen. So don't look for logic: there isn't any. These decisions are not being made by women, and they should be.'

After nullifying the spurious medical concerns, the roundtable committee drafted a motion. 'It looked like one of those UN motions—whereas this, whereas that, we call upon you to do that,' Dodd says. The motion travelled up the chain and was endorsed. The hijab ban was eventually lifted in 2014 after further advocacy and the slow turning of cogs it takes to enact such change.

As far as Dodd is concerned, 'The most important thing is that at grassroots level and every level above that, women and girls from those cultures can know and feel that football's door is open to them.' Given there are some 800 million Muslim women in the world, that's a sizeable number of women for whom the door is opening. Still, Dodd notes, 'These things have a lead time. If you're not allowed to wear a hijab in a World Cup or the Olympics, then how many countries where women predominantly wear the hijab are going to progress to that level of football? How long does it take after you change that rule for women and girls from those cultures to really feel like the door is fully open to them? Then how long does it take to progress to the level where their national team is playing in a major tournament such as a senior World Cup?'

That lead time is already proving shorter than predicted. We saw the first steps realised, coming full circle, in 2016. 'When the under-17s Women's World Cup was held in Jordan in 2016, the host nation appeared in the opening match with two players wearing a hijab,' Dodd says. 'That was, quite fittingly, the first instance of a player wearing a hijab in a global tournament—in Amman, where we'd had the roundtable discussion five years before.'

In 2022 we saw the Iranian team—the team whose forfeit had brought the hijab ban concerns to the fore—competing in the 2022 AFC Asian Women's Cup. In a best-case scenario, and in contrast to the furore that had had to be navigated, the hijab simply formed part of Iran's uniform and barely warranted being commented on. The same year, we saw the Afghanistan national women's team restart its training in Australia, having sought asylum after the Taliban regained control of Afghanistan. Neither the Taliban nor any purported hijab 'safety' issues have been able to prevent Afghan women from playing football. Indeed, women who wouldn't be able to play, had that rule not changed, are showing that the participation door referenced by Dodd is open and they are walking through it.

8

2015:
IT'S NOT ABOUT THE GRASS

WERE YOU TO read only the newspaper headlines in 2015, you'd think the world's top female footballers were griping about inconsequential grass. Were you to lean in, though, you'd realise they were doing nothing of the sort. The turf war that revolved around 2015 Women's World Cup host nation Canada staging the tournament on artificial turf wasn't about turf at all.

The artificial-turf issue initially flew under the radar, perhaps because it wasn't well publicised, perhaps because players hadn't fully realised its implications, perhaps because the tournament was years away and surely common sense—a return to real grass—would prevail. When it became apparent that they would need to push back on the decision, players from around the world, led by the USWNT, wrote to FIFA to ask it to reconsider.

Moya Dodd had been co-opted to the FIFA Executive Committee in 2013, kicking off a 'three-year adventure on the inside' that included serving as deputy chair of the 2015 Women's World Cup organising committee. That role included helping to address the artificial-turf concerns and mitigating the decision's worst outcomes. 'I didn't like the idea of artificial,' Dodd says. 'Certainly my own experience playing on artificial was from a couple of decades earlier when it was truly terrible, unplayably bad. It's better now, but it's still … I don't like it better than I like grass. In fact, I think I'd actually prefer bad grass to artificial simply because of what artificial does to my knees these days. So I was not a fan of it, and when I went inside FIFA, I was like, "What the …? Why is this on artificial?" and got the answer that it was locked and loaded and wasn't going to change.'

To be fair, Canada had been transparent about the turf plan from the outset. Also, it had been the only bidder for the tournament. Had FIFA asked Canada to change the grass and the host nation refused, FIFA didn't have other options to leverage. Dodd did investigate what it would take to put real grass on top of turf, but it was clear it wouldn't be viable in the timeframe. 'There were numerous issues with it. If you put out a grass pitch, you have to let it settle,' she says. 'It seemed impossible to do that. Also, some stadia did not get much sunlight. Some players reported that grass on top of turf can slide around like a floormat. All the games were double-headers, so there was a lot of wear and tear. If you got into trouble with a grass pitch, there wasn't time to repair or replace it.' So she did the only thing she could: she worked with others to ensure that the artificial turf was of the highest quality and was consistently implemented on both the training and match pitches.

After being told FIFA wouldn't be budging, the players' next step was to file a complaint with the Human Rights Tribunal of Ontario. If you ask the players, they'll tell you turf tears skin. On-pitch temperatures burn feet soles. The hardness of the surface changes the way the ball bounces, affects joints and hampers recovery. Worse, given the high incidence of knee injuries already plaguing female footballers and the untested grip and slip of the unfamiliar surface at a senior football tournament, players both privately and publicly wondered if such a pitch could even be downright dangerous.

FIFA argued that such claims were anecdotal at best and disproven by studies that showed artificial turf to be equivalent to real turf. But what FIFA failed to realise or recognise was that the player pushback wasn't about the grass at all. Asking the world's best female footballers, for whom peak Women's World Cup performance would mean obtaining potentially crucial and otherwise scant pay and sponsorship, to play on a surface that had never seen a tournament of this calbire wasn't just odd: it was galling.

Shifting the women's game's top tournament from real grass to artificial grass was illustrative of the nonchalance with which female footballers have traditionally been asked—nay, *expected*—to accept second best. Whether actual or imagined, such a risk would never have been tabled, much less taken, with the men. (Canada will be co-hosting the 2026 Men's World Cup. Unsurprisingly, it will be on real grass.) 'I think it was part of a broader conversation around equality and fairness and respect. You wouldn't test it in a Men's World Cup,' PFA co-CEO Kate Gill says. 'That wouldn't even be a conversation that was had. So why is it acceptable in the women's domain? It's just disrespectful.' Subsequently, the human-rights complaint's central argument was that the artificial turf decision was discriminatory based on gender.

Time ultimately defeated all action. FIFA argued that it didn't, as Dodd had found, have time to change the pitches. Nor was there time for the lawsuit to wind its way through the legal system. When the tribunal rejected the players' application to fast-track the complaint, the players had little choice but to withdraw the application and prepare for the tournament. The alternative of boy-cotting the event was understandably a bridge too far for players who had spent their entire careers aspiring to play in it and who were aware that the quadrennial playing window was too narrow and too integral to miss.

'Going into it, having not really ever played a lot on it before, we were concerned about the change of surface from an injury point of view and a performance point of view,' former Matildas physiotherapist Kate Beerworth says. The AIS provided the Matildas with a specially installed artificial-turf pitch to prepare on so they were as familiar and comfortable with the unfamiliar, uncomfort-able surface as they could be.

One challenge that quickly became apparent was that artificial turf is hotter—way hotter—than grass. There can be a difference of more than 10°C between air temperature and a watered artificial pitch—20°C if it's unwatered. 'The summer months training on the new artificial turf at the AIS will stay with me for a long time,' former Matilda Ash Sykes says. 'The heat that comes off it is intense.'

'We trained the entire six-month period prior to the tournament in Canberra on the artificial. Our feet were absolutely blistered,' former Matildas captain Melissa Barbieri recalls. 'You know when your feet go white and shrivelly in the bath? When your foot is so melted that you get blisters?' The players had to get special socks to prevent slipping. Also, none of the Australian-made boots specifically met the artificial-turf specifications, and the boots the players ended up having to get were less than ideal. 'I looked like the umpire from an under-12s cricket team' is how Barbieri describes it. 'And the turf burn. All the reasons you play football, [such as] sliding—all those options were taken off you.'

'There's a hesitancy to go to ground,' former Brisbane Roar player Rebecca Price, now an academic, explains. When slide tackling will likely involve removing layers of skin, you rethink the need for it. Indeed, USWNT player Sydney Leroux posted a now-infamous image on social media showing the graze-meets-rash-meets-bruising she obtained by slide tackling on artificial turf. In a tweet using the polite hashtag #realgrassplease, her teammate Kelley O'Hara responded with the suggestion that Leroux 'should probs tweet that to FIFA'.[1]

'I absolutely hated playing on turf,' former Matilda Laura Brock says. 'It's super hard on your body. My back and knees were often in pain. Also, as a centre back there are times where you need to make sliding challenges to save your team, and doing so on turf left me with carpet burns up my legs. It was awful. Not to mention the fact that it changes the way you play, the pace of the ball is different, the ability to get underneath a long pass and "chip" to a teammate is difficult, passes would bobble instead of skid, your first touch felt different from grass and often ran away from you.' Then there was the heat. 'I distinctly remember in our final match, the quarter-final against Japan, I had to take off my boots at half-time and pour water on my feet because they were so hot and running around out there was genuinely painful.'

Ultimately, and invoking complex emotions because as much as you wanted a good outcome, you also wanted the players to be vindicated for their concerns, everyone's worst fears weren't realised. Injury analysis showed that the artificial turf didn't especially appear to pose a risk other than through skin injuries. (But skin injuries still really, really sting.) Sykes perhaps sums up the experience of it: 'It took a while for my body to adjust to the surface—like, it made you more sore for a while because it rebounds differently to grass—but once you got used to it, it wasn't so bad.'

The tournament itself went pretty well. *FourFourTwo* again featured the Matildas' campaign as a cover story, this time brought to life by editor Kevin Airs.[2] More broadly, television viewership exceeded 750 million and more than 1.3 million people attended matches in person. The tournament had been expanded to feature twenty-four teams (up from sixteen), including eight first-time qualifiers: European teams Spain, Switzerland and the Netherlands; African teams Cameroon and Côte d'Ivoire; Costa Rica and Ecuador from South and Central America; and Thailand from Asia.[3] The Matildas felt that increased attention and expectation, and the opportunity it presented. 'Canada 2015 seemed to hold a lot more pressure,' Tameka Yallop explains. 'The women's game had become a lot bigger and more publicised across the world since 2011. You could feel that this was the opportunity we'd been waiting for to push women's football into the homes of Aussies and make a name for the Matildas.'

Sykes sensed that shift, too. 'The game has grown a lot since 2015, so playing in front of big crowds is something all the players are experiencing more often. But at that time, walking out to the bench in front of 34,000 US fans was new for me and so energising. To see the way the US team, and even their fans, carried themselves was a good learning experience. They were so confident. It seemed like they were always in control through the tournament and like they hadn't even considered the possibility that they could walk away without winning it. I remember a moment when I came off the bench trying to run past Julie Ertz to pressure a ball that was going out for a goal kick. She wasn't fazed at all—bumped me out of the way so calmly.'

* * *

Most of the talk about turf had dissipated by the time the finals rolled around. The much-anticipated Japan–United States final rematch demonstrated a reversal of the 2011 fortunes. This time the United States came away victorious 5–2 after Carli Lloyd became the first player to score a hat-trick in a Women's World Cup final (including the fastest-ever goal scored in a final, just 2:35 into the game).

The 2015 win made the USWNT record three-time Women's World Cup champions and the world's most successful women's football team. On its return home, it became the first women's team to receive a New York City ticker-tape parade. US president Barack Obama invited the players to the White House (an invitation that would play out very differently in 2019 when Donald Trump was president). In a serendipitous wider cultural occurrence, the USWNT winning the Women's World Cup dovetailed with the US Supreme Court determining that the US Constitution protects the right to same-sex marriage.[4]

The Matildas performed admirably, too. They opened their 'Group of Death' campaign strongly against eventual winners the United States, giving them an almighty scare before going down in a result not befitting the close contest: 3–1. They bounced back with a 2–0 win over Nigeria, then a 1–1 draw with Sweden to progress to, and meet Brazil in, the Round of 16. They defeated Brazil 1–0, becoming the first Australian team, women or men, to win a World Cup knockout stage, but eventual tournament runners-up Japan proved too strong in the quarter-final.

Barbieri hadn't actually been sure if she would make the 2015 team given she was one of the older players and was a few months post-partum, and there wasn't a maternity-leave policy or solid support structures to help players return after having a baby. 'I was trying to show everyone I was capable even though I'd had a baby,' she says. 'I knew if I just turned up every day, I would have done everything I could. I couldn't have done anymore, no regrets. Then I made the team because I did what I said I'd do: I just turned up every day.'

Turning up meant having to make sacrifices. Barbieri's family stepped up to enable her to travel back and forth to interstate camps for days at a time: in the absence of a formal parental policy, she and teammates such as Heather Garriock had to compartmentalise their playing and familial commitments. Garriock's career ended prematurely. She never retired. She was never thanked for her career. She was simply never called back up. With the PFA's help, she took legal action to try to ensure that subsequent generations would not have the career-ending maternity experience she had. She didn't earn a single cent from the action and it cost the PFA in the vicinity of A$50,000 in court costs, but her case likely inspired improved maternity policies across all women's sports.[5] Certainly Katrina Gorry's pregnancy and return, which came almost a decade after Garriock's and Barbieri's experiences, was better handled.

Recent maternity leave aside, at thirty-five Barbieri was the most senior Matilda, something she was regularly reminded of. 'You get continuously told it's the next generation's turn, and I was happy to accept that,' she says. But Casey Dumont had torn her ACL and Lydia Williams was just returning from tearing hers, and the other younger goalkeepers were less experienced and consistent. 'It does mess with you,' Barbieri says of the question of whether or not to retire. But she turned to her trusted inner circle of people who had her best interests at heart and would also tell her the unvarnished truth, and they told her to persevere. That perseverance paid off when she was selected for her fourth Women's World Cup.

Sykes' selection experience, too, was one of perseverance: 'It was a rollercoaster! There was a period of about four years where I thought my opportunity of getting another call-up to the Matildas was gone. I had a lot of work to do to improve, but sometimes it felt like I was still getting overlooked. So I just kept working on my game in the background and trying to force my way into squads whenever the chance came up. Luckily, as sometimes happens, a change in coach meant a better opportunity for me to get called up again.'

That meant the artificial pitch was not her primary concern. 'I was more focused on trying to make it through each camp and get a call-back for the next week. Because I wasn't really an entrenched member of the squad, it felt like at the end of each weekly camp I'd be waiting by the phone to see whether I was still in contention for the Women's World Cup or whether I was going back to looking for another regular job. When I got told I'd made the squad, it was mainly a massive feeling of relief. The coach who let me know even remarked that I hadn't been at the top of the list at the start of the process but somehow I kept managing to rise a bit, improve, find my role in the squad, and make it onto the plane to Canada.'

The team might have had a decent tournament, but the locations posed some logistical challenges. For many fans, the prohibitive distance between game locations made Canada tricky and expensive. The Matildas' results meant fans travelled from Edmonton to Moncton, a 4554-kilometre or roughly six-hour flight across the country, only to have to return to Edmonton for the Matildas' next match. Kyah Simon's family actually hired a van and drove the whole way there and back.

Coffee, unsurprisingly, was the priority no matter which town everyone was in. Vitor Sobral recalls arriving in Winnipeg. 'We need coffee because we're Australians, and so we look up "Best coffee Winnipeg" and end up at this cafe. The whole team's there, and the families, and the other journos. That happened everywhere we went.' They also likely gathered as a group in the various locations because the tournament awareness hadn't entirely broken through in Canada, a country where football has to compete with more established sports, such as ice hockey. 'In Canada, no one really knew the World Cup was on,' Sobral remembers. 'They would say, "Are you here for the FIFA?"'

Avoiding the prohibitively long distances remains one of the potential improvements people identify about that tournament (and what needs to be avoided as much as possible in 2023—such as making players and fans traipse to and from Perth and Sydney). The same goes for really ensuring that the entire country is aware the tournament is on. Then again, Clare Polkinghorne's family managed some inventive cost-saving measures. 'In Winnipeg, we had fifteen travelling in our group and needed an easy way to the game,' her brother Tom explains. 'Turns out limousines aren't that expensive in Winnipeg, so Dad found a business card in the hotel lobby for a limo driver who picked us up for $75 and dropped us to the game. It was cheaper than the bus and we got dropped off in the VIP zone because of the car.'

Clare Polkinghorne was actually both captain and injured for most of that Women's World Cup. 'The weird thing when you're injured and you have people there watching is that Clare felt bad,' Tom says. 'You know, "You guys have come all the way over to watch me and I'm sitting on the bench." That wasn't something that crossed our minds, to be honest. But in saying that, that was probably the most important World Cup we went to for her ... You're there for different reasons. It would have probably been worse if we hadn't been there for the Canada World Cup when she was injured than for Germany where she was playing every game.'

Former Matildas coach Tom Sermanni was at the tournament, too, although not in the capacity most had expected. Having moved to coach the USWNT in the years between the 2011 and 2015 Women's World Cups, he'd been blindsided with a sacking in 2014, less than eighteen months into the job. Then, in a meeting of the worlds, he was called up to assist former New Zealand coach John Herdman, who was tasked with steering home team Canada through the tournament.

It was a change in pace and responsibility for Sermanni, and one not entirely unwelcome. 'The one thing you learn when you are an assistant coach is you sleep a lot better,' he laughs. The two coaches had different but complementary styles, which allowed Sermanni the freedom to be himself while also seeing things from a different perspective. 'I really learned from that World Cup. People say you never stop learning ... and you actually don't. You can stop *wanting* to learn, but I felt that I took away a lot of things from that World Cup that have benefited me since that time.'

Have such learning experiences meant coaching has become easier for him over the years? 'No. I thought it would,' Sermanni says. 'When I was a younger coach and saw older coaches, I thought it would be easier because you've put in time, got your experience, established your credibility. It's not. You feel the same pressures. Probably when you start out, you don't know what you don't know. When you get to my age, you know what you don't know.'

★ ★ ★

Although it attracted all the initial headlines, it wasn't just the turf that posed gender-based issues. The FIFA prize-money issue wouldn't truly catch fire until 2019, but in 2015 it was definitely smouldering. The Cliff Notes version was that the 2015 Women's World Cup bestowed US$2 million on the winning team; the 2014 Men's winner was gifted US$35 million. Meanwhile, the teams eliminated at the group stage in the 2014 Men's tournament each received US$8 million—that is, the worst men's teams in the tournament were paid four times what the best women's team was in 2015.

When these disparities were put to them, the (mostly male) administrators invariably trotted out the standard line: the Men's World Cup, then up to its twentieth iteration, was a vastly more mature, marketable and commercially robust product than the fledgling Women's World Cup, which was only up to its seventh. Lacking from such justification was any acknowledgement that the reason women were only up to their seventh tournament was because male administrators had prevented them from officially launching FIFA Women's World Cups until 1991, and that without some concerted intervention, women would never be able to catch up.

Also playing out in the background to, and threatening to eclipse, the tournament was a corruption scandal that skittled FIFA's most powerful men. In the month preceding the 2015 event kicking off, the FBI and the US Internal Revenue Service (IRS) arrested and indicted fourteen FIFA officials—and later another sixteen—under corruption charges that included wire fraud, racketeering and money laundering. It's estimated the officials had collectively received bribes in the vicinity of US$150 million. Dodd was one of three FIFA executives to decline an expensive proffered gift watch. (The US$29,000 women's version Dodd politely turned down was even more valuable than the US$25,000 version offered to the men—a price difference potentially attributable to the fact the men's version didn't have diamonds around the bezel.)

The tournament's first press conference was dominated by questions related to the unfolding scandal, including whether Canada had paid bribes to host the event. For the record, the answer was no, Canada had absolutely not done so. (It was an odd question. There had only been one bid. What purpose would bribes have served given Canada had no competition?) It was a frustrating start to the tournament as many pondered if men's actions would, yet again, obscure women's football.

Unlike the turf war, the corruption scandal created some golden opportunities. FIFA president Sepp Blatter elected not to attend the tournament, citing travel concerns (which could arguably be read as concerns about travelling to a country with an extradition treaty with the United States). His absence meant that the FIFA symposium held at each tournament was able to enact real change. Dodd explains: 'At the end of every symposium there would always be a call to action, and usually Sepp Blatter would go to the front and say, "Ladies, shall we ask for the percentage of the grants to be spent on women's football to be increased from 10 per cent to 15 per cent? Shall we ask for that?" They would all clap and he'd go away and make that happen. In my view these were fairly marginal improvements. They might have sounded big on the day, but actually over four years they were fairly marginal.'

Dodd saw an opening. 'I was [developing] a plan to lobby more extensively for reforms on gender issues. We used the opportunity of the symposium to have the room pass much more robust calls to action around the inclusion of women in governance and the proper resourcing of women's football at a participant level, and the proper commercialisation and marketing of women's football around elite competitions.'

As part of this, she tabled a proposal that posited that gender balance would generate governance improvements and 'a culture that is less prone to corruption'. (Research supports this. Such a best-practice approach and cultural change promotes transparency, accountability and diversity, and helps to restore trust and faith in professional sports organisations[6]—all elements that mitigate potential corruption.) The symposium supported the plan, which Dodd was later able to leverage when it got to the pointy end of getting the reforms across the line: it wasn't just her supporting it; hundreds of member associations did, too.

There was more. 'Funnily enough, the reforms were something that FIFA itself adopted as part of the narrative,' Dodd says. 'That was quite unexpected, because the raids and the vote on the reforms were probably eight months apart. During that time, first the CEO of FIFA, the general secretary, was stood down, then Blatter was stood down, and the place was being run by lawyers and corporate communications consultants who were quite open to the idea of these reforms and who seized upon them as positives to show that FIFA was putting itself on a better path. I mean, FIFA had the FBI looking over its shoulder all of this time, so to say, "Yes, we are reforming ourselves, yes, we are improving, we will do better" was exactly what FIFA needed to say at the time. So I found myself fronting press conferences and being given the microphone to talk about these issues, which I never expected to happen—*never* expected to happen.'

It was a pretty remarkable result, even if the general punter wasn't aware of the innovative work Dodd was doing—and doing as one of just three women temporarily co-opted to the FIFA Executive Committee, the first women in its 108-year history. The three also received a late call-up to present the trophy and medals at the 2015 Women's World Cup final, presumably because FIFA needed the good PR of having women leaders visible at a Women's World Cup, and because they were short on officials and needed to deflect from the notable absence of Blatter and co.

Still, to the general fan Dodd was just another representative of an organisation mired in a corruption scandal and with a black mark against its name for such sins as artificial turf and unequal prize money. 'There I was in the line-up to shuffle out onto the field, and I'll never forget it—this line of blue suits [of FIFA officials] walks out onto the field and everyone in the stadium boos us. So if you want to know what it's like to be booed by 50,000 people, I can tell you,'

she laughs. 'It was what the rank and file Canadians, or Americans—
because there were a lot of them in the crowd—thought of FIFA,
and they were letting us know. Fair enough.'

Did she feel that she was actually one of the good guys trying
to change it from the inside? As in: 'Boo them, but don't boo me'?
'You have to take what comes, really,' Dodd says. '[There was an
assumption that] if you had joined FIFA, you must be part of the
problem. People who knew me and people I knew and worked
with outside FIFA knew differently. But you can't stop and have
that conversation with every person in the world who thinks FIFA's
bad, or you'd never get anything else done.'

★ ★ ★

So 2015 was rife with themes of grass, greed and prize-money
discrepancy. That trifecta would have been enough, but there was
more to play out, specifically for the Matildas and their pay, playing conditions and recognition (or lack thereof). In addition to
joining women footballers from other countries to push back on
the artificial-turf decision, the Matildas stood up an additional two
crucial times that year, bookending the Women's World Cup and
inspiring enormous strides in women's sport.

The first hint came after the Socceroos' January Asian Cup win.
Headlines and social media posts congratulated them on being
the first Australian team crowned champions of Asia. Except they
weren't: the Matildas had achieved that feat five years earlier with
their thrilling, rain-soaked penalty shootout win against North
Korea. It was a sobering reminder that men constantly occupy the
central, blinkered position in the collective historical and media-
coverage consciousness.

A number of fans 'fixed' the headlines and shared posts on social
media flagging that, while it was a fantastic achievement for the
men, the Socceroos were actually the first Australian men's team
and the second Australian team to win the tournament. 'We were
so proud of them, but then we were shunted out of history,' Barbieri
says of that moment. 'Words matter, and yes, it sounds like seman-
tics, but really it makes such a difference. It costs nothing. It costs

absolutely nothing, and when you get those things right it makes a world of difference.'

The other crucial time the Matildas stood up that year marked a sliding-doors moment in the rights and history of women's football—or, rather, of women's sports: the players went on strike over the conditions under which they were having to operate.

The under-resourced generations before them had literally had to pay for the privilege of playing for their country and were widely known to have forked out cash hand over fist to pay for flights and more. But the current generation of Matildas were essentially having to do the same, just less visibly, as the pay rate they were on—A$21,000 per year—hovered around Australia's poverty line. That meant the players were living much the same way the previous generations had: delaying major life milestones such as moving out of home or buying property, working multiple casual jobs, relying on the support of partners and family. (A related issue is that this, too, meant the game was accessible only to players and players' families who could manage to scrape together enough to afford to support the pursuit. So through affordability attrition, players and their families were likely to be, at minimum, middle class. At a mercenary level, it's unclear just how many extraordinarily talented players missed out on representing Australia and being venerated by fans because of purely socioeconomic factors. At a moral and ethical level, it's unclear how many women missed out on the potentially life-changing benefit of football, whether at the elite or even social level, simply because they couldn't afford to play.) In short, the Matildas appeared to have a dream job, but their circumstances were tenuous and unsustainable—especially as the public and the federation expected them, as an elite team, to achieve professional-athlete results.

The strike came off the back of arduous collective bargaining agreement (CBA) negotiations that ultimately broke down. The Matildas were wedged by an impossible and cascading trifecta. They were no longer contracted. Because they were no longer contracted, they were no longer being paid; nor would they have been medically insured had they been injured in the course of their national team duties. So they faced physical risk on top of their financial one. To ask them to fly to the United States to play two friendlies against world champions the USWNT was ecstasy and agony: the chance to test themselves against the best women footballers in the world, tempered by the precarious pay and medical insurance issue. 'They asked us to play those games without being paid for two months,' Barbieri explains. 'Players had to move back in with their parents and put stuff in storage. We couldn't afford rent or food. All of us were on bare minimum money and they wanted us to jet off to America to play two games.'

This two-game friendly ask also occurred after the team had forgone other incomes, such as more lucrative overseas contracts or stable full-time jobs in other industries, in the 2015 Women's World Cup lead-up. 'They didn't want us to take any overseas contracts before the World Cup so we could basically spend six months training together,' Barbieri says. Sounds sensible, especially given everyone's nervousness around the unfamiliar artificial surface—except the FFA was essentially asking for full-time commitment from the players without full-time remuneration. As Barbieri explains, 'You had to say no to a lot of things because you didn't know where you'd be with the national team. You couldn't get a job, you couldn't get a second job … I wasn't on contract, so I had to do that six months on a per diem. You know, if you didn't go on camp, you didn't get paid. We all made sacrifices. Whether you were contracted or not, you made sacrifices.'

So players were experiencing unsustainably lean times before their two months of even leaner, unpaid times. The Matildas went on strike, sombrely fronting the media in a park near the FFA's Sydney headquarters. FFA staff could likely have watched the press conference from their office windows.

With goalkeeper and PFA ambassador Lydia Williams as spokesperson, the Matildas outlined their requests. The logical asks, which centred on creating a sustainable foundation, included adequate conditions and standards suitable to a high-performance environment: appropriate medical care, accommodation, insurance and travel conditions. These were uncontroversial but nonetheless make-or-break elements that were standard for men. Despite being paid poverty-line-level income, all of the players were, for example, having to pay their own top-tier medical insurance. Some were also having to pay their own gym memberships, which they needed for strength, conditioning and rehabilitation, as no gym facilities were made available to them.

The Matildas also asked for adequate pay to reflect the full-time, professional-equivalent training load they were already completing—A\$21,000 was, in the long term and even often the short term, unaffordable and unsustainable. Such low pay essentially rendered their football career a side hustle and forced them to rely on family or seek out other sources of income to top up—or prop up—their football one. So basically they were requesting pay, conditions and security to enable them to perform their job, irrespective of their pre-existing socioeconomic standing. They also requested a commitment to supporting the women's game to ensure the longevity and success of women's football in Australia, to treat it as a sport to be invested in, not as a box-ticking corporate social responsibility initiative. Again, a sensible, realistic ask.

'Upon reflection, it was the time for this to occur,' Gill says of the strike. 'Everything aligned: the CBA had expired, management was refusing to even engage with players, the US were standing there waiting for us to go and play against them. It was like this was the opportune time to do this and to get an impactful response.'

Still, it was stomach-churningly scary, and the enormity of what they were risking was unparalleled. There's only one national women's team, and you're either in it or out of it. The risk of non-selection—and specifically the risk of non-selection because you're seen as being the worst thing a woman can be: 'difficult'—can mean the difference between realising and not realising your dream. That's before you factor in pressures adding to selection availability and complexity, such as a narrow window of age opportunity and being injury-free. Under such circumstances, it's understandably very difficult to say no if you are selected, no matter how poor the conditions and pay.

'The position you're in as an athlete is so precarious,' Gill says. 'If you disagree with management ... Yes, there should be footballing reasons as to why you don't play, but that's not always the case because it's so contextualised, everything is intertwined. Ultimately one person decides if you do or don't have a contract. And they don't have to justify their decision.'

Although excruciating to have to turn down playing the ultimate in friendlies, the Matildas knew that if they had gone on the US tour, they would have lost any and all (albeit meagre) leverage, and the CBA likely would have either stayed unsettled or been settled overwhelmingly not in their favour. The FFA would have known, too, that the lure of being a Matilda outweighed the physical, mental, financial and emotional costs required to pursue that dream, and the cycle of undervaluing and underpaying the Matildas would have continued. So, like the stand the players had had to make around the artificial turf just months earlier, a stand that wasn't really about turf at all, this stand transcended recompense. 'You're essentially fighting for your livelihood,' Gill says. 'The power imbalance and notion of gratitude are hard to grapple with and ultimately mean that you aren't entering into a fair fight.'

It's difficult to know what the correct approach was given it's impossible to play out both scenarios and choose the optimal one. Certainly the improved conditions they subsequently obtained suggest that the strike was the right move. But the opportunity to play the United States in the United States wasn't an opportunity frequently available to the team. Garriock, for example, considers that perhaps it could have been handled differently. She's well-positioned to make that assessment given she was instrumental in negotiating earlier gains the team made.

Sports broadcaster Stephanie Brantz sums up the conundrum: 'I was proud of them for standing up for what they believed in, but equally I felt that the exposure they would have got playing in the US would have been fantastic.' She ponders whether it would have been more viable to act at a time that would maximise pressure and media attention, reminiscent of the action the USWNT had taken in the 2015 Women's World Cup lead-up and would take in the 2019 one, too. 'I mean, if I was going to strike, I would have done it before a major tournament,' Brantz says. 'I would have waited for the next major tournament and made a stand. But that's just me, and I wasn't a player, and I wasn't not getting paid for what I did.'

Worth noting is that the Matildas had been playing for exposure and asking nicely for decades. If you omit the emotion and pride involved in representing your country, this was essentially an employment contract dispute. There aren't a lot of industries where an employer can ostensibly require full-time commitment and results that meet or exceed KPIs without comparable conditions and pay.

The Matildas didn't know what the response would be, either from the FFA or the general public, and some of the players temporarily went offline and avoided making further comment as events unfolded. 'The moments after the press conference were a bit strange,' Yallop says. 'It's always hard to anticipate how people are going to react, especially those who don't know that much about what you do and how much you sacrifice. We definitely found comfort and confidence in the support we got from each other. Standing as a collective was so important and we all looked out for each other like true teammates during that time.'

Brock says similar: 'The strike was a bit of a whirlwind, to be honest. I just remember how important it was that we stuck together as a team and made a collective statement. I think it played a critical role in the progression of our sport, but it definitely wasn't easy. I was often so nervous I felt sick. I'm a bit of a people pleaser and feeling like we had to leave staff in the dark about our decision, to make sure the right message came out at the right time, was horrible.'

Sykes was similarly terrified, especially as she felt her position within the Matildas squad was anything but cemented. 'I felt super conflicted about whether we were doing the right thing and how it looked to the public. I still felt new to the squad, and didn't actually get many more opportunities to play for the Matildas after that point, so the selfish part of me was worried about missing an opportunity to play in a big tour to the US. But the reception was positive and, looking back, I'm proud to have been part of it. The women's game has come a long way even in the time since that moment in 2015, and I'm really happy for the players who get to follow not just the few of us who took a stand at that time, but also all the other pioneers of the game before us who had done similar things and more. It taught me a lot about when to draw a line in the sand and how to respectfully take a stand for what is right and what is necessary.'

Lisa De Vanna was the only player to cross the metaphorical picket line, but ultimately her outlier stance didn't disrupt the strike's message or outcomes as the strike struck the perfect PR chord with the media and the public. Although they hadn't yet been voted Australia's most beloved sports team (that would come in 2019), the Matildas were well known and well respected. 'I felt like that was probably one of the biggest strengths, timing-wise,' Gill says. 'The Matildas had created enough of a name for themselves to have that fame, for the public to know who they were and what they were fighting for.'

The shock and exasperation that resulted when it became known how inadequately the Matildas were paid were perhaps best summed up in a *Junkee* headline that won the internet that day: 'The Matildas Have Gone on Strike Because, Oh My God Can We Just Pay Them Properly?'[7] Journalist Sam Squiers was equally direct in an editorial on her website, *Sportette*, entitled 'Don't Let the Matildas Strike Be in Vain'. In it she called out the FFA's empty-pockets argument by saying it hadn't done enough to fill said pockets by generating revenues or promoting the women's game.[8]

The much-needed, albeit nominal improvements yielded by the strike included a salary range between A$30,000 and A$41,000 a year, depending which tier players were on, supplemented by training-camp and match-day per diems. While still comparatively low wages given that the average Australian full-time earnings were and are around double that, the gains made the difference between players being able to continue training and representing their country and having to make tough either/or decisions. (Indeed, while Yallop couldn't possibly have predicted it exactly at the time she participated in the strike, the advantages gained then and since are ones she was already directly benefiting from. Born at just the right time to push for and begin to receive these improvements, and to have same-sex marriage recognised, she has been able to marry as well as start and support a family with her partner, former Football Fern Kirsty Yallop, while still playing.)

The strike, along with the turf and first-Asian-champions push-backs, had a common throughline: expecting the women footballers to accept whatever was offered, however unreasonable, would no longer be tolerated. The Matildas took a stand to prevent a stasis or slippage in rights, and increase safety and respect for themselves and future generations. And although they were going it alone, they did feel as if they had some support, including from the USWNT. 'Their encouragement definitely helped us to make a stand,' Brock says, 'and ultimately a lot of good came from it.' (One upside of the strike was that the union approached Barbieri to tell her story—as a paid speaking gig, of course. 'They loved the story,' she says. 'They totally backed us.')

Through the strike, which was essentially 'crash or crash through' in ethos, the Matildas achieved the latter. They also opened the door to previously uncomfortable, if not taboo, pay parity and gender equality conversations not just for themselves but for all partici-pants in women's sports. 'They gave other sports the confidence to make noise' is how Gill summarises it.

'I think fundamentally through the Matildas' or the football push, and the recognition from Football Federation Australia at that time, the other codes couldn't *not* do something,' former Matilda Julie Murray says. 'I certainly think football has led the charge. And it's given players and women the confidence that we can actually make a difference. Because again, I think that they recognise it's not just a difference for them, it's societal change and it needs to happen. Then you have all these other movements within politics talking about the way women are treated ... and just not accepting it, basically. I guess they caused a groundswell across the board.'

Indeed, the Matildas made enormous strides and opened the door for other women's sports to walk—*run*—through behind them in subsequent years. The pressure those emboldened rival codes applied after having been given a leg up arguably in turn forced the FFA to up its game. As a code that recruits players with similar technical skills and athleticism, the AFLW had already poached former Matildas goalkeeper Brianna Davey and was looking likely to steer the next generation of potential Matildas towards its domestic competition. Suddenly W-League pay, which had remained almost non-existent and largely stagnant for the league's first decade, was increased and then increased again. (The AFLW's 94 per cent pay increase in 2022, which set annual pay rates between A$39,184 and A$71,935 depending on the player's tier, raised the bar higher again in what will hopefully become a women's sports salary arms race.[9])

Pay parity and true equality didn't come in 2015, though—it would take another four years and being out the other side of another Women's World Cup for the Matildas to achieve that. But the groundwork had started, and the signalling of what would (or would not) be acceptable long term in terms of pay and conditions for women's sport began in 2015.

9

2019:
TIME'S UP

STANDING IN THE half-time toilet queue at the Australia v Norway Round of 16 match in Nice—because there's always a queue for women's toilets at women's sporting events—was a bashful young fan wearing a polka-dot French women's supporter jersey and a tiny homemade sandwich board. The jersey she was wearing came in a girls' and women's cut Nike had specially produced for the 2019 Women's World Cup. The sandwich board comprised low-resolution, watermarked Australian and Norwegian jersey images that looked like they'd been ripped from a website. The young fan had laminated those images and strung them over her shoulders in a show of neutral support.

Small but significant, her gesture illustrated the great gains women had made and the bright future women's football had. Here was a young girl who knew about women's football, was able to play it, was able to buy an appropriately sized supporter jersey of her national team, and was watching women play in a World Cup in her home country. None of that had been guaranteed a few decades or even a few years before.

★ ★ ★

Dual US and UK citizen Evie Chamberlain literally moved countries, from Scotland to Switzerland, to pursue a dream job of working in marketing and promotions for FIFA. Her first days were at the 2019 Women's World Cup. 'I arrived in Zurich on the Sunday, and on the Monday I got my phone and laptop. On the Tuesday at 7 a.m., I was on a train to Paris. So I was totally confused, mystified, overwhelmed,' she says. 'But the second we arrived in Paris, you could feel the joy and excitement. I do think there's some kind of extra optimism around the women's events ... For the men's stuff, they're patriotic, they want their team to win, but it's almost like it's only the football. But for the women's events, it feels like more.'

For Chamberlain, whose own experience came from playing in high school, unaware that becoming a professional footballer was even a possibility, working for the world's governing football body on the biggest women's football tournament in the world was well worth upending her life for, even if it wasn't as glamorous as it sounds: 'I lived out of a suitcase for three, four months. I didn't get the rest of my stuff until October. There were some things where I was like, *This is a bad choice; I should have put more pyjamas in here.*' But, as she puts it, 'It was just such a joy to see the fans, the excitement they were feeling, listening to their conversations, hearing people having discussions where they were talking about football and their team and not saying "the *women's* football".'

★ ★ ★

Kate Jacewicz has broken plenty of new ground in Australia, not least becoming the first woman to operate VAR and referee in the A-League Men's, but she sees herself as just one woman chipping away alongside rather than out front of others 'eking' out a football officiating career. 'I feel like I'm a part of history,' she says, 'and I'm doing my part as well as the other women [who] are doing it.' A moment with a fan and their father made her realise that, just as she'd looked up to referees such as Tammy Ogston before her, there were aspiring referees looking up to her.

Jacewicz was outside the referees' hotel headquarters when a girl and her father approached and asked if she was officiating that evening. 'Apparently she was a young, aspiring referee and her father took her around to see the referees,' Jacewicz says. That's some sophisticated ambition—refereeing isn't something traditionally chosen as a pathway at a young age—and some equally impressive parenting to nurture it. 'It was very cool to be talking to a young fan. I really felt that honour. They came and watched my game that night. I gave them my email address if they needed advice, and they emailed the very next day.'

* * *

Stephanie Brantz was at the 2019 event covering Australia for FIFA TV. Although she'd worked in and around women's football for years, 2019 was her first Women's World Cup on the ground. 'If you're not throwing money at the players, you're hardly sending a massive media team over, either,' she explains. 'I came very close to going to Canada as part of a tour group, but for whatever reason it didn't work out. I think someone looked at the distances and went "This is really expensive. So maybe not."'

The 2019 logistics were, Brantz says, hilarious. Trains were the primary transport mode, with a hire car at each end. 'I remember arriving at the train station in France looking for a big trolley to load our stuff on because we had all the camera equipment. We had seventeen bags and a team of three. How do you work that out? You need two people to push the trolley, but you need someone to stay with the stuff you can't fit on the trolley, and someone to stay with the stuff you dropped on the train platform. It was just like, "Oh my god." That was actually the trickiest part of our trip: manoeuvring stuff through France.'

Also, the work that went into capturing key, but quick, footage was enormous. 'Match days were interesting. It was jam-packed because you'd be there hours before, you'd have to film the team arrival.' That arrival is a fleeting but significant moment. 'You'd be liaising with the media team from your country to find out when the bus was going to arrive, because you only get one chance to get a bus coming in. So all those little bits and pieces that people don't notice when they're sitting at home watching the pre-game show and the team arrival happens—they don't realise how much negotiation goes into finding out when that's happening.'

★ ★ ★

Events manager Rebecca Yolland has Brexit's delay to thank for her ability to swing a last-minute 2019 Women's World Cup gig. That the UK took longer than expected to extricate itself from the European Union enabled the British–Australian passport holder, who'd been studying French due to a bit of an obsession with the culture, to realise some longheld dreams. First, to work on a French event. Second, to work on a Women's World Cup.

Yolland's late call-up was a whirlwind. 'It was a very short contract, and I didn't get a lot of information to start with … Also, my interview was in French so I wasn't 100 per cent sure I'd understood everything correctly,' she says. 'Thankfully I had!'

While Yolland's previous experience included working across a number of operational areas for events that included the 2014 Men's World Cup, two Men's Asian Cups, the 2018 Commonwealth Games and the Australian Grand Prix, her Women's World Cup gig was as a floor manager in Infotainment, a role not standard in her wheelhouse.

'Infotainment is everything entertainment-wise 'in bowl' [AKA inside the stadium],' Yolland explains. It combines a lot of fun with important information relating to the event, match and/or venue. The team creates and follows a callsheet that coordinates ground announcers, giant screens and the stadium sound system to share interviews, team line-up information, fan giveaways, sponsor ads, etc. It also plays a crucial role in the team walk-out, kick-off and announcements for goals, cards and substitutions. 'The idea is everybody's aligned and the overall match runs like clockwork.'

It's not a small job, and one where people know if something's up. 'In back-of-house operational roles, it's arguably easier to shift gears to rectify possible problems,' Yolland explains. 'However, when live and in front of thousands of people, if something doesn't go to plan it needs to be managed on the spot to the second, often involving other areas. There's a lot less room to move and the show must go on!'

But Yolland ultimately found the gig fun. 'We worked with Ettie the mascot, did games and giveaways. We were always looking for good opportunities. You could see the impact in firing up the crowd, especially those hardcore fans who got to the stadium early, and we'd be daring them to yell louder than the opposition while they could see themselves on the giant screen. They really got into it!' The VAR was in also play—one of the first times it was used—which represented new considerations. 'You had to figure out where to stand so you could see what you needed to see, but not be in the way of VAR or anyone else—it was quite tight!' she laughs.

The 2019 Women's World Cup work was a stepping-through-the-looking-glass moment for Yolland, who'd attended the 2007 Women's World Cup in China as a spectator. She'd been living in Beijing and she and her Hong Kong–based friends fleetingly appear on screen in the *Never Say Die* documentary.

Akin to the actions of the Croissants a generation before the Croissants, they had created green cardboard signs to which they affixed yellow cardboard letters and kangaroos. They'd cut those out in an arts-and-craft production line on the train to the game. The signs, which bear the quintessentially Australian words 'bonza', 'noice', 'you little ripper' and 'bloody beautiful', were likely slightly befuddling to, but a great talking point for, non-Australians; more importantly, they were an effort likely well appreciated by the Australian contingent.

To find herself pitchside, working on the event she'd once experienced as a fan, and to be practising her French—at times 'Franglish', but persevering in building her solid linguistic base—was a pinch-me moment. Particularly as even she, an experienced operator, could sense the 2019 tournament was bringing something different. 'There was a real pride to be a part of it. You could feel the connection within the venue team. There was a sense of being a part of something bigger, something special,' she says. 'You definitely could see how much people cared and how much they loved it.'

★ ★ ★

Player agent, manager and women's football advocate Fatima Flores attended the FIFA legend VIP events as former New Zealand player

Kirsty Yallop's plus one. Having grown up getting up in the middle of the night to support her beloved Real Madrid, being in a room filled with the world's best male players was unimaginably exciting. 'For me walking in, obviously I was crying, jumping, laughing, everything in one, but I had to contain it,' she says of her internal elation and outer professionalism. 'We noticed, though, after the initial excitement, that there were so many men at the Women's World Cup.'

Yallop played in a legends game and she and Flores attended workshops and the opening ceremony. 'There were some amazing people,' Flores says of the VIPs they met. 'But a lot of the other women legends, we all hung out because, well … we felt like the male players were elite superstars and we're just, "Here we are."' The women were humble, approachable and often fairly anonymous even to football fans like Flores, because their careers had played out with little to no promotion or media coverage. 'I felt I *should* know, I *want to* have known of you. But how was I supposed to?'

★ ★ ★

The 2019 Women's World Cup's climactic close involved a trophy presentation during which a stadium full of women's football supporters chanted in deafening unison, 'Equal pay! Equal pay!' The unwilling recipients of those chants—chants that became an almost physical wall of sound buffeting their bodies—included FIFA president Gianni Infantino. He was the man tasked with handing the Women's World Cup trophy to the winning team, the USWNT, while maintaining the party line that FIFA's prize money parity cupboards were bare.

Former AWSA board member and long-time football advocate Kerry Harris was the person who inspired the 'equal pay' clarion call that reverberated around the stadium and the world. 'I'd like to say it was a planned strategy, well thought out with measurable outcomes,' she says, 'but it was the total opposite of that. I was in the merchandise queue at the final and ahead of me was a USA fan from the American Outlaws fan club. On the back of her T-shirt she had written #EqualPay. It got me thinking, *How do we amplify that message?* and the idea of a chant popped into my head. Sadly, I didn't get her name, but knowing she was from a fan club I figured she would be able to galvanise a large group to get the chant going. So I tapped her on the shoulder, told her my idea, and the rest, as they say, is history.'

★ ★ ★

Twenty years on from the iconic '99 tournament, two years on from the #MeToo and Time's Up groundswells, and staged approximately six months before COVID-19 upended the world (and women's sport, and mass gatherings in sports stadiums), the 2019 Women's World Cup ratcheted women's football up another level. It was the tournament that embodied and illustrated the complex mix of euphoria, admiration and frustration being in and around women's football entails. From providing on-pitch performances so skilful and thrilling that they attracted more than a billion tuned-in eyeballs, to players becoming accidental activists addressing off-pitch issues ranging from gender-based discrimination to homophobia, it was a tournament that had everything. It also signalled that women were done with having their polite requests rebuffed: they were requiring proper progress.

Women's sport has traditionally received minimal mainstream media coverage. There's less coverage in terms of frequency, quality and length. The tone is often patronising or infantilising. Such 'gender-bland sexism' positions women's sport as inferior to, and less exciting than, the more established, better-remunerated men's equivalent.[1] But 2019 at least partly challenged that. Players leveraged their platforms and the unrivalled media spotlight to call out inequity; fans used their voices in stadiums and online to echo and amplify that pushback. Online, in pubs, and while gripping safety straps on the buses and trains travelling to the stadiums for games, supporter-jersey-clad fans of all countries and backgrounds held informed, intercultural conversations that segued between discussing such substantial, substantive topics as pay and prize-money parity and lighter, friendly-banter-based topics of teams' likelihood of winning. Combined with the heightened, interest-piquing football skill beamed around the world by major media, players, fans and administrators alike could sense and see it: something had shifted.

The high-stakes, high-publicity advocacy commenced long before the tournament began and would continue long after it finished, with players leveraging their platforms to raise awareness of issues and push back. The first signal of the tournament's Time's-Up tone and the organic but loosely unified and timely gender-equality themes that would infuse every tournament element perhaps came from a stylised video with a sobering subtext released by the German team. In the professionally produced 90-second video, an artefact of the wider collective mood irrespective of players' and fans' country of origin, the two-time Women's World Cup and eight-time European champions listed and skewered the biases and dismissal the team had faced. Those included trolls' suggestions that women's place is in the home, not on the football pitch. As in, cooking, cleaning, bringing up kids. Speaking directly to camera, some of the players asked whether we knew their names before noting, in what we could say is reminiscent of the Matilda Effect, that they played for a country oblivious to their identities and therefore contributions. Posed sipping from delicate tea cups, pinkies raised, with tinkling backing music that contrasted with the rest of the video's frenetic sounds, players also referenced Germany's 1989 European Championship win, for which the players mind-bogglingly received impractical and ultimately offensive tea sets instead of any kind of cash prize. (That's not just a practice relegated to the 1980s. The Matildas did not receive any prize money for their 2010 Asian Cup win: instead, they were given plasma-screen TVs, which sounds generous until you consider that TVs weren't the most practical item for players who were living a fairly transient existence pursuing northern and southern hemisphere football seasons.[2] You could say, though, it was a step up from being traded for a TV, which is what happened to former Matilda Alison Leigh Forman.)

The second sign that women were done with being ignored came in the form of a more serious shot across the bow by reigning world champions the USWNT. After years of asking and negotiating—more than twenty years, in fact, as the '99ers had been having equivalent conversations—the USWNT launched a class-action lawsuit to sue US Soccer three months out from the 2019 Women's World Cup.

The premise was that US Soccer had engaged in 'purposeful gender discrimination' for failing to enact equal pay for comparable work. The USWNT had a point. Ranked first in the world, its achievements and accolades are so lengthy that one needs to truncate the list and even then take a breath before rattling it off. In short, the USWNT has won seventeen major tournaments: four (of a possible eight) Women's World Cups, four Olympic gold medals, and nine Confederation of North, Central America and Caribbean Association Football (CONCACAF) Gold Cups. Yet the USWNT earned less than half the salary of the US Men's National Team (the USMNT), a team that at the time hadn't made much of a mark in the football world. So the USWNT, regarded as a powerful leader both on the pitch and in the gender-equality advocacy space, had been rendered powerless by US Soccer's and FIFA's refusal to invest properly in the women's game.[3]

The story US Soccer had long peddled was that the women's team wasn't bringing in enough money to warrant parity. The thing is, it wasn't true. US Soccer's own financial statements clearly showed the USWNT to be earning the organisation money while the USMNT cost it.

US Soccer failed to voluntarily rectify—or even suggest it might rectify—the pay disparity. In fact, it doubled down. So, in a move that showed that if US Soccer wasn't going to get there on its own, the USWNT would leverage the law (not to mention the attendant media interest and poor PR) to make it do so, the USWNT lodged a wage discrimination complaint with the Equal Employment Opportunity Commission (EEOC). Suing its employer heading into the two's busiest and most entwined work period lobbed an elephant into the room and ramped up the pressure on the team to win. But staying the course spoke to the severity of the issue and the lengths to which the team was having to go to be heard.

For the Matildas' part, their 2019 tournament and its preceding months were equally tumultuous, albeit ending with less favourable results. Less than six months out, and at a time when the team should have been refining combinations and building for a June peak performance, it was rocked by the sudden removal of Alen Stajcic, its coach of four or so years. No information or explanation was (or, more likely, could be) made available. In its absence, disproportionate attention fell on confidential team surveys focusing on player welfare amid a reportedly dysfunctional team environment. So the Matildas' preparation was marred by speculation and distraction as media and fans alike sought to answer a single question: Why had Stajcic been sacked?

The question remains unanswered, and no one emerged from the incident unscathed. Even now, anyone even tangentially related to the situation understandably continues to keep their head below the parapet. Although absolutely wretched for everyone concerned, it's important to note that senior management and boards don't tend to make decisions rashly or lightly. Likewise, the high-pressure nature of the job means that coaches are removed with regularity should results be unsatisfactory or should bodies decide to bring in different coaching styles and expertise. While an equivalent of Stajcic's removal is ideally never to be repeated, it's worth acknowledging that a substantive, future-focused takeaway is the need for a coach succession plan. The vacuum left after Stajcic's departure, the absence of a clear plan to fill the position and the lack of information forthcoming from the FFA undoubtedly left space for rumours to fill. Imagine if, for example, as per the German model, there were women candidates who'd been mentored and developed through dedicated women's coaching programs and who were genuinely ready and supported to take the helm. Imagine if we had shifted focus from why an incumbent coach had been removed so close to a crunch event to ensuring that such pre-tournament transition tumult never happened again.

New Zealand's own Women's World Cup preparation faced similar interruption when in 2018—roughly a year before the 2019 tournament was due to kick off—coach Andreas Heraf was removed following allegations of bullying and intimidation. It was an uncomfortable situation for former Football Fern Sarah

Gregorius for myriad reasons. Having been heavily involved in the New Zealand players' union and the CBA negotiations, she was well-versed in the team's rights and felt a responsibility to look out for her teammates. Complicating that was the fact she had to take action against the very coach who had convinced her to come out of retirement.

'Part of my motivation [for coming out of retirement] is that we'd got a new CBA in place, and I'd always felt I wanted to help the team out in terms of understanding this new era of rights and what New Zealand owed them in terms of obligations that was different to how things had been in the past. I had been so involved in the process, was still so close to the team, and obviously the coach thought I could make a football contribution as well on the field, so I came back with the idea of *I'll just play an off-field leadership role*,' Gregorius says. 'Then everything went down with the coach. He turned out to be unequivocally the wrong person to be leading us.'

Gregorius advised her teammates on, and participated in, a formal process to address players' concerns. 'Basically the coach was found to have engaged in bullying and harassment behaviour, so we were completely vindicated as to why we had to go through that process, and we got the right outcome. But it's not a process I ever want to have to repeat. It was unbelievably difficult.'

Tom Sermanni stepped in as interim coach shortly before the 2019 tournament. (He initially signed up to go to the World Cup, then was extended to the Olympics, then was extended again when COVID-19 delayed the Olympics. It was, he says, 'the longest short-term contract'.)

'In comes Uncle Tom at the end of it,' Gregorius continues. 'We probably couldn't have had a better person come in and take the reins after all of that. He knows football, he knows women's football … he's people-driven. He's got that character, he's got that warmth. So at the end of all of that to have a coach with his experience and with his manner come in and take the team, it was another good outcome at the end of a very difficult situation.'

Sermanni's entry, a casual barbecue on the beach, provided an opportunity for the team to reset. The team had had a facilitated debrief day, a rare but much-needed day away from playing football, before joining Sermanni. 'He came along and said, "Look, I acknowledge that I wasn't here, like didn't go through all this with you, but I'm here, I'm with you now, take what you need to get back together as a squad, and you have the support of the new staff coming in." He did all the right things, and then we're just having a barbecue on the beach with him. It was just really what we needed. We're like a little family. I know a lot of national teams say that, but we really are. A lot of us have known each other since we were teenagers. A bit like Uncle Tom. He just came in at the right time and he did the right thing and we had a family barbecue.'

The team's improved outlook was apparent in the players' and teams' demeanour in subsequent months. One particularly illustrative social media post, captioned 'Move over [Thor actor] @ chrishemsworth. There's a new hero in town', depicted Sermanni—'Thormanni'—kneeling, fist to ground as Hemsworth's character does, and New Zealand players jumping backwards in response to the awesome power Thormanni's move unleashed. Sermanni didn't quite understand the plan when the players suggested he strike the pose. But, ever willing to not take himself too seriously and to facilitate opportunities to raise women's football's profile, he duly obliged. After some photoshopping to add some light-changing effects to depict the power transfer, New Zealand Football published the light-hearted post to great reception.

Coach investigations and removals aside, both teams' pre-tournament distractions ultimately proved to be lesser issues as the rise of European teams and other wider issues overtook the coach dramas once the event kicked off. The 2019 tournament was only the Netherlands' second Women's World Cup appearance, and Australia and New Zealand both arguably wished it hadn't happened at all. Australia was absolutely dismantled by the Dutch team in a pre-tournament friendly—an early warning of the gains European teams had made and were about to unleash. New Zealand, for its part, must have been rueing lost chances as it had the Dutch on the ropes in the opening group-stage match but lost 1–0 in the final few minutes. The team continued its tradition of testing but not quite defeating teams that would go on to win or finish runners-up, and retained and extended its unwanted record as the team with the longest winless streak in the Women's World Cup. Italy, full of largely unknown debutantes due to it being the team's first appearance in twenty years, was not expected to trouble the top-10-ranked Matildas, but it proved the group-stage gauge of women's football development. With a 2–1 loss that put them on the back foot from the outset, the Matildas' plans were in disarray. The Italy game wasn't the tournament start Brantz or her FIFA media counterparts following the Italian team expected either. She and the Australian crew were, she says, 'shell-shocked afterwards. It was kind of like, "No, no, no. We don't want to go home after the group stage. What is happening here?"'

With their tournament progression now shaky, the Matildas faced arch rivals Brazil. In a heart-stopping, must-win match so deafeningly loud and so punctuated by fans' high-pitched whistling that players couldn't hear each other on the pitch, the Matildas overcame a 2-goal deficit to defeat Brazil 3–2. The long-time rivals had more in common than their confusingly similar green-and-gold supporter colours. Both were succeeding or failing on the skill and determination of their committed but underpaid, undersupported players, and both were grappling with the surge of European teams that had the investment they lacked.

Capturing the euphoria and the heartbreak—including the vulnerable, private moments players have with their families in such a public arena—was photographer Rachel Bach. 'The atmosphere was really distracting,' she says of the Brazil game. 'I remember being tuned into the crowd in a way I hadn't been in other games … The hostility was electric. Because our colours are so similar, it was interesting to figure out who was supporting who.'

That pressure-cooker environment yielded some of the best moments and photos of the tournament. 'I have a lot of weird superstitions when I shoot, and one of them is about moving,' Bach explains. She elected to stay put in the Brazil game despite having the option to head to the other end at half-time. Heeding her superstition paid off. Chloe Logarzo scored to ignite the Matildas' comeback against Brazil by levelling the score 2–2. Bach was perfectly placed to capture Logarzo's iconic goalscoring celebration and her own favourite image from the tournament: Logarzo standing tall, hands on hips like Superwoman, the number 5 written on tape wrapped around her wrist. The pose was a heartfelt gesture to teammate Laura Brock, who'd been ruled out with a foot fracture on the eve of the event but who'd continued her pre-match ritual of singing Alicia Keys' 'Superwoman' to Logarzo to pump her up for the game. (Using technology to overcome geographical logistics given she was no longer travelling with the team, Brock switched out *a capella* in the change room for *a capella* over the phone.) Logarzo, who wears custom shin pads featuring family and friends to signal how much they too are part of her football experience, perhaps understood better than most what it was like to have to watch a World Cup from afar. She watched the Matildas play in the 2015 World Cup, a tournament she might have been in contention for, while instead absent from the game and very alone in an overseas bar. That distance was pivotal in helping her realise that being a Matilda and playing in the biggest women's football tournaments was very much where she wanted to be. She, like Brock, ultimately understood how hard-won being part of the national team is and how fleeting and quickly extinguished national team dreams can be. 'I vowed to the girls that I would remain in France as long as they did and would be cheering them on all the way, and that is exactly what I did,' Brock says of her efforts to support from the stands and await her chance to go out on a high, which she later achieved via the postponed 2020 Olympics. Of the Brazil game and Logarzo's touching tribute, she says, 'That game had my emotions on a knife edge.'

The tournament's theme was 'Dare to Shine', a sentiment players took to heart. In her goalscoring celebrations, Megan Rapinoe took up space and invited and soaked up adulation. Logarzo's Superwoman pose was similarly one of strength, of soaking up the recognition she deserved. Bach says, 'I think probably what I was thinking when Chloe scored and turned almost directly towards me was *Oh my god, is this really happening?* I couldn't believe what

I was seeing and the luck I had being in that spot. That whole game, that whole experience, I was shaking. I don't generally do a lot of editing while I shoot, but that game, that Chloe celebration photo, was probably the first time in the tournament that I got out my laptop and edited a photo during a game. I thought to myself, *You're breaking all your rules, all your superstitions—this might come back to bite you. If Brazil wins, this photo doesn't mean anything.* I think that's a big thing about photography and those moments: when the story changes, there's only so much a photo can mean. So that whole experience was insane but it was probably one of my favourite parts of the whole trip.'

Upping the media-attention ante after that game was Matildas captain Sam Kerr. Fed up with trolling on her social media that veered from unhelpful criticism about how she was playing to outright homophobia, she mentioned off the cuff but on camera that her haters could 'suck on that one'. The statement, which she issued after proving her trolls wrong with her on-pitch prowess and which the host-broadcaster newsfeed beamed around the world, sparked controversy about appropriateness. It also exposed what few in the media and beyond understood players were going through. Some media commentary in the days afterwards—invariably mostly written by men—suggested that the 'millionaire Matilda' was being precious. Then Kerr shared screenshots of some of the social media abuse she regularly received, much of it homophobic. It was revelatory.

Kerr's pushback arguably occurred at the beginning of a wave of elite athletes—specifically elite women athletes, such as Naomi Osaka and Simone Biles—valuing their mental health and showing courageous vulnerability previously unseen from athletes whom most assume are superhuman and have it all. Kerr's comment also inspired empathetic fans to seek out a local screenprinting shop to make 'Suck on that one' tribute shirts they proudly wore for the rest of the tournament.

The Matildas then turned their attention to the last and most pivotal group-stage match against Jamaica. A first-time qualifier after being disbanded twice and resurrected thanks only to the advocacy of Bob Marley's daughter Cedella, the lowest-ranked tournament team was not expected to stretch the Matildas.[4] But, as Italy had already proved, such teams can prove to be bogeys. As it turned out, even though the match lacked the rivalry of and technical elegance of the Italy and Brazil matches, it delivered key moment on top of key moment. Kerr led by example to score 4 goals to secure the Matildas' Round of 16 berth, and Lisa De Vanna notched up an incredible 150th cap—one shy of then record holder Cheryl Salisbury.

Karly Roestbakken, a cusp player who narrowly missed out on being selected for the 2019 Women's World Cup and would have been forgiven for sitting at home in Australia eating her feelings as the event kicked off thousands of kilometres away in France, had received a fairytale call-up. The team was short on defenders due to injuries to the likes of Brock and Clare Polkinghorne, so Roestbakken was teleported from non-selection to Starting XI in the space of a dreamlike few days. She debuted in stoppage time against Brazil and started against Jamaica.

'It was such a surreal moment. It's everyone footballing dream to play at a World Cup so to get the call-up was just such a special moment for me and my family. Even just being in contention, that was huge, and then to get the call-up was even better of course. It didn't really hit me until the tournament was over. First making my Matildas debut, but to do it at a World Cup was really something special,' Roestbakken says. 'It was a happy time for me, I had worked so hard so to get recognised for that was an honour. Loz [Brock] was amazing as usual. I felt gutted for her but her support was something I couldn't have asked for. I knew I had really big shoes to fill, and I just wanted to do it for her.'

While that story was incredible, spare a thought for the overlooked players. Gema Simon, for example, was vying for one of those defensive positions but remained on the bench the entire tournament. (And even for Roestabakken herself. Her call-up was shortlived as she, too, suffered a foot bone injury that took her out of the game for a sustained period of time—so the cycle continued as she, as the injury replacement, too needed an injury replacement. 'My journey so far has had some really big highs and quite a few lows. But that's how it goes in sport, you never know what will happen. Going from a major tournament, breaking into the team, to suffering a pretty serious injury was really hard. It put me out of the game for a really long time, and I was away from home as well, which made it a lot harder. I missed things I have been working towards for a long time. But in saying that, it has made me grow even more as a person. It's definitely tested me but it has made me stronger. It's made me [want to] work harder and get back to playing football consistently. I love it, and I wouldn't want to do anything else. It's the most fun thing in the world, and there are still goals I want to achieve so that's what has driven me.') Spare a thought, too, for Brock. 'I think I spent the most part in disbelief,' she says. 'This was meant to be my final chapter with the team, and it didn't go to plan at all. Let me just say that once I actually left the team I cried ... a lot! The most was during the first game's national anthem, when I was still feeling shell-shocked and confused as to why I wasn't standing beside my teammates.'

Brantz ran into Brock shortly after the start of the match when she had ducked out to the FIFA TV team's hired van to grab some gear. 'I said, "Are you OK?" She was like, "I was OK until the national anthem." It was heartbreaking for her. She wasn't dropped—she was injured, so she had to withdraw. I just thought, *That's when it gets really tricky. Your family's flown over to see you play, you're expecting to be on the pitch.* She would have been starting. And all of a sudden that dream, in the blink of an eye, is gone.'

The FIFA TV crew shoots the team's tournament headshots. Those images are made available for media use and are projected on the stadium screens as part of announcing the Starting XI. As a FIFA TV crew member, Brantz had early but unconfirmed indication of Brock's agonising injury. 'On one of the days, Laura Brock hadn't come through yet, and I was thinking, *Where is she?* And then we had another shirt brought in. I was like, "What's going on here?" Then of course Karly Roestbakken had been brought into the squad. We had to shoot her picture, but Laura still had a fitness test to go. It was all this very fine juggling, and again you're never going to say anything, especially when you know the players. You felt desperately heartbroken for Laura, but what an experience for Karly.'

Brock admirably cheered on her team from the stands. 'I made the decision early on to support Karly as best I could and focus my energies on being there for her and the rest of the girls. That shift of focus definitely helped me to get through and increased my bond with them. When they told me my jersey was hung in the change room, I was incredibly humbled by how amazing my teammates and staff were to include me like that. It's so easy for an injured player to feel ostracised and on the outer, but I very much felt a part of their journey through that tournament.'

The Jamaica match also saw Brock's teammate and close friend Aivi Luik make her Women's World Cup debut after almost a decade persevering beyond missing out on the 2011 tournament. The 24th-best player in Australia when the Women's World Cup only allows a squad of 23, she had been overlooked for not one but two Women's World Cups before finally making the 2019 squad at age thirty-four. Exuding a luminosity reserved for elite athletes who spend all their time training outdoors and fuelling their bodies with dietitian-approved wholefoods, Luik is the kind of person for whom you assume things are going pretty well. But she is one of many players we hear very little about—good enough to be in consideration to represent her country at the world's pinnacle tournament, but not quite good enough to cement a spot. There are hundreds of players like her for whom Women's World Cup selection is so close and yet so far.

'In 2011 I was twenty-six. All my life, all I'd wanted was to compete in the World Cup. Every moment of football was a lead-up to that point, so I was so devastated when I got cut,' Luik says. 'For a long while after, just the mention of the World Cup was like a knife in the heart. Maybe some people won't get that, but I reckon there are plenty of athletes who know exactly what I'm talking about: years of dedication, desire and dreaming came to a halt.

'In 2015 I was thirty. In my mind, if I was ever going to make it, this was it. But I didn't. It was almost equally as horrible as the first time—feelings of loss, disappointment, of not being good enough and more. The recurring thought of *That was my last chance* was pretty devastating, too.'

Yet Luik persisted when other cusp players, worn down by the grind, the omissions and the lack of pay, fell away. She worked to improve her skills and versatility. She also shifted her focus. 'I just let go and played football. I think it was an unconscious way of protecting myself. The 2019 World Cup was never really in my thoughts. I was just focused on club football to that point, on doing my best there and enjoying it, and I think that showed in the way I was playing. Of course, in a small corner of my mind there was a part that hadn't given up hope and believed there was a chance, but only up until a short time before selection was I in the mind frame of *Hey, I might actually be going*.'

At thirty-four, an age where most players would be retiring by will or by force through injury or non-selection, Luik realised her Women's World Cup dream. 'Maybe unsurprisingly, I don't remember being told I had made it,' she says. 'I suppose that's how things go sometimes—you remember the painful experiences more than the good ones. But being in France was amazing. It was a feeling of accomplishment, of *Finally I got here*.'

Luik was substituted onto the pitch against Jamaica and played for a total of three minutes—an emotional, incredible 180 seconds, the significance of which was cognisant only to those who knew her backstory. ('It's moments like that I absolutely feel that pressure, because I'm acutely aware how fleeting these moments are and how important they are, and I just know there's a good chance they won't be captured,' Bach says of photographing Luik's debut.)

And so the Matildas made it to the Round of 16, where they faced Norway. The sudden-death match ended in 4–1 penalty heartbreak, and the historical footnote version is that the Matildas couldn't edge past the Norwegians. This was despite circumstances favourable to the Matildas specifically, albeit unfavourable to women's football as a whole: Norway was missing Ada Hegerberg, the best female footballer in the world at the time, who had opted out of the tournament and vowed never to play for the national team again. (In a cryptic statement most women would nevertheless comprehend, Hegerberg had said that one day the 'men in suits' would understand. Fortunately, she returned to the squad in 2022 after reaching an agreement with the Norwegian governing body. Unfortunately, Hegerberg's wasn't an isolated issue. French captain Wendie Renard and the entire Canadian national women's team had to take similar stands in early 2023.)

The 2019 Women's World Cup became the first where an Asian team did not progress to the quarter-finals, a sign of how European teams had surpassed Asian ones in investment and results. That was little comfort to Australia—or New Zealand, for that matter. Oceania-based New Zealand's tournament was similarly tough, except its exit was at the group rather than knockout stage. Throw in turmoil with the previous coach and a qualification route via Oceania that was basically a walk-up start, and the preparation was not ideal. Sermanni says, 'Assessing our performances, I thought we overperformed in the first game and underperformed in the second game. We couldn't back up because of the effort required in the first game. And the third game still frustrates me to this day because, again, it's a game that, if I'd had a bit more time getting the team together, we could have, *should* have won, that we lost.'

The New Zealand squad was also decimated by two tournament-ending injuries to two key players. Meikayla Moore ruptured her Achilles in a training warm-up and CJ Bott broke her wrist during the group-stage game against Canada. Also, New Zealand encountered teams with the aforementioned vastly superior resources, investment and development. 'The challenge is only going to get tougher and tougher for teams like New Zealand now that the rest of the European world has woken up to women's football,' Sermanni says. 'The depth in the squads and the lack of money to prepare teams is a challenge. And while Australia's geographical position isn't the best, New Zealand's is worse. And it has a smaller population, with multiple sports like netball and women's rugby, in particular. Those two sports are vying for the best athletes. So there's challenges for New Zealand. And they're aware of it.'

That Women's World Cup exit would be Gregorius's third and last. Fittingly, her family was there, as with her 2011 debut. 'In 2019, after we got knocked out of the tournament by Cameroon, that was heartbreaking. I remember going over to where my mum, dad and two brothers were and crying with them. I just needed it, you know? My brothers are quite big dudes and so they make a bit of a wall around you, and then I was just hugging my mum and dad. It's that kind of stuff that is the most precious, because you get to share, and because the emotions are really difficult to prepare for. You feel you're so close to, on the one hand, absolute misery and, if it goes slightly different, absolute joy.' (Bach would attest to how central family is to players' tournament experience. The question players most frequently ask her is 'Do you have any of me with my family?')

Shortly afterwards, Gregorius accepted a job offer from FIFPRO to take on its women's football advocacy at a global level. Her football retirement didn't go quite according to plan. 'Yeah, it was really awkward,' she groans at mention of Sermanni's story about her two attempts at her second retirement. 'I sat down with Tom and told him, "Look, I'm going to retire but I've been in this team for ten years. I'm very, very close—I'm two games away from 100 caps. What do you reckon?" He was like, "All right, we'll get you to 100 caps and then this can be your last tour." I said, "I don't really want to tell the team. I just want them to able to focus. It's not a big deal, and I'll just go quietly into the night." He was like, "Yeah, OK, that's fine."'

Her roommate, Rebekah Stott, was one of the few who knew about the plan. She asked if Gregorius was sure the number wasn't ninety-seven. 'I was like, "Shut up!"' Gregorius says. 'This was half an hour after I'd talked to Tom.'

'We were sitting there trying to count them up,' Stott says. Sure enough, Gregorius was on ninety-seven caps, not ninety-eight. She had to fess up to Sermanni: 'I counted wrong.' He was amused, and called Gregorius up for one game at the Algarve Cup so she could obtain her final, 100th cap.

'The first game in the Algarve Cup was against Belgium and it was going *fine*,' Gregorius says. 'We were up 1–0, and obviously the idea was for me to come on at the end of the game and get that cap, and happy days. Then our centre back got sent off and Belgium equalised, and it was getting towards the end of the game and we were hanging on by the skin of our teeth, trying to get a result.

I'm warming up and also thinking—maybe I said it to him—"Tom, maybe this isn't the game for me to get 100 caps—it's getting a bit serious, a bit tense out there." But he didn't care. He put me on in the eighty-fifth minute. It ended up being a 1–1 draw. Because we were at the Algarve and [under tournament rules] there was no extra time, it just went straight to penalties. They had to have a winner.'

Ali Riley told Gregorius she had to take a penalty. 'I was like, really?' Gregorius says. 'After this game, I know I'll be nobody to this team. She's like, "You're definitely taking one." So my last kick of my international career for the Football Ferns was a penalty against Belgium. I scored, and we won the penalty shootout.'

It's a fun story, but also a meaningful one. Gregorius is the first to acknowledge that she was fortunate to be able to go out on her own terms: 'To be able first of all to pick my moment is a privilege in itself. To not have it decided for me through injury or deselection or whatever was unbelievable ... I know I'm one of the lucky ones. It's an absolute fairytale. I don't know what I did to deserve it, but I'm so grateful it worked out that way. It was just perfect: 100 games, last kick a penalty, and starting a new life in a wicked city in a job I love was an absolute dream.'

Gregorius also has a story or two to share about Sermanni. 'His first tournament was the World Cup qualifiers in New Caledonia. A bit of a relaxed setting, right? I think it was the half-time talk of the match against Tahiti, everyone's sweating bullets. We were up by a few goals at this point, quite comfortable, but it's still World Cup qualifiers. We get back to our little change room in this poxy little stadium in New Caledonia and we've got our ice towels around our necks trying to get our body temperature down. Tom walks into the half-time team talk, into the dressing room, with a coconut in his hand and a straw he's drinking from. And he delivers his team talk holding a coconut, sipping on the straw, and telling us what we need to do for the second half to continue on in the tournament.'

Same tournament, different game: 'We get into half-time and we're like, "Where are the lollies to get the glucose levels back up?" There was only one bag [left]. Our team doctor was like, "Tom snuck in and ate the other two bags." So for the rest of the tournament they had to hide the half-time lollies from Tom because he has a bloody sweet tooth and would go ferreting around for our lollies. If it wasn't the half-time coconut holiday drink, it was the lollies,' she laughs. 'So that guy, before he starts telling stories about players, he needs to watch himself!'

★ ★ ★

Having commenced legal action against its federation just prior to the event, and with players such as Rapinoe prepared to speak publicly about pay parity and other gender-based and LGBTIQA+ issues, the USWNT was at the pointy end of the 2019 tournament's seismic cultural and awareness shift. Rapinoe and her teammates were all beneficiaries of the Title IX public policy, enacted in 1972, that prevents gender discrimination in education or feder-ally funded activity, including sport. Having fostered a generation of sportswomen with 'an appetite for' and expectation of equality in, for example, education, opportunity and resourcing, this policy acted as a catalyst for the equal-pay advocacy.[5]

Rapinoe, in particular, became a lightning rod for conservatives' ire, not least because she pointed out that it wasn't scientifically or statistically possible to win tournaments without gay team mem-bers. Obviously, LGBTIQA+ people exist in all parts of society and particularly in women's football, which has traditionally provided a more inclusive environment.[6] The USWNT itself had five out players and an out coach at the time of the 2019 tournament. Also, Rapinoe, who deemed herself a 'walking protest' in relation to US president Donald Trump, declared she was 'not going to the fuck-ing White House' if the team won.

While these were likely burdensome distractions at a time when Rapinoe would have wanted to concentrate on the game alone, women's sport and politics have never been mutually exclusive. When you're a woman trying to play a male-dominated sport, when you're seeking to overturn systemic pay disparity structures that hamper women's ability to participate in said sport, and/or if you also happen to be openly gay, controversy and politics tend to find and follow you. You could say that women's football is full of accidental advocates who embrace activism to varying degrees while simply trying to carve out a space adequate to play the game.

Still, with the weight of the expectation that the USWNT would win the Women's World Cup resting largely on Rapinoe's shoulders, it would have been understandable if she'd buckled under pressure and slowed down a little. She turned thirty-four during the tournament—an age that, although not even remotely old, is certainly towards the end of a player's typical career arc. But Rapinoe was in a league of her own; it may not have been possible for any other player to have stood out or owned the tournament more. At its end, she was awarded the Golden Boot for being the tournament's top goalscorer, and the Golden Ball as its best player. Instead of humbly deflecting attention and admiration and diminishing her efforts, as women are so often acculturated to do, Rapinoe welcomed and encouraged the adulation, hands on hips or arms raised, hailing the crowd, chin out and chest puffed in deserved pride.

Attracting slightly less attention than the likes of Rapinoe and the USWNT, but doing equally consequential work, was Australia's player union, the PFA.

The PFA was seeking pay parity on three converging fronts: first, at the domestic (W-League) level through negotiating equivalent hourly rates and conditions to the A-League; second, at a national team level by negotiating for the Matildas' pay and high-performance conditions to match those of the Socceroos; and third, by taking on FIFA over its gender-based discrimination regarding Women's World Cup prize money. It was an ambitious but much-needed trinity.

On the tournament's eve, the PFA and the FFA got the first across the line, jointly announcing that W-League and A-League players would receive the same hourly rate. Although the overall pay disparity would continue due to the different season lengths, the hourly rate was now equal and W-League players would also receive a base-level season payment of A$16,344—a 33 per cent pay increase.[7] (Those were huge strides. Even as recently as when Gill had started at the PFA in 2016, it was contractually feasible to pay players nothing. She herself was paid only $5000 when she was Perth Glory's marquee player in 2014/15.)

With that first crucial increment achieved, the PFA could turn its attention to the national and international level. That meant calling in internationally based Australian help. Human-rights lawyer Jennifer Robinson's involvement actually came long before the Women's World Cup and not through women's football at all. It came through consulting on Hakeem al-Araibi's incarceration. (She makes clear that she consulted on his initial arrest but was not and is not part of al-Araibi's legal team.) Al-Araibi, a talented footballer who had successfully sought asylum in Australia after being persecuted in his home country of Bahrain, was arrested and detained after travelling to Thailand on his honeymoon. It was a trip the Australian Government had told him was fine. Amid efforts to get FIFA to pressure Thailand to relinquish al-Araibi, who was in grave extradition danger, conversations between Robinson and the PFA turned to broader but related principles.

'It was in those initial conversations about FIFA and human rights that we started to talk about the obligations of major sporting organisations, the role that sport can play in progressing human rights, the important cultural role that sports heroes and players and sporting bodies play in our society, and the impact those bodies can have in furthering human-rights conversations and using the platforms they have to speak out about human-rights issues,' Robinson says.

The conversations naturally progressed to discussing less explicit but just as significant issues, such as FIFA's lowballing of the Women's World Cup prize money. But al-Araibi's circumstances were pressing, so the gender-based discrimination discussions were deferred. Once al-Araibi had been freed, PFA CEO John Didulica called Robinson and said, 'Would this be a case you'd be willing to run?'

FIFA is no stranger to human-rights violations claims, but those claims have traditionally related to, for example, the poor treatment of workers building stadiums. 'On that front there had already been quite a lot of discussion about human rights and FIFA, and what FIFA was doing to ensure that its brand and the World Cup were not marred by the human-rights violations in the country they were visiting in general,' Robinson explains, 'but also specifically around the building of facilities and the event itself, and how workers were being treated in that context.'

Robinson is characteristic of people whose work involves encouraging countries and organisations to heed legally, commercially and politically inconvenient things such as human rights. She pragmatically recognises that if the legal, moral and ethical imperatives alone aren't enough to motivate FIFA to do the right thing, the additional risk of brand damage might. Still, no one had yet taken on FIFA directly about the Women's World Cup prize-money parity issue.

On paper, the heart of the prize-money issue is that FIFA is saying it is on board with equality, but in practice, not so much. To poorly paraphrase Robinson's and the PFA's legal analysis, FIFA has voluntarily pledged to respect and protect all internationally recognised human rights (think the Universal Declaration of Human Rights and the Convention on the Elimination of All Forms of Discrimination Against Women). The PFA was arguing that FIFA was breaching its human-rights obligations by discriminating against women based on their gender. Ergo, it had failed to follow its own rules.

FIFA had actually announced it was doubling the prize money for the 2019 Women's World Cup, which suggested it was making strides towards enacting the equality it espoused. But the new prize purse, totalling US$30 million, equated to just 7.5 per cent of the prize money paid out at the 2018 Men's World Cup. To bring the 2019 Women's World Cup money level with the Men's, FIFA would have had to pour in an additional US$336 million, which sounds like a lot until you realise, as the PFA pointed out, it's less than 6 per cent of FIFA's revenue for the 2015–18 period.[8] Rubbing salt into the wound, FIFA had already announced that the 2022 Men's World Cup prize money would increase exponentially again, from US$400 million to US$440 million. 'They were saying, "Look, we've doubled the women's money",' Robinson says, unpacking the mathematical reality. Doubling was important, but it didn't address the discrimination or even represent a step towards greater equality: the gap between the women's and men's prize purses had, in fact, increased by US$27 million.

'This issue had been boiling away for a while,' Moya Dodd says. 'FIFA had said that it was going to increase the prize money sometime before the tournament but it wasn't clear by how much. And I went public pretty early and said, "You should, at a minimum, increase it more than you increased the men's prize money last time, because you're then in a position of actually narrowing the gap between the two." We all accepted that $300 million or so is a big gap, but I said, "Surely you don't want to be in a position where the gap got wider on my watch. Surely you want to be in the position where you can say you're the guy who started to close the gender pay gap."'

'They were patting themselves on the back for having doubled the women's prize money,' Robinson continues. 'When it was pointed out to them that the gap had in fact increased, they didn't provide any justification for that further discrimination.' There were no budget pressures FIFA could point to to excuse it. Even if there had been, Robinson notes, that doesn't absolve FIFA: equality is a right. And just as many people were now watching the Women's World Cup on TV as the Men's. Also, in any event, you can't use past discrimination, such as the failure to provide women with equal platforms and commercial opportunities, to justify ongoing discrimination.

Around the time of the tournament, FIFA reported a cash-reserve buffer of just under US$3 billion—a confounding 66 per cent more than it had estimated.[9] That prompted two questions: first, how could FIFA have so significantly underestimated its buffer, and second, how much did FIFA not care about women's football or the related optics to not, upon recording unexpected surplus, top up the Women's World Cup prize purse? It was a missed opportunity to surge the women's game and its own reputation forward.

'There are so many layers to it,' PFA co-CEO Kate Gill says. 'For us, it was asking the question: If you really do care about the women's game, where do you sit on the scale of remunerating them as you would the men? To be fair to the Men's in itself, there's no mathematical equation as to why its prize purse is worth more than $400 million. Yes, there are commercial rights attached to it, but no "This is a percentage of the commercial rights". It's just a number.'

The issue is more dire when you compare the circumstances that underpin professional footballers' club-level playing conditions. The 'too long; didn't read' version is that for most men, playing in their national team is a bonus as they are already well remunerated at club level. For women, it's the opposite: national-team payments might be their main football income, meaning that the trickle-down from FIFA is an important boost for their federation's national-team funding. (A related issue is the federations aren't necessarily obliged to distribute the prize money to the women's teams—in the absence of clear parameters outlined in such documents as CBAs, the money can go into a pot that just as easily ends up funding the men's programs.) 'What is so striking about this is you see FIFA making general statements about FIFA supporting gender equality,' Robinson says. 'Female players are often dependent on the prize money they receive at these tournaments to maintain their ability to play the sport they love and to play it professionally, and yet FIFA is underpaying the women's teams.

'When we were preparing the case, we looked at some heart-breaking examples of women who were having to work part-time in cafes and in other jobs to sustain their ability to play for Australia. We anonymised them because we didn't want any of the women to be identified and singled out—we didn't think that was fair. But for the purposes of the potential case against FIFA, we prepared case studies of the women players who were unable to commit to the time and travel required without financial assistance because they weren't being paid enough or earning enough through prize money to play professionally. This is our national team and there are Matildas who can't afford to do what they do. That is unacceptable. The Matildas are, or at least were in the year of the Women's World Cup, Australia's favourite sporting team, yet there are women on that team who can't afford to be there.'

Robinson notes that pay disparity exists at all levels of the game. But, as she points out, it's about benchmarks and perception: FIFA is the standard-setter. If FIFA, which has the resources and the influence to fundamentally change the landscape, elects not to enact parity, what message does that send to less powerful, less well-resourced bodies? 'It's why taking on FIFA is so important, in my view,' she says.

So, with FIFA not willingly implementing prize-money parity, and with no hint of plans to change that in sight, the PFA deemed legal action ambitious and nerve-jangling, no doubt, but absolutely warranted. Besides, as Robinson notes, their case was feasible: 'The great thing about the statute is there is a remedy ... FIFA must be accountable to its statute like any organisation in the world. So it *is* possible to take action against FIFA.'

The PFA wrote to FIFA, asking for the prize-money issue to be explained and rectified. It asked again, and then asked another few times. Then, given it had received no adequate response or resolution, the PFA sought to leverage FIFA's own dispute-resolution mechanisms. FIFA Women's World Cup regulations 8(1) and 8(3) mandate first mediation and then, failing a satisfactory outcome through that avenue, arbitration via the Court of Arbitration for Sport (CAS). In short, it requires the parties first to get into a room to try to negotiate. If that mediation fails, the only recourse is for an aggrieved party to go to the neutral CAS in the neutral country of Switzerland for a final, binding determination.

The PFA may have been leading the campaign, but it wasn't alone. A bunch of other countries sent letters of support. Those included Norway and New Zealand, both of which had already enacted pay parity at a national team level. (Curiously, the USWNT wasn't among the supporters.) Robinson says, 'I felt very proud working with the Matildas and the PFA, representing little Australia, taking on FIFA for women everywhere.'

Still, it was a tricky task made trickier because the PFA needed to be considerate of other countries' and the global player union's wants, needs and politics. Also, the FFA was concurrently trying to garner support for Australia and New Zealand hosting the 2023 tournament, presumably with or without prize-money parity.

With issues such as these, there's the legal case but also the public understanding and poor optics that apply essential additional pressure. In some ways, the PFA was doing the legal work but also the PR work: here's what you need to know; here's why it's outrageous. 'With any of these cases internationally, particularly where it's so political and where FIFA has a brand to protect, there is a role for public advocacy,' Robinson says. The 'equal pay' chant at the tournament final was evidence of that. But with the exception of players like Rapinoe speaking out, players were publicly fairly muted in their advocacy.

'As we were getting into learning about this and being at the World Cup, I had two feelings about it. There were isolated incidents of women speaking out, like Marta did about the obstacles that women faced, but otherwise people weren't saying much,' Robinson notes. 'The gender pay parity didn't get as much traction as I thought it might. I think there must be a lot of pressure on women players who are in these teams not to speak out. Even the Australian women's team, who we were representing, I don't think any of them said anything themselves during the competition. I think that was a missed opportunity, because you had this global platform to talk about it. My questions are: What are the pressures on the players that prevent them from speaking out? What are the consequences for them if they were to?' Robinson has identified the precarity of the players' financial positions or potential effects on their careers and selection.

She recognises that it is, of course, easier for women with more power in the game, such as Rapinoe and Marta, to speak out, and that any obstacles women face to speak out should be addressed. 'It's interesting. I really thought this issue would gain more traction and attention because people love the Matildas and love women's football. I think it's a very important issue—women should receive the same prize money as men. The fact that it hasn't had a lot of media coverage is a real issue, because it deserves it and I think more adverse publicity for FIFA about its clear discrimination against women would help to progress the issue.'

FIFA never responded to the PFA's mediation request, which arguably triggered the PFA's arbitration right. But the PFA held off on pulling the trigger. Global player union FIFPRO has formal structured channels in place to work with FIFA, so, having taken the first decisive steps and mapped out a plan for taking on FIFA, the PFA passed the baton to FIFPRO to continue the fight.

'We felt they'd taken on a lot of our arguments, a lot of our rationale and logic, and were advocating with FIFA directly on a range of issues,' Didulica says—for example, to have pregnancy and maternity leave embedded at an international level, a policy that came into force in 2021. (Approximately a year later, Icelandic captain Sara Björk Gunnarsdóttir became the first player to enforce the terms of that policy after she successfully lodged a claim against club team Lyon for not paying her during her pregnancy.) 'Once we had some satisfaction that it was a standing item they were prosecuting with FIFA, we reluctantly said, "All right, the ball's in your court, but we'll be watching. And your carriage of this now is without prejudice to our rights to reactivate the case in the future."'

In the interest of women footballers and the sport, the PFA is playing the long game. 'While we haven't directly litigated around prize money, although it is a case I think we could win, it's achieving other incremental gains,' Didulica explains. 'The stakes are so high that if you get it right, the uplift to all footballers will be astronomical. If you lose that case, you lose all future leverage. So you're trading that off with OK, how do we put institutional pressure in all the right places? I think for me that's where we landed. By not testing the rights of law you actually put yourself in a stronger negotiating position, because if you run a case and lose, that's it, the horse has bolted. But if you've still got that in your pocket and you use it to leverage other outcomes, that compounds over time. That's where the focus was.'

While Australia didn't achieve prize-money parity at the 2019 Women's World Cup, it did achieve pay parity at a national team level soon after. Two out of three, with the ambitious third still a possibility, isn't bad.

The announcement of a groundbreaking CBA that brought the Matildas' conditions and pay to the level the Socceroos were accustomed to came in early November, a few months after the Matildas' bruising 2019 Women's World Cup campaign. The equal-pay pressure had been building for some time. The USWNT had been fighting its federation since about 2015, and Norway and New Zealand had implemented equal pay in 2017 and 2018 respectively.

Norway's and New Zealand's models were predicated on taking money from the men's pot to increase the women's. Australia's CBA tried something different. 'This wasn't a social mission around gender equality,' Didulica says. As Gill puts it, 'We understood that equity was what we were looking for. It wasn't about bringing the Socceroos down to the level of the Matildas—it was about improving the Matildas' standards to where the Socceroos' were. So that was the starting point, and then it was working back from there: OK, how do we create a model that achieves that?'

The PFA and FFA looked to two innovative sources for inspiration and guidance: Ruth Bader Ginsburg, and a Swedish concept called *jämställdhet*.[10] Didulica and Gill had actually strategised and refined their CBA approach during a visit to the iconic Paris bookstore Shakespeare and Co. while they were at the 2019 Women's World Cup. It was from the unusual bookstore, which provides accommodation among its bookshelves to artists and intellectuals at night in exchange for a few hours of help in the store during the day, that Didulica bought Gill the Ruth Bader Ginsburg biography.

Ginsburg was famous for tackling gender discrimination through novel cases and arguments, not least of which was that, as Gill and Didulica point out, gender stereotypes and related division negatively affect everyone. Famously flipping the model and using the test case of a widower who was the primary carer for his newborn child after his wife died during childbirth, Ginsburg argued that pensions traditionally granted to widows (that is, women) should also be extended to widowers (that is, men). 'We got talking about some of those concepts. It's not about treating the sexes or the genders differently, it's about how equality improves the lot of both,' Gill says. 'That's the model we needed to create. It wasn't about taking money from one pot and redistributing it to the other. That wouldn't have helped anyone. It was about resetting the model and aspiring for both cohorts to build.'

Jämställdhet entered the picture as a principle of 'progressive equality'. Gill and Didulica explain that regressive equality would have been lessening the Socceroos' conditions or landing on a middle ground where each team 'kept a foot on the throat of the other', to reference Ginsburg's famous *Frontiero v Richardson* phrase.[11] So they devised a model that paired remuneration, performance and commercial interests with core values of partnership, equality and investment.

When the various stakeholders started having those conversations around equal pay, Didulica said, 'Guys, if we do this, things like the World Cup will be easier to win, the biggest corporate partners in the country will come on board ... [Australia has since co-won the 2023 Women's World Cup bid and major naming-rights sponsors, such as the Commonwealth Bank, have signed on.] Whether or not these things are solely responsible, they're certainly contributing to a narrative that allows us to go to big companies and to FIFA and beat our chests and go, "Hey, we're walking the walk."'

Like all aspects of women's football, the disparities are greater than just wages. The inclusion of improved conditions was central to the negotiations. 'We were intentional about how that would look for the support services that wrap around both our national teams,' Gill says. She gives the example of how the Matildas were, until recently, travelling economy class while the Socceroos were travelling business class. This disparity extended to support staff: the Socceroos had a technical analyst, a dietitian, a sports psychologist and more, while the Matildas operated with a skeleton staff who doubled up on jobs. 'We drilled down and got really prescriptive and said, "If this is happening on one side of the table, why isn't it happening on the other?"'

'The way players have been remunerated historically has been for their labour. But the value of their labour is inextricably linked to the value of the product,' Didulica says. 'We had to justify that the value of the product of women's football was as powerful as the men's. That was a leap of faith, because it wasn't quite there yet.' As he notes, women's football has always been treated like 'bonus steak knives': 'It's always been something that's thrown in as a consolation prize.'

Although the national team CBA is essentially an employment contract, the negotiations 'transcended a purely employment discussion'. 'I don't think anybody said, "No, we don't want to do this,"' Didulica says. 'It was all about making it a priority. And once we made it a priority, I like to say that everybody sat on the same side of the table and projected forward rather than sitting across the table from each other debating or arguing the cost. We'd been able to convince each other it was the right thing to do and make it happen.' That pay-parity impossibility had become an affirming inevitability.

'While the World Cup [prize-money parity] wasn't going to happen, it was clear to me the tipping point had been reached,' Didulica explains. 'In my mind, for us to have gone in on a CBA that wasn't equal pay would have condemned the sport for a generation, because the opportunity was there at that time and if we hadn't seized it, it would have gone backwards.' Such an approach was always, he says, 'about making the sport stronger and creating a halo for the game that no other sport could have'.

In a quirk of history, the Matildas had gone backwards before. There was a brief period, former Matildas manager Jo Fernandes recalls, where with the stroke of a pen and the acknowledgement it was 'the right thing to do', FA administrator Alan Vessey had granted the Matildas the same per diem as the Socceroos. The Matildas had only started being paid a day rate a few years earlier, and Vessey's update saw their day rate more than double. But that parity wasn't sustained. This time, though, things were different. As Tameka Yallop, who'd been involved in the Matildas' 2015 strike, noted, this negotiation had implications beyond women's sport: 'We had the support of our men's team, which spoke volumes, and not only that, we felt we were fighting for equality not just in sport but across all industries in Australia. This time around we knew we were fighting for a large part of the population and for people experiencing exactly what we were. We knew we had so much support.'

How the PFA kept the 2019 CBA under wraps until the very last moment is quite remarkable but utterly vital. 'Until we had a signed agreement we didn't let ourselves think for a moment it was going to be done,' Didulica explains. 'These things can be derailed so quickly. All you need is one misleading media story.' So, he says, keeping shtum from their end wasn't difficult at all.

'The end result was fantastic,' Brantz says of the now-heralded CBA. 'It's still not quite where I think it should be, because we talk about equal pay but there's a little fine print there. You know, equal pay, but when they play. Or how does it work, because they're certainly not getting hundreds of thousands of dollars from their club like the men are, and how does that measure up in the grand scheme of things? So there's a way to go, but they now have a career path. I think prior to that, it was probably difficult for players to even consider giving their life over to football and still being able to eat and rent a house and live, basically. You play for the love of the game, but there comes a time when, in your late twenties, if you have nothing to show for playing, you have to make really difficult decisions. And also, you can't commit all your time to training and strength and conditioning and all the things we see happen now, which have resulted in a marked improvement in the standard of the women's game, until you treat it like a professional game. That's the difference they made. We started to see the ability of these players to dedicate a large portion of their lives to football. And it's really made a difference.'

It really has. Fine print that can be refined in subsequent iterations aside (because this was the first CBA step, not the last), cementing the groundbreaking CBA lifted a weight and created career paths previously unavailable to women. It wasn't—isn't—a case of job done, though.

10

TOWARDS 2023

WHEN AUSTRALIA AND Aotearoa New Zealand jointly won the 2023 Women's World Cup bid in the middle of the COVID-19 pandemic, the ecstatic players and staff who led the bid—in their excitement temporarily forgetting about social distancing measures—sprang from their chairs and hugged in celebration and relief. The footage of that moment, which featured players and administrators channelling their anxiety and adrenaline into prodigious leaps as soon as the announcer uttered the first syllable, 'Aus', captured the tension and emotion that had underpinned the bid process.

Hours before that famous leap, bid organiser Jane Fernandez and her peers created a similarly Instagrammable moment. As the last light of the sun disappeared, the Opera House sails lit up with projected contrasting action images. On one sail, current Matildas captain Sam Kerr backflipped in high definition and full colour. On another, in black and white organic film clarity and tones, there was an action shot of inaugural national women's team captain Julie Dolan.

Dolan didn't have any forewarning of the Opera House plan. She wasn't even sure she should accept the invitation to attend: 'Walshy's [Sarah Walsh] really cagey, you know. She sort of indicates,

"Yes, Julie, you need to be there." And sometimes I think, *Oh god, they don't need me there.*' Fortunately, Dolan went. The emotion is evident in her voice as she relives the moment more than a year on from seeing her image materialise on the Opera House sail. She likens the aftermath to the out-of-body experience you have when paramedics give you emergency pain relief for a serious sporting injury 'and you have this silly grin on your face and you're laughing a bit too much, your head's not really with the program, so to speak. I walked around like that for days.' (It was likely an equivalent experience for another former Matilda: in a meeting of worlds, those projections signalled the progress women's football had made since Thea Slatyer had abseiled down those same sails working her high-risk part-time job to fund her playing career.)

Kim Anderson, who oversaw the bid's communications strategy, says it was special, too, for the bid staff and made the bid announcement seem real. 'I think in the frenzy of just trying to get it done and do all the things that you have to do in the lead-up to something like that, that for me was the first moment where I went, *Oh wow, this is happening tonight. We're going to find out. Win or lose, glory or failure.*'

It had been a serious undertaking to realise the Opera House images. The sails are not a flat surface and are extremely public—you're either on the Opera House or you're not. So at 3 a.m. the night before the announcement, the bid team and the projection technical team ran through the loop a few times to confirm it worked. They then headed home to get a few hours' 'rest'.

'The bid team said they were working with Tourism New South Wales and doing a lot of work behind the scenes with them, because I asked if they'd been inspired by Phar Lap on the Opera House,' Dolan says. Her Phar Lap comment is particularly telling given that female horses have long received more media coverage than women athletes, but apparently Phar Lap wasn't the impetus. 'What a dedication to the women's game,' Dolan continues. 'Amazing and overwhelming, emotional, all those adjectives. There aren't enough of them.'

FA kept the images scrolling for the rest of the night so they were visible from a multitude of Sydney aspects, including the equally iconic bridge that connects the city's north and south. FA staff had invited Dolan to stay for the announcement itself, but perhaps needing some time to process what she'd just witnessed or a moment to feel the full force of the feelings it invoked, she graciously thanked them for the offer and turned homewards. Going from having few images from her playing time and even fewer people watching her play to seeing her image projected on one of Sydney's most treasured and visible landmarks was a little overwhelming. 'I remember driving back over the Harbour Bridge on the way home and I saw the image,' Dolan says. 'I nearly drove off the bridge.'

Dolan phoned Fernandez on that drive home, once she was safely away from bridge verges. Fernandez was on the chartered bus transporting staff back to the office to await the vote results. She recalls Dolan telling her, '"I don't know how you guys have done this but, thank you so, so much." She was like, "I don't think you guys really understand what it means and the impact it's going to have."' Then, Fernandez says, Dolan told her, 'So you better bloody win.'

★ ★ ★

Knowing the outcome now makes the 2023 bid seem like a certainty, but it was far from that. A record ten countries had nominated to host the tournament—a far cry from the lone bidder for, say, 2015—although natural attrition and COVID saw that number shrink. It came down to Australia and New Zealand versus Colombia. Scoring a 4.1 on a 5-point scale on the bid technical report, compared with Colombia's 2.8, put Australia and New Zealand's bid in the lead heading into the final vote. In a reverse of the underdog status the two countries were used to, they were firm favourites.

The technical score, an imperative first hurdle, allowed the bid writers to feel cautiously optimistic. They had deliberately crafted a bid that equally weighted the social and commercial outcomes. That commercial viability was, Fernandez says, what put Australia and New Zealand in pole position; FIFA has since told them as much. 'We did a lot of work during the bid on the social and economic benefits of hosting. Then, post-winning, there was another economic and social report written, and that tied into

Football Australia's development of the Legacy '23 plan. We all know that yes, there's the social elements, but the economics are just as important, because for governments to invest, they also want to make sure there's an economic return ... The fact that we had the Australian government's support up to A$94 million, for FIFA that was like *Oh wow, OK, fantastic, this government is really keen for this tournament*.' The legacy piece was similarly strong, concentrating on, as Fernandez phrases it, 'development *of* football and also development *through* football'.

However, a good technical-report result does not necessarily translate to votes. If the failed 2022 Men's World Cup bid taught us anything, it was that it's not definite until the votes are in. So FA's senior executives advocated with their voting constituents right to the last minute. 'On the bus from the hotel to the Opera House, the FA admins—Mark Falvo, Chris Nikou and a few other guys—were non-stop on their phones still trying to win,' Dolan recalls. 'They just *did not* take the phone off their ears. That continued for the rest of the night. These guys worked tirelessly to garner more votes for Australia, because at that point, when we left the hotel, it was looking pretty shaky because England had backed Colombia.' (So much so that someone asked tongue-in-cheek if anyone had UK football patron Prince William's phone number so they could advocate with him.)

Having been part of the unsuccessful 2022 bid, writer, author, editor and FIFA whistleblower Bonita Mersiades, whose work had contributed to exposing the FIFA corruption and governance issues ahead of the 2015 arrests, watched the 2023 bid unfold from afar. 'I was absolutely confident that Australia and New Zealand would win the right to host the 2023 [Women's] World Cup. The deal was done late in 2019 around the time of James Johnson being appointed as CEO, was sealed at the time of the Asian Football Confederation elections a few months later, and was delivered once the president of the AFC convinced the other Asian bidder, Japan, to withdraw. On this occasion, the deal-making worked in Australia's favour. While we are all happy with the outcome this time around, it's a pity that FIFA and global football administration continue to make decisions based on deals rather than merit. While we had a strong merit-based joint bid in any case, and we will deliver an outstanding tournament, the decision-making process suggests that little has changed in terms of the culture of FIFA.'

In the end, the vote was too close for comfort but unarguably clear: Australia and New Zealand secured 22 votes to Colombia's 13. Australia and New Zealand, in need of some good women's football news specifically, and good non-pandemic news generally, erupted in celebration and pride.

★ ★ ★

Speaking with Fernandez, you get a sense of how powerfully the lessons learned from the failed Men's bid informed the Women's bid—it walked so the Women's could run. 'Having been part of that process put us in such a strong position. Because we'd participated in a FIFA process before, we'd written bid books, we had strong relationships with governments …' she explains. 'And I think the other thing that helped us was that because governments had gone through the process, they understood and were much more open to "This is the FIFA document, this is the FIFA agreement, we understand it's not negotiable really, so either we're in or we're out." It made it a lot easier. It wasn't easy, but it made it easier because they understood.'

Wanting to avoid a 2022 bid repeat also urged them on via a last push that Anderson describes as a 'whirlwind': 'The only thing I imagine it's parallel to is a political election campaign, and I guess to some extent that's what we were running.' The media blitz she coordinated in those final days was comprehensive. 'We had players doing breakfast shows, news, sports media all over the place. We had the lighting of the Sydney Opera House and Sky Tower in Auckland. We were trying to get all of our ambassadors on social media to really try and make noise in that lead-up. I'd been talking to [former Socceroo] Tim Cahill in the middle of the night about what he could post on social media to then waking up in the morning and trying to do breakfast slots. So it was everyone, and we obviously had the strength of former Matildas and Socceroos, media personalities, political figures, entertainment figures, community bid champions across Australia and New Zealand. Everyone was doing their bit.'

They received above-and-beyond support and uplift from unexpected quarters. 'It's not like we had a big media budget to target people,' Anderson explains. 'I saw Russell Crowe talking about it on his social media and I was like, "Did anyone contact Russell Crowe? Because I didn't contact Russell Crowe, but now he's tweeting."' (As in the Russell Crowe Thea Slatyer had provided protective detail for, now a Matildas fan voluntarily using his profile to elevate and amplify the campaign.)

After the Opera House projections but before the host country announcement, the bid team had sports presenter and journalist Tara Rushton facilitate a live Facebook event with players and executives to try to give fans a transparent, climactic window into the final bid moments. 'Then in the room itself was another whole thing again,' Anderson says. She's talking of the private meeting a core group had with FIFA and Australia and New Zealand's competitor, Colombia. 'But no one could see that, so I was on WhatsApp with the players telling them what was happening, trying to give them updates: here's where we're at, here's when we think the announcement's going to be—there wasn't a set time, it was whenever it fell into the meeting. Everyone else is on this blank YouTube channel waiting for the announcement to start.'

It was intense. Rushton recalls exchanging nods with the others as she took her seat in the room with the YouTube channel feed, which was set up in a socially distanced front-facing classroom layout. 'There was a buzz in the air, an energy—excitement: tick, anticipation: tick—but also nerves. It felt like grand final day. Everything you had been working towards all season (including [through] a very long pre-season) was about to come down to this moment … But the moment we were all building towards felt "big". It was weighty. It was major. If it all "worked out", football in this country [Australia] would never be the same again.' Alanna Kennedy specifically recalls how anxiously hushed and still the room was as they strained to hear the result, and the contrasting eruption when the winning bid was announced. 'Before [FIFA president Gianni Infantino] even finished, I jumped out of my seat and the room erupted. I turned and hugged Steph [Catley] and Lyds [Lydia Williams], and everyone in the room was just so happy and elated. A lot of people had worked extremely hard to make it possible, so it was a really special moment to be able to be with them all and see them get the win.'

'The funniest bit for me was looking back at the photos from the room. Obviously there's the iconic video of us all celebrating, but I look so pale. I clearly needed sleep,' Anderson says. She wasn't alone in that—almost everyone I interviewed who was there recalls being decidedly edgy and peaky. That's relevant given that activities and attention accelerated after the announcement: 'I tweeted some of the stuff live immediately in the room. And then the media frenzy started and went through until 3 p.m. or 4 p.m. the next day.' Adrenaline and elation carried them through.

★ ★ ★

If the suspenseful last few days felt long, the bidding build-up had been even longer.

Characteristic of their footballing histories, both Australia and New Zealand had initially commenced the bid process individually but amid friendly rivalry. However, FIFA's mid-bid decision to increase the number of teams from 24 to 32 substantially increased the logistical complexity. It was quickly apparent that neither country alone had enough available stadiums to host the requisite matches within the requisite timeframe: 64 matches contested by 32 teams in a roughly thirty-day period. The Australians had actually already considered a partnership, but after examining the requirements for a compliant bid (that is, one that met all FIFA's specifications), they knew they could go it alone and had headed down that path—until the number of teams and the footprint (that is, the minimum requirements for number and quality of stadiums and other infrastructure) changed. Both countries knew a co-confederation bid would solve the scaling-up problem, so they merged their respective bids and sensibly relaunched 'As One'.

'We'd written all the bid book chapters. We were ready to go to print,' Fernandez says of how far the Australians had progressed before the pivot. 'I knew that once the expansion of the tournament happened, there were further conversations [about] what would strengthen the bid to the Asia-Pacific. The decision hadn't yet been made. I remember saying to some of the bosses of Football Australia, "If we don't start preparing another book now, assuming that's where we land, we actually won't be ready."'

With that second option not yet confirmed, and having bedded down what appeared to be the final Australian version, Fernandez took a moment out to have lunch with Jill Davies, the 2023 bid book's overall author and editor and also the woman behind the successful 2000 Sydney Olympics bid. That's when Fernandez got the call. 'I said, "Don't tell me now,"' she laughs, wanting to enjoy a brief respite before putting her shoulder back to the wheel.

A frenetic couple of months full of workshops and meetings and rewriting later, they finalised the coauthored bid book under the collaborative brand. With that shift, Australia and New Zealand's would be the first proposed bid to play out featuring two host countries from two different confederations. Fernandez notes it was just as well they had started early, because the deadline extension was only two months.

Anderson didn't mind the pivot, despite the additional workload it entailed. The 'Limitless' and 'Get Onside' strategy pre-dated her. The shift gave her the chance to conceptualise an entirely fresh campaign to help shape women's football's upwards trajectory. 'If I was working on the Men's World Cup, that would be amazing, don't get me wrong. But how do you really innovate in that space?' she asks. 'It's a mature product, and I guess because women's football isn't quite at maturity, we're on that accelerating curve and haven't quite reached the crest of the wave. It's ours to write the history and create the moment.'

Part of that shaping involved crafting a mascot to provide tournament and cultural cut-through. Anderson was working on the mascot at the time of our interview. 'Again, that's a really cool opportunity to think about how you bring these two distinct but similar cultures together in one mascot. It's not the simplest of exercises.' She's not wrong. As she points out, Australia and New Zealand don't share many, if any, native animals or plants. The outcome, announced in late 2022, was a penguin named Tazuni. Her name is a portmanteau of 'Tasman Sea', the body of water that abuts the two countries, and the key tournament value of 'unity'. She is modelled on the genus *Eudyptula*, endemic to Australia and Aotearoa New Zealand. Interestingly, unlike Adriana Lima, the supermodel ambassador FIFA later recruited, Tazuni also represents realistic proportions and body positivity: she has hips and thighs.

★ ★ ★

The bid marked the culmination of a very different pathway for dual citizen and player ambassador Rebekah Stott, whose allegiances and playing experiences spanned the two host nations. Her tale perhaps illustrates the winding-path, bittersweet complexity that infuses every women's football experience. Just as she should have been celebrating her best-case Women's World Cup scenario and turning her focus to 2023 playing preparation, she underwent the most wrenching of plot twists. It wasn't her first, but it was a biggie.

Stott's first fork in the road had come when she was just seventeen through the decision about her senior playing pathway. New Zealand–born, Australia-based Stott, who describes herself as 'half Kiwi, half Aussie', was offered the chance to play for her birth country. New Zealand was a way behind Australia in its football development, but, unlike Australia, was heading to the 2012 Olympics. Stott was faced with the choice of joining a team that was less likely to win games but that would, with less competition for spots, probably provide her more game time. The decision was agonisingly difficult. FIFA has rules about players committing to a country and sticking with it—once Stott was capped at a senior level for a given country, the allegiance would be fairly permanent, regardless of whether that country continued to select her.

Stott, who was undeniably talented but who hadn't yet fully developed as a player, had some tough competition, with an influx of prodigious young Australian players such as Kerr, Catley and Kennedy who would quickly go on to become Matildas golden-generation greats. As with any elite sport, there were no fairytale-ending assurances. Wanting the best for her whichever path she pursued, Australian coach Tom Sermanni gave her sage advice: get confirmation that New Zealand is definitely going to play you.

Ultimately, Stott took up New Zealand's offer. 'I'm so happy with my decision. I don't regret it at all,' she says, more than a decade on. 'If I look back on my career, some of my best moments and best memories have come playing for the [New Zealand] national team.' Stott has also enjoyed the best of both worlds, playing in the W-League/A-League Women's and overseas, alongside or in friendly rivalry against her Australian peers. In a twist of full-circle fate, Sermanni became her coach again when he temporarily coached New Zealand from 2018.

Stott's dual allegiances, profile and popularity made her one of the ideal ambassadors for the 2023 bid, which she undertook alongside longtime friends Catley, Kennedy and Williams. But the lead-up to 2023 was unimaginable. For her, playing selection and allegiances were no longer a concern: playing at all became one. After eight months of a diagnostic journey that traversed Australia and the United Kingdom and played out in the middle of COVID-19, Stott learned she had Stage 3 Hodgkin lymphoma.

Some of the diagnostic journey unfolded during the 2023 bid campaign itself. 'I remember we were at the Opera House—this is before the actual announcement—and a week before that I had gone to see my doctor,' Stott explains. 'I'd had a biopsy on my neck, and I actually got the call with the results while we were standing outside the Opera House. But those results were quite inconclusive.'

It must have been a peculiar and perturbing experience to be taking such a sombre phone call amid the final hours of bid promotion and subsequent exhilaration—even more so given the call didn't answer her questions. 'I remember the phone ringing, and I'd been waiting for that call,' Stott says. 'So I walked away from everyone and took it. I was a bit like, *Oh god, what's going to happen? Could this be bad news?*' It would take many more months and while she was in the United Kingdom playing in the FA Women's Super League for her to finally obtain the answers she needed. 'It was', she agrees, 'a very long diagnosis process.'

So instead of undergoing concentrated 2023 tournament preparation, and while the rest of the world entered into tournament attendance planning and anticipation, Stott veered into chemotherapy treatments and fundraising to raise awareness about, and beat, blood cancer. After an arduous treatment schedule, and a little over a year before the 2023 tournament kicked off, she was told she was in remission. From there, coupled with the jumble of emotions and exhalation of held breath that comes from successfully navigating a cancer treatment regime, she returned first to the A-League Women's domestic competition and then to the Football Ferns. She was back on track for 2023.

★ ★ ★

Matilda Elise Kellond-Knight's best-laid 2023 plans were similarly derailed. Kellond-Knight was a player who for more than a decade had been the kind of figure around whom there was no question she was on the plane to any tournament in which the Matildas were involved—and not just on the plane but one of the players consistently anchoring the Starting XI.

Her recent issues began with an ACL injury she sustained in 2020. 'That's how it started. Just an unfortunate turn of events,' Kellond-Knight says of what unfolded over the next two years. 'I did my knee on the back of COVID. We were meant to start, then the season didn't start. We were up and down with training and whatever. We finally started in July of 2020, and in the second game I did my knee.' She outlines two key challenges that compounded that injury. 'One, I got stuck in the country, so I was stuck in Sweden—Australia wouldn't let me home [due to COVID-19 border closures]. Two, Australia wasn't operating—I couldn't have got surgery at home anyway. So I was basically stranded.'

Kellond-Knight had the surgery in Europe, but her post-surgery complications went undiagnosed for a year, and she spent a seven-month period where the pain she was experiencing was so intense that she couldn't walk. 'No answers, a million doctors, a million scans, no answers, stopped being able to walk, chronic pain,' Kellond-Knight runs through the list of what she went through. Those of us removed from Kellond-Knight's day-to-day existence knew it wasn't good, but we perhaps didn't understand how significant it was. 'I never wanted to talk about it because it really damaged my mental health so bad[ly],' Kellond-Knight says of that time. Also, as she notes, injuries like this aren't isolated. 'I don't like to talk about injuries and things like this too much, because it's a part of the game. If you've played for as long as I have—I've been in the game at that level for sixteen years—you're going to cop something eventually.'

Still, this injury broke the mould. 'I did my ACL in 2011. I know how shit of an injury it is. But this was next level. This was unbearable nerve pain. And people just kept saying, "There's nothing wrong with you," which is the worst part. So yeah, it just added on another whole mental complexity too because I thought I was imagining the pain, and I'm in ten-out-of-ten pain.'

Despite the agony, Kellond-Knight was determined that she, not the injury, would dictate her playing future. 'It would have been so easy to just stop trying to be an athlete, accept that this was going to be my new normal. But I just didn't want that to … I just see so many players who are forced to retire through injury and I'm like, no.'

The turnaround came when she found a surgeon who 'came up with a theory about what was going on because my symptoms didn't make any sense', Kellond-Knight says. The surgeon identified and neutralised much of the source of the pain by removing a nerve from her knee.

With some answers around her injury and with the borders now open, Kellond-Knight returned home to undergo rehab that saw her slowly but steadily improve. Then, in the last stages of a friendly played in late 2022, crowd and camera attention turned to the sideline to see her jersey number go up on the fourth official's board. With the match paused, Kellond-Knight subbed onto the pitch, 475 days after her last Matildas appearance.

'Yeah, I felt it, and I think that what's was the biggest surprise,' Kellond-Knight says of the surging crowd support. She'd been missed, even if she hadn't been aware of it until she made her return. 'It was a significant milestone. I didn't think I'd play football again, so to put on the green and gold [was] maybe unexpected, but I was grateful. I just had so much gratitude. Just to be able to walk. Playing football is another thing, and then playing for Australia again … I just went through such a bad period of having so much pain and not being a functional human anymore that it feels a little bit surreal.'

Given the scale of recovery involved, Kellond-Knight's pathway to a 2023 appearance was far from assured. Her interview occurred before she experienced the hammer blow of rupturing her Achilles in early 2023. At the time, she was preparing for whatever the tournament might bring. Her approach, albeit no long applicable to an on-pitch role, and no doubt difficult to reckon with, may still be relevant but require emphasis on the initial elements: 'I just take one day at a time, so we'll see what happens. The main thing is to just enjoy what I'm doing so if that's contributing to 2023, then yep. If it's not, that's also good.' With Kellond-Knight having demonstrated her resilience to adversity, we can only hope we'll see her involved in or around the 2023 tournament in some capacity.

★ ★ ★

Esteemed New Zealand–based chief operating officer Jane Patterson joined the team and injected fresh eyes and expertise shortly after the successful bid campaign wrapped. Like Stott's and Kellond-Knight's, her path was uncharted and unplanned. 'I was living in the UK and had returned because of COVID to see my family,' she explains. 'But I had left my partner and my life in England and come home with one suitcase, literally.'

The opportunity to join the team was one she never thought she'd have. She had embarked on a career working on the world's biggest sporting events. 'I never thought I would get the opportunity to live that in New Zealand, given the size of New Zealand and the size of our stadiums and infrastructure,' she explains. So, until then she had necessarily based herself overseas.

Patterson, whose accomplishments are so great that in 2016 she was awarded the Order of New Zealand Merit in recognition of her services to sport, put some feelers out once Australia and New Zealand won the bid. New Zealand Football offered her a contract for the initial operating phase (IOP) based on her vast experience. So it turned into Patterson going to visit her parents for six weeks, to having a contract until the end of the IOP, to having a contract until the end of the tournament and the knowledge that 'I needed more than a suitcase of clothing and to put my roots down in New Zealand'.

Moving countries is no small feat, not least in the middle of a pandemic. It couldn't have been easy to duck back to the United Kingdom to grab a few things. 'I haven't been back,' Patterson says simply. 'My partner moved back here a year later and brought an extra suitcase with some things in it. Because otherwise I begged, borrowed and ... Thankfully my sister and I are only a couple of years apart in age and we're the same size, same size feet, same size body, so she sent some work clothes to me and I made do and got through.'

Planning an event involving two isolated island countries with some of the most stringent COVID quarantine rules in the world added another layer of complexity. An obvious difficulty was that it delayed site visits from FIFA teams with football-specific expertise that didn't then exist in New Zealand, where sports expertise is concentrated in netball and rugby. Less obvious was that lockdowns meant staff had to be hired and onboarded and then had to work remotely, even if they were just down the road from each other.

The COVID hurdles even prevented Fernandez and Patterson from meeting in person until early 2022, despite the fact that they are doing mirror jobs and speak multiple times a day. This might be the first Women's World Cup largely planned in lounge rooms by people who never or rarely met in person and who were quite possibly wearing pyjamas during meetings. It is also the first Women's World Cup executed by two women who share the same name: Jane. 'It is funny,' Patterson agrees. 'Both Janes, both COOs [chief operating officers], and having birthdays three days apart.'

The two solved any potential 'Jane' confusion pretty quickly, as Patterson explains. 'In my first week in the role, I didn't know Jane very well. We were sitting in a number of meetings and people would say, "What are your thoughts, Jane?" and we'd both go to answer. That's really difficult on Zoom anyway, because you can't make eye contact like you would across a table. So very quickly, probably at the end of my first week, I said, "My name was shortened to JP when I was at university and I've still got loads of friends who call me JP. Can I suggest that I become JP and you're Jane?" And we did that, so I sign off my emails Jane or JP depending on who I'm writing to. But everybody knows me as JP now. I don't hear "Jane" anywhere across Australia or New Zealand.'

11

LEVELLING UP

FOUR WORLD CUPS on from her 2003 Women's World Cup appearance, Tal Karp guest-commentated the 2019 tournament for Optus Sport. 'There were a lot of realisations during my time in the studio in the early hours of the morning in June,' Karp says. 'The first is an obvious one, and that was that my experience, both on and off the football field, wasn't unique. I had this overwhelming impression as a kid that I was different. Playing football meant fighting my way into boys' teams—in my neighbourhood, football wasn't something I saw women do.

'Watching on from the studio in Sydney, I heard tale after tale of women like me who had fought for their right to play—who had faced far bigger battles than mine in their home countries—and who had made it to compete at the highest level. Knowing about stories like that would have made a huge difference to my seven-year-old self. It made me really appreciate the power of the World Cup as a platform to share stories and drive change.'

Karp's second realisation was that the stories she encountered extended past the fight to play: 'In my era, we were so busy just trying to squeeze in the door and find a place on the pitch that other questions of equality were beyond contemplation. We were so grateful to play for our country … Feminism felt like a bit of a dirty word back then … Watching on as the competition played out, I was struck by the many tales of activism—Ada Hegerberg boycotting the World Cup, the US team filing a lawsuit against its federation for institutionalised gender discrimination, and tens of thousands of fans chanting "equal pay" while the US team waited to accept their trophy.'

That equal-pay notion also applied a new lens to Karp's experience. 'During my time playing for the Matildas, I was just so grateful to play for my country and be supported to travel overseas when those in the generations before me had to pay to play, and even sew the Australian emblems on their own outfits. I was studying for a Law degree at the time I was playing, but even so, concepts such as equal pay didn't resonate with me. We didn't expect equal pay. We didn't expect to stay in quality hotels like the Socceroos did. That teammates would return from international tournaments to join the Centrelink queue was just how it was back then. As I mentioned earlier, I lived in seven different houses in three years because I couldn't afford the dead rent when we travelled. Boxing my life up so regularly was the bane of my existence, but it was just how things were. It was part and parcel of being a Matilda.'

Cast about and you'll quickly find equivalent examples of human-rights challenges in women's football, both within and beyond Australia before, during and after Karp's era. For while women's football has made huge, accelerated strides in recent years, we're still facing many of the same issues more than two decades on from Hillary Clinton's 1995 human-rights speech. Those issues are iterative, Whac-A-Mole-like and wearyingly familiar to the women who've had to tackle them again and again. Case in point: the lack of opportunities and the outright refusal to include women in the game that prompted New Zealand women's football matriarch Barbara Cox to twice bring cases to the New Zealand Human Rights Commission (NZHRC).

The first time Cox went to the commission was to address a known football-playing gap. Eleven was the arbitrary age dictated by the rules for when girls' and boys' playing pathways diverged, but twelve was the minimum age to join women's teams. That meant Cox's daughter

Michele, then eleven years old (and later a Football Fern), was simultaneously banned from playing with the boys' team she'd been part of for approximately four years and prevented from playing in the women's league. Cox won the case, but Auckland Junior Football (JFA) dragged its heels in implementing the ruling that allowed girls and boys to continue playing together, so Michele never saw the benefit of it. Fortunately, the girls who came after her did.

The second time Cox went to the NZHRC was around 2000, after, akin to Australia, the New Zealand women's football association was absorbed into the men's equivalent. The intent was that the men's association would bolster the women's, but the predictable reality was that the funding, resources and focus were redirected to the men's game, and the women were excluded from decision-making roles and processes.

'At the 1999 general meeting they resolved that we would have to join with New Zealand Football,' Barbara recalls. 'And we couldn't get anyone on the board.' New Zealand Football did set up a women's football committee, 'but it was basically a Clayton's committee, because everything we said and did was totally ignored.' The committee didn't have any funding and couldn't make budget decisions, and women at all levels left the throttled women's game out of frustration. In the end, Cox and three others (one woman and two men) lodged a complaint with the NZHRC on the grounds that New Zealand Football was neglecting the women's game.

'It was quite horrific, but you know, funnily enough, it was actually fun,' Cox says of the contests she's endured to advance women's football. 'The thing is you had a sense of purpose,' she clarifies. 'But that human-rights thing was quite unpleasant, dealing with people who should have known better ... We had all of the written evidence in front of us, we'd done surveys, and it was almost as if they were affronted that we were questioning them ... I couldn't work out how educated people on the board couldn't actually see. It became a fight—us versus them—instead of "Let's see how we can improve things."'

★ ★ ★

No doubt seeking to rectify such issues, the 2023 bid organisers commissioned Griffith University human-rights academic Professor Susan Harris Rimmer to produce what she believes is the first independent human-rights assessment for a Women's World Cup written by a woman and focused on the obstacles women face.

Harris Rimmer's report identified respecting sexual orientation and gender identity, protecting against homophobic or racist chants, and gender discrimination as some of the key tournament-specific considerations. It recommended that the event be framed as contributing to recognising and elevating women's rights, and that its impact be measured not just in quantitative ticket sales and broadcast figures but in qualitative measures of how it inspired people.[1] In short, the report recognised, as the PFA and others had before it, that women's participation in sport isn't just about enjoying sport: it's a fundamental human-rights issue.

FIFA later commissioned the Australian Human Rights Commission (AHRC) and the NZHRC, in consultation with experts such as Harris Rimmer, to consider human-rights risks related to the 2023 tournament. The usual suspects featured: discrimination based on gender and sexual preference, and pay. Like the PFA and Jennifer Robinson had in 2019, the report noted the absence of concrete human-rights commitments despite FIFA's articles 3 and 4 stating it will adhere to the relevant charters. Also listed were threats to players' mental health and physical safety, the latter being through career-ending injuries attained through a workplace that is not women-specific.[2]

The report identified, too, the absence of clear guidelines and opportunities for transgender women to participate. It highlighted that FIFA retains gender-verification regulations despite stating in 2019 that it would remove them.[3] A hallmark of attitudes that infused previous Women's World Cups, including the 1991 one Heather Reid referenced, the regulations allow for mandated, intrusive, gender-determining physical examination and medical history review. (To be fair, the complexity around trans athletes' inclusion extends far beyond football, but it does require urgent policy development to facilitate consistent inclusion across all sports at all levels.[4])

Of course, the issues identified in both Harris Rimmer's and FIFA's reports are vast. As the FIFA report acknowledged, it's unlikely FIFA or the local organising committee will be able to solve these entrenched problems before or during the 2023 tournament.[5] But it did identify and recommend some key actions to generate a robust legacy, including striving for gender equality; facilitating an accessible, inclusive space and tournament free from discrimination, abuse, violence and harassment; and fostering partnerships with, opportunities for and representation of First Nations peoples.[6] The latter is something we're already seeing hints of, including through the organisers commissioning artworks by First Nations artists and the standard inclusion of traditional place names.

Significantly, the report recommended that the tournament endeavour to provide players with the same conditions as men for their World Cups and that the organising parties develop robust plans to address the prize-purse inequity.[7] The appointment of Australia's Sex Discrimination Commissioner, Kate Jenkins, as a tournament ambassador signalled the seriousness with which organisers interpreted that instruction. Likewise, with the USWNT achieving pay parity on 22 February 2022—an auspicious date befitting such a momentous achievement—prize-money-related gender discrimination is the final major outlier. All eyes are now on FIFA.

For the record, Jenkins, a long-time women's sport advocate, didn't play it cool and say she'd check her diary when she was approached to be an ambassador. She had been a bid ambassador, then worked on the FIFA human-rights assessment as part of her Sex Discrimination Commissioner day job. 'I have been super busy and it is no coincidence that this is one of the things I most wanted to do this year. It just felt like a really substantial opportunity,' she says of prioritising fitting in the ambassador role. 'I hope to contribute on the back of something really positive towards change, because a lot of the work I do is off the back of something really terrible having happened.' Indeed, Jenkins is the person who is normally called in when something has gone very, very wrong. Her day-to-day work includes writing reports and making recommendations to address such issues as workplace sexual assault and sexual harassment.

At first glance, Jenkins' ambassador role is a comparatively fun job, but it has a serious, iterative human-rights undertones, too. When we spoke, the United States had just celebrated fifty years of Title IX and its related gender equality advancement. A day later the US Supreme Court published its judgement overturning *Roe v Wade*, comprehensively destabilising such gender equality gains.

Thinking back over the preceding years, which included her examining abuse claims in the sport of gymnastics, Jenkins acknowledges that the work she's done in the gender equality space has embodied 'real tension between progress and exposing real detriment'. But she maintains a steadiness and perspective. Not even a fire drill rattles her. Her schedule is so packed that she squeezed in our interview while waiting to board a flight. 'I'm not even at work and I have to do fire testing,' she laughed when the whoop interrupted her.

Citing the first woman jockey to win the Melbourne Cup, Michelle Payne, as an example, Jenkins acknowledges that there are plenty of unacceptable challenges women in sport have to face to succeed. But she also sees the Women's World Cup as an unrivalled opportunity to advance gender equality. She references a recently completed trip to New York where she met with activist and #MeToo founder Tarana Burke. 'I was there just when the Johnny Depp decision had come down[8] and [Burke] said that many people were saying, "#MeToo has failed. This case is a really terrible thing. Amber Heard lost. People aren't believing women." And her next comment to me was a great reminder: "If you think that one case that doesn't go your way will stop what is basically a whole movement, you're misunderstanding the nature of the change we are going through." I think in that big way, that's how I feel … particularly in the time I've been in this [Sex Discrimination Commissioner] role, I think there's been change.' She terms it 'a compounding momentum that is tipping the balance'.

Jenkins notes that Australia's timing for hosting the Women's World Cup is impeccable. 'When I started [as the Sex Discrimination Commissioner] it was before the [Harvey] Weinstein things had happened,[9] and a lot of my work has been both to do the work and know what's going on, but also to be looking at the signals in society, at what other people are doing, at when the opportunities or the moment arises—even the bid for the World Cup with New Zealand. It was another of those things where the time was right. But [even when] the time is right, you need lots of smart people pushing forward. My sense is to get to a moment—for example, last year when the federal parliament asked me to lead a review of sexual harassment, sexual assault and bullying in the parliament. Five years earlier I would have said there's no way that would happen. So there are really good reasons to feel optimistic.'

Jenkins points to the frequency and normalisation of such issues now being reviewed and reported on. 'There's the WA review of mining. There's one about the legal sector. There's one about the [Country] Fire Authority … It's almost daily now. Five years ago I don't think anyone could have imagined this would be a daily news topic. So my sense is that for a while we've had not enough progress, and we're having some acceleration now and we just have to keep pushing really hard. The World Cup is such a great, positive moment in the middle of that change in Australia, and our [2022 federal] election and the improvement of the number of women in our parliament … All of those are pointing to a change, and the balance is tipping.' The FIFA prize-money parity may well be one such issue where the scales are starting to right.

For her part, Jenkins sees her ambassador role as a 'mutually agreeable' one for her to hold, particularly as it enables her to cross paths with people she otherwise wouldn't, and to introduce the people she does tend to come into contact with to the incredible world of women's football. 'It's a conversation starter no matter what,' she says. 'It's a really helpful kind of role to have to find places to talk about it. So from my point of view it's quite flexible, and I'm happy to do whatever will have the most impact.'

★ ★ ★

Speaking of impactful, whether they are working on the 2023 tournament delivery or plying their volunteer trade at the grassroots level, anyone who's spent time in and around women's football can rattle off the big-ticket items 2023 needs to deliver. Prize-money parity is the obvious target, but 2023 will have a bunch of jobs. If they had to be distilled down to one, it's to simultaneously elevate women's football while shoring up its foundations. One obvious means of achieving that will be to increase and normalise women fulfilling leadership positions, particularly when it comes to administration and coaching.

The appointment of Jane Fernandez and Jane Patterson as co-chief operating officers has brought a wealth of experience to the 2023 event. Having two women at the helm is appropriate, but still unusual. Case in point: FIFA missed a golden, Bechdel-test-passing opportunity to appoint an incredibly capable woman as tournament CEO. Women have been excelling in this space for decades with meagre resources and against the odds. It's puzzling that one of these proficient women wasn't allowed to unleash their potential with all the resources and odds in their favour, and also, particularly given current discussions around gender equality, that a man would consider it appropriate to occupy the position. It was a move akin to former prime minister Tony Abbott appointing himself Minister for Women.

That said, the women who *are* in the space are doing innovative things. Patterson wants the 2023 tournament to be remembered as an event that shifted attitudes to women's sport. Likening this aim to how the London 2012 Olympics broke new ground for the inclusion and elevation of Paralympians, her hope is that 2023 'shifts the needle' in women's representation and media coverage. 'I often look back on 2012 and Paralympic sport, and [London 2012 is considered to have] completely changed people's thoughts and observations and respect for and *everything* for Paralympians. They became athletes, not "para athletes". That's one of the great legacies of London 2012. So I look at the FIFA Women's World Cup and say we're hosting the largest female sporting event in the world and it has got to be a watershed moment not just in the history of women's sport in Aotearoa New Zealand, but an opportunity to really radically move the dial for gender equality.'

It's a lofty but realistic goal. New Zealand is hosting three Women's World Cups in three years: cricket (March–April 2022), rugby (October–November 2022) and football (July–August 2023). There's also the International Working Group on Women & Sport (IWG). Patterson and her peers—cricket's Andrea Nelson, rugby's Michelle Hooper and the IWG's Rachel Froggatt—have a 'Big Four' WhatsApp group. (Fernandez has an equivalent Australian group with peers working on events such as the 2022 FIBA Women's Basketball World Cup.)

'We talk on that most weeks, certainly every second week,' Patterson says of the WhatsApp group. They meet regularly at a pub, too, to informally share information and ideas, and have a collaborative comms plan to release information at complementary times, thereby enabling each tournament to maximise its media coverage and promotional opportunities. They have nominated key staff to a 'bench' who can be subbed in if another event's staff catch COVID and have to self-isolate. The four have a no-poaching pact, too, working to accommodate later starting dates so people can finish out each contract and don't leave one of the other events in the lurch. They're also providing concrete career opportunities for women. 'We are aiming—and we're on track right now—for a 60:40 women-to-men workforce,' Patterson explains.

Some of that 60:40 workforce is made up of administrators whose invaluable work imperceptibly turns women's football's cogs. Football administrator Helen Tyrikos aptly describes these women's contributions: 'There are ten women, at least. There are so many people behind the scenes who have contributed to players being in the spotlight for Australia. Half the time you don't even know who they are, and they don't get the acknowledgement they deserve.'

Alongside Tyrikos herself, Jo Fernandes is one such administrator. Fernandes has been involved at crucial touchpoints in all the recent Women's and Men's World Cups. Equipped with a sports science degree, she initially thought her career path would involve being a 'lab rat'. (Fascinatingly relevant to her subsequent career, Fernandes's Honours degree revolved around one of the very first studies into hot–cold recovery techniques.) Fernandes spent more than a decade managing the Matildas and forging plenty of new football administration ground in contract roles as an AFC match commissioner and FIFA general coordinator (GC). While she says 'nothing was by design', her strategy of saying yes to career opportunities helped her break new ground. Without her, the Matildas wouldn't have made their flights or had the necessary accommodation or food. Without her, match days and their surrounds wouldn't have run smoothly. If Fernandes did her job well (which she did), we likely never knew she was there. Few would know, for example, that she was instrumental in the delivery of some of the 2015 and 2019 Women's World Cups' key matches.

In 2015 Fernandes was a GC—the most senior person at the stadium and the person with whom the buck stops for everything before, during and after a match. The job included facilitating the United States–Japan final. As part of that role, she and her team were advised to prepare for the attendance of a senior US official. The official's identity was cloaked in secrecy until the final moment— you can only imagine the security arrangements involved—and Fernandes and her team privately wondered if it might be Barack Obama, a known USWNT supporter.

'In the end it was Joe Biden, who was vice president back then,' Fernandes says. Given it wasn't Obama, Biden's visit didn't especially register with Fernandes; she had plenty of other things to think about to deliver the final. 'I didn't remember the name until later,' she explains. 'When Biden was made president last year, I was like, *Huh*, and I pulled up a photo. They're on the pitch, the Bidens and a couple of others, with the team. He came down, and apparently it's mayhem when the [vice] president leaves the VIP area, the bubble, to come down onto the pitch. But of course we were oblivious because we were getting ready for the presentation ceremony and all the medals and so on, and we just let them do the security thing.'

Fernandes was one of two women appointed as GCs for the Men's World Cup in its 2018 iteration—a trailblazing crossover appointment. She levelled up as a GC again in 2019, overseeing not one but two stadiums, and three of the biggest matches. 'That was another great experience for me, to have to do two venues in one tournament. You leave one venue [Montpellier after the Round of 16] and then you have a whole new venue team to get to know and deliver maybe the most important games in the tournament: the two semi-finals and the final,' she laughs.

Given that she'd overseen the 2015 final, Fernandes had assumed she was out of the 2019 running. The announcement was made while she was preparing for a GC function, and she emerged from the shower to a flurry of congratulatory messages. Eventually, someone registered her confusion and asked, '"Haven't you looked at your emails?"' They informed her she had the final—she was gobsmacked.

Fernandes is the 2023 tournament's Head of Competition, which is, in many ways, the culmination of all the skills she's been developing in her previous roles: venue coordination, match commissioning and general coordination, sports administration, team management, and event delivery. For this role, she's overseeing aspects that include hotels, training sites, medical teams, competition zones and referees. 'We call them our thirty-third team,' she says of the referees. 'They're the biggest team of all, actually.'

Having carved out a less-trod career path, Fernandes is acutely aware of the shortage of women in senior administrative roles and an understandably ardent supporter of any and all steps to remedy that. 'There are very few female presidents at any level, not just at national level but at association level and club level. There are very few female CEOs across the game when you look across those levels,' she says. Altering that is relevant, she says, 'because once you start to get that balance in the boardroom and at senior executive level, the conversations start to change.' That means more than token appointments: it means fundamental, culture-shifting progress across all aspects of the game. She sees the Women's World Cup as a contributor to this. 'The idea is that we have a wholistic approach to diversity and inclusion and gender equality right across the game out of the Women's World Cup. I'm not asking too much, am I?' she laughs.

For her part, the similarly last-named Fernandez, Fernandes's administrative peer and another part of that 60:40, has been part of increasing women administrators' profile, albeit inadvertently. 'It definitely wasn't deliberate. It just sort of happened, and I couldn't stop it,' Fernandez laughs. She's referencing the media interest she has experienced, at least part of which was precipitated by the fact that she's the person leaping—almost levitating—front, centre and higher than just about anyone else in the iconic bid-announcement photo. The image blew any anonymity aside and, like Fernandes, she understood that by making her private profile more public she might inspire other girls and women to pursue sports administration.

More recognisable to the general public than her peers, but increasingly plying her trade behind the scenes, is former Matilda Sarah Walsh, now Head of Women's Football, Women's World Cup Legacy and Inclusion. Walsh is tasked with realising much of the gender equality and inclusivity Fernandes and Patterson speak of.

The length of her job title is matched by the vastness of her deliverables, but Walsh is perhaps well placed to achieve those KPIs because she's experienced just about every aspect of football and knows its power and potential. Her early-teen playing pathway involved having to seek special dispensation to continue playing on the boys' team. It was followed by a national team career that paralleled the beginning of semi-professionalism through player contracts. That career was interrupted and punctuated by three knee reconstructions and incalculable numbers of other knee surgeries that would have ended most players' careers. But Walsh persevered and was one of the first Matildas and journeywomen to spend considerable time being paid to play overseas.

Walsh's playing career spanned the eras of no media coverage to some media coverage (including the *Never Say Die* documentary in which she features), and she understands its uplift. She studied marketing concurrently with the final stages of her playing days, and took up opportunities that harnessed her lived football experiences and her media and marketing skills. Having transitioned from playing into commentating and then administrating, Walsh is, alongside her contemporaries Kate Gill and Alicia Ferguson, one of the first former Matildas to forge an uninterrupted, sustainable, multifaceted football career.

'I'd like to say it was deliberate, but it's not actually how I operated,' Walsh says. 'My skills in long-term strategic planning and building process to deliver have somewhat progressed since I played. Training as a player, it was literally all about the process. Essentially, before you thought about your Sunday game, you had to think about and get through two training sessions. You had to focus on your process and your role and what you could control … I had to adjust the way I worked in the business world to focus more on the long term. To say that it was deliberate? No.'

That's an interesting juxtaposition given that Walsh is, perhaps more than anyone working on the 2023 tournament, required to actively consider its longevity. But it's perhaps that ability to adopt both a long-range and a day-by-day approach that simultaneously equips her to tackle it. Rather than be overwhelmed by its scale, she's approaching it as she would as an elite athlete: day by day, trusting the process, focusing on what she can control, and keeping the end goal in sight. Walsh's guiding principles are 'Are we heading towards what we said we want to do?' and 'How am I going to feel at the end?' She points to both the 2000 Olympics and the 2015 Asian Cup and the infectious enthusiasm and inclusivity they inspired. Her goal is to ensure that an equivalent ethos infuses the 2023 Women's World Cup.

Walsh is on her way to achieving that. Every announcement signals the advances women's football is making under her tutelage. They range from the implementation of the National Indigenous Advisory Group (NIAG), which recommends authentic ways to incorporate respectful recognition of and opportunities for First Nations Australians, to ambassadorships that include Australia's highest-ranking official tackling sex discrimination. Included in that work, too, has been the inception of the ParaMatildas, the Australian national team for women and girls with cerebral palsy, acquired brain injury and/or symptoms of stroke. Walsh is also working to provide opportunities and safeguard the game for migrant, refugee and LGBTIQA+ players.

While that's a lot, Walsh is clear in her focus. As she indicates, we've got over the 'why' of women's sport and it's now about opportunity: 'Honestly, the thing I want to do is start moving away from conversations about barriers into action and delivery.'

★ ★ ★

That action and delivery, as well as that concomitant visibility and invisibility, are evident in the refereeing teams striving for tournament selection. It's well known that players spend four years preparing for tournaments, ensuring they're at peak fitness and skill sharpness to improve their chances of representing their country. What's less known is that referees and other match officials—the often maligned and overlooked contributors integral to game delivery—spend an equivalent amount of time training and preparing.

Five Australian women vied to be part of 2023's 'biggest, 33rd' team. Three factors boded well for their selection. First, 2023 is a bigger tournament, so FIFA would need more referees. Second, VAR isn't yet ubiquitous in women's football, so referees with VAR experience, such as Kate Jacewicz, were arguably in a good (but not guaranteed) position. The third factor was that there may have been some strength in numbers as the five women worked together to test and improve their skills and support each other through the process. Team Australia hoped for some hometown advantage as they gunned for all five to be selected in what Jacewicz thinks could have been a Women's World Cup first.

FIFA could have selected all five team members (there are more than 150 contenders in total): Jacewicz and Lara Lee as referees, Sarah Ho and Joanna Charaktis as assistant referees, and VAR candidate Casey Reibelt. It could have selected one, or even none. In the end, it opted for three of the women—Jacewicz, Reibelt and Charaktis—as well as male referee Chris Beath, who had most recently appeared as the only Australian referee at the 2022 Men's World Cup. In 2023 he'll be a video match official.

Regardless of final selections, the training the referees and assistants undergo is immense. Indeed, if there's one thing Jacewicz says is not often discussed about participating in the candidates' program, it's that it's hard work: 'It's a complete and total investment of your life.'

The Women's World Cup selection process starts in an Olympic year. That's when FIFA announces a candidate longlist. The match officials spend the next three years being assessed as FIFA seeks out the best of the best. Throughout the selection process, the match officials complete fitness testing akin to the beep test most players know and dread. But the tests are customised for their specific on-pitch roles. The referees complete the YoYo, which involves running in more of a zigzag to mirror referees' in-game movements. The assistant referees' Assistant Referee Intermittent Endurance Test (ARIET) involves every second run being sideways as if running the line. 'It's an awful test,' Jacewicz says. 'I think we [referees] have to run for about eighteen minutes. The ARIET lasts for eight minutes, but it's a painful eight minutes.'

Even within the tournament, there's scarcely any rest. 'Any FIFA tournament we go to, we're at a separate hotel from the players. Breakfast, lunch and dinner are provided and we each have our own room. I'd hate to see the bill,' Jacewicz says, but she appreciates that they are treated as professionals and given accommodation to help them rest and perform well.

A typical Women's World Cup tournament day would see the officials have breakfast by about 8.30 a.m., be on the bus by 9 a.m. or 9.30 a.m., and then head to the training pitch. There they'd have an entire football field set up and they'd cycle through fitness tests, drills and VAR practice, with players there to do simulations. 'Sometimes you can kind of figure it out from the way it's set up: today they're doing handballs, free kicks ...' Jacewicz explains. 'By lunchtime we finish. We go back to the hotel, shower, have lunch and some free time. Then we're in the classroom, depending on whether we're in the tournament. Sometimes we get a treat and go to a game in the stadium. Otherwise, we're in the training room watching the matches on the big screen. That's every day on repeat for a month.'

Overseeing the month-long training and preparation in 2023 will be a sixth Australian and a highly experienced match official, Allyson Flynn, who was an assistant referee alongside Jacqui Hurford in 2011, and who also officiated at the 2015 tournament. She will be responsible for the referee contingent and while she won't be undergoing the training and testing her five constituents will be, she'll be extremely familiar with the process (and the pain). This role, a marked change from her usual pitchside officiation, represents an unrivalled home-country work opportunity.

★ ★ ★

If circumstances had been different, former Matilda Sonia Gegenhuber would have loved to pursue coaching post-playing. But the pathway and remuneration weren't (and arguably still aren't) yet there. 'There's no money in coaching, and I played football for ten, fifteen years and didn't make any money,' Gegenhuber explains. 'You can't get to thirty years of age and go, "OK, I'm going to go coach for another ten years and not make any money." I mean, you're thirty. You're behind the eight ball already with regard to money coming in ... So there's a time when you go, *I love doing this, but I need to do this, and if I've got time I'll do a little bit of that.*'

The coaching figures paint an equivalent picture. Just nine of the twenty-four teams at the 2019 Women's World Cup fielded women head coaches. Five of those nine successfully progressed their teams to the knockout rounds. The 2023 tournament will hopefully bolster and exceed those coach figures. New Zealand appointing Jitka Klimková as head coach means it's off to a good start. Australia has Melissa Andreatta, Rae Dower and Leah Blayney in assistant, technical and youth development roles, so we may see one or all of them hold the top job in coming years. Sports psychologist and coach Tanya Oxtoby, a former Perth player who is currently assistant coach at Chelsea, may well one day be in the mix. Oxtoby, who is an Aboriginal woman, is arguably walking the path Karen Menzies didn't get to walk. The number of women in coaching positions, and the developmental pathway to get them there, will undoubtedly be scrutinised in and around 2023, for coaching, like administrating, is an obvious area in which to make gender equality inroads.

Barbara Cox points to the opportunity FIFA has to be the catalyst for improving coaching opportunities for women, just as it has for refereeing: 'This is the way I think FIFA can lead. They made a conscious effort, an official measure, to make sure women were refereeing at women's events. We've seen a career pathway develop for women ever since. And yet we haven't seen commensurate input when it comes to women coaching, because they can't control that. That's up to the countries, other than FIFA maybe saying that every federation, every team that goes to a tournament has to have a certain number of women on its staff in technical roles—and meaningful technical roles, not just sitting on the bench filling [a quota].'

That's something Walsh and her Legacy '23 team are undoubtedly conscious of as they consider such substantial developmental and legacy challenges. As will be the newly appointed Football Australia Women's Football Director Raeanne (Rae) Dower, for that matter. For while it's tempting to push for women to be installed in senior coaching roles, stat, it's likewise necessary to ensure women aren't elevated to those positions only temporarily through the 'glass cliff' phenomenon[10]—that is, where they're awarded senior positions only during times of downturn and when the white males who traditionally hold those roles are abandoning ship. If the women save the situation, happy days. If they fail, as they're often set up to do, they are viewed as expendable and blameable, and are rarely given another chance to prove themselves. A solid, steady career-development program to increase women coaches' opportunities, experience, networks and profile would help budge the entrenched assumption that coaches are male, and/or that only hard taskmasters are cut out for being coaches in elite football environments, and would ensure women's longevity in the game.

Dower's own career trajectory has involved making inroads as a player and coach at grassroots and elite levels. As that conversation-shifting expert now in the decision-making room Fernandes mentioned, Dower has almost unrivalled insight into the challenges women face to carve out a fully professional coaching career. But she is also perfectly positioned to help advocate for, and establish good policy around, women coaches' training, mentoring and employment conditions.

'We've been working on a specific development initiative, High Performance Women Coaches in Football, to address the critical shortage of women coaches, especially in the advanced pathways,' Dower says of her initial undertakings. 'We're excited to roll that out in 2023, in a FIFA Women's World Cup year, and challenge some myths and misconceptions around women coaches. We want to ensure we provide the coaches with what they believe they need to be successful and ultimately use data and facts to change the narrative.'

With Dower at the apex, and taking an evidence-based approach to dismantle myths and build new foundations, we're soon more likely to see more women in meaningful technical roles and shifting the coaching gender stats. We're also more likely to see women more smoothly transitioning from playing to coaching.

Former Matilda Catherine Cannuli and her efforts are examples of that greater transition and permanence Dowers' oversight and the narrative- and system-changing policies she and Walsh and their peers will help foster. Since finishing playing, Cannuli has spent time coaching Western Sydney Wanderers in the A-League Women's. One of her proudest achievements is mentoring other women to pursue football past their playing careers. 'I genuinely think that if we don't tap other females to be involved in the game, either in coaching or admin roles, they will be lost to the game,' she says.

Cannuli herself was almost a casualty even as a player because of lack of pay and career-path options: she juggled multiple jobs in her family's business to cover her costs. Paid W-League contracts came into effect the year after she retired. Fortunately, she pursued coaching options even as she necessarily hung up her playing boots. She's also supplemented that with commentating gigs. Still, as it stands, even though former players like Cannuli are starting to forge coaching and administration careers, it isn't entirely easy to do so. Cannuli jokes that while she found you used to have to crack out your 'boxing gloves' as a woman player in order to advocate, you need 'bigger gloves' to advocate as a woman coach.

★ ★ ★

If there were any doubts about the vast, invaluable impact Australia and New Zealand's successful 2023 Women's World Cup bid would have on future female football generations, the Darebin Falcons junior women's football team quickly dispelled them with their video tribute. Seated on socially distanced plastic chairs on their club's training pitch, the players in their early teens re-enacted their female footballing heroes' tense moments prior to the announcement, and the springy, spontaneous leaps that followed it. The goalkeeper, cast to type, massaged her temples to mirror goalkeeper Lydia Williams' tense pose. Another sprang vertically from her chair like defender Alanna Kennedy. The organic and heartfelt video signalled that these young women could, unlike generations of female footballers before them, envisage a future where they could be a Matilda or a Football Fern.

A multisport club for women and girls, Darebin perhaps embodies all the things women's sport in Australia should aim for: an inclusive, collaborative environment for women and girls to give sports a go, and a place where football is housed and encouraged alongside, rather than competing against, sports such as Australian Rules (AFL). Located close to the custom-built facility the Matildas will soon call home, the club saw the 2023 announcement as a big leap in the validation of girls' and women's sport and wanted to celebrate that. It filmed and posted the short video with the junior women's football team thinking it would garner a few views from club members. The club didn't expect the Matildas social media accounts—or ABC TV's *Insiders*, for that matter—to share the video. In fact, it almost didn't film it given the COVID logistical challenges of social distancing and not hugging. 'We were like, "Should we do this?"' club vice president Jasmine Hirst says. Fortunately, the club decided it should.

An unexpected boon from the announcement of their viral feelgood video is that the Darebin Falcons secured a promise from the local council to upgrade lighting facilities on another reserve to extend the club's capacity. It wasn't the plan, but it's an exceptional outcome. Darebin has just one pitch for all its football teams, and is conscious that the 2023 tournament is likely to result in an influx of more girls and women wanting to play. Like all clubs grappling with limited facilities, the last thing Darebin wants is to have to turn players away.

Once you've completed the 'normalise women in senior leadership positions in terms of administration, refereeing and coaching' items on the women's football to-do list, infrastructure in the form of women-specific amenities is the next 2023 legacy item that leaps off the page—especially if FA realises its goal of achieving a 50:50 participation rate by 2027. The 50:50 participation rate is ambitious at first glance, but particularly so given that roughly 50 per cent of girls quit sport in their teens.[11] Realising this goal would equate to an additional 400,000 women and girls playing football and a significantly increased requirement for facilities. Currently, just one in five football facilities are adequately equipped for girls and women.[12]

'I like the ambition of 50:50 by 2027,' former Brisbane Roar CEO and 2023 bid consultant Eugenie Buckley says. At the same time, she acknowledges the implementation challenges it entails. 'That covers everything from "Do we have enough pitches to actually support that growth?"—because presumably the 50:50 is not the men decreasing, it's the women increasing. So the considerations become "Are there enough coaches, are there enough referees, where are the venues, are there enough venues, are they located in growth areas of the population, are they the right standard?" That's a lot of work that needs to be done in a short space of time.'

While change rooms are the physical embodiment of creating dedicated space for women in football, 2023 represents an unrivalled opportunity to carve out less tangible but equally imperative space through elevated visibility and media coverage. That's a departure from, and potential eradication of, the 'If you can't see it, you can't be it' effect imposed on previous generations.

In an inadvertent but excellent pop-culture-led outcome countering the Matilda Effect, girls who grew up watching Gillian Anderson play scientist and FBI agent Dana Scully in *The X-Files* were inspired to pursue careers in STEM.[13] The movie *Hidden Figures* showed women of colour that they, too, can work at NASA.[14] The Matildas and the Football Ferns are now inspiring girls and women to pursue careers in football—inspiration that will hit warp speed in 2023. Representation matters.

Prior to this Matildas cohort, few female fans had women heroes in a football context. We know, for example, that many sought to emulate male players and even aspired to play in Men's World Cups because they couldn't see any female football heroes. The current generation's visibility has dramatically shifted the lever and encouraged a swathe of girls and women to pursue, proselytise and drive women's sport, from social participation all the way to the elite level.

The Commonwealth Bank, a sponsor of women's football and cricket, has reflected that in its 'The Game Changers' ad campaign, which features Ellyse Perry and Sam Kerr, two of Australia's highest-profile team-sport athletes, irrespective of gender. The ad's faux press-conference question to Perry about changing the game leads to a sequence of grassroots players and Kerr playing football and cricket and more, the culmination of which is a return to Perry, who says, 'I'd say we're *all* changing the game.'

That visibility is relevant not just for inspiring girls and women to play, although it's potent for that, too. Certainly, you can't be what you can't see. But neither can you support something you can't see. Lack of media coverage is the most frequently cited reason why people don't follow women's sport. Such lack of coverage reinforces gender bias and hinders commercial and sponsorship opportunities.[15] Worse, the lack of audience is attributed to lack of viewers and fans pulling their weight as opposed to the primarily white male sports journalists, editors and producers whose gatekeeping fails to prioritise equal or fair coverage of women's sports.[16]

While media coverage has improved in recent years, the gains are tenuous. This was evidenced by the COVID-19 pandemic, which derailed sport altogether as competitions ceased worldwide. The pandemic-induced complete absence of sport presented an inimitable opportunity to examine and potentially reset media coverage. That reset didn't happen. As research lead-authored by *Siren* co-founder and research fellow Dr Kasey Symons found, even when they couldn't be played or watched, men's sports dominated headlines as media regressed to familiar (read: men's-sports-focused) reporting patterns as media scratched around to collate highlights packages and listicles. For women's sports, it was tumbleweeds.[17] Likewise, governing bodies went above and beyond to get men's sports back up and running, including, in the case of sports like rugby league, creating a geographic 'bubble' to house the players and keep the competition running. Women's sports and seasons were left to languish. It was a brutal reminder that when things get difficult and money gets tight, all resources and focus are funnelled to men's sport.

Absent the urgency surrounding getting men's competitions back up and running, women footballers went on average 250 days without a game, and minutes played for national teams reduced by 56 per cent.[18] It wasn't just the lack of games, but the lack of ability to train and the fragmented nature of the training when players had to train alone for a team sport—it was almost a return to the past when players completed their training with individual programs in isolation. Such long layoff periods were then followed by intense patches of injury-risk-increasing activity through games played in a condensed, congested timeframe.

Sarah Gregorius believes that we're yet to see the long-term impact of the pandemic-induced cessation of games on both players and women's football as a whole. Women's football was booming after the 2019 Women's World Cup before COVID kneecapped it, she says. The pandemic-related interruptions adversely affected not just the players but also an industry trying to emerge and develop in its own right. Granted there's no optimal time for a pandemic, but Gregorius points out that COVID-19 was particularly devastating because we were only just starting to address some of the fragilities of women's football in terms of professionalisation, pay parity, gender discrimination and media coverage. The pandemic provided a stark reminder of the undercurrents of scarcity and precarity that infuse women's football.

Pandemics aside, a 2021 New Zealand Sports Women Leadership Academy report recommended a three-pronged approach to progress women's sport's visibility and profile, much of it wresting and facilitating crucial self-determination for women. The prongs entailed empowering women to own and tell their own stories through their own social media; encouraging collaborating with allies such as national sporting bodies to improve, extend and amplify outcomes; and championing sportswomen through improved media coverage.[19] Notably, while major media is in the mix, it's not the primary mechanism and therefore not the gatekeeper.

Such a social-media-led approach enables distribution and audience-building independent of major media intermediaries deeming women's stories coverage-worthy, and helps counter the power and media coverage imbalance.[20] It also cuts through the chicken/egg scenario where the lack of investment, match broadcasting and media coverage is used to justify the lack of investment, match broadcasting and media coverage because the market and audience purportedly aren't there. (Spoiler alert: they are.) Case in point: that fanbase facilitated FIFA selling more tickets on the first day of its pre-sale for the 2023 tournament than it sold in the first week for the 2019 tournament, with the number of ticket sales later exceeding 500,000 tickets sold to fans from more than 120 countries more than 180 days out from the tournament.[21] But there were subsequent hiccups that showed FIFA wasn't yet aware of the 'sleeping giant' that is women's football support. When Australian fans complained about missing out on tickets due to the general ticket sales window opening at a time that favoured international time zones (that is, in the middle of the night Australian time), FIFA admitted it was 'caught off guard' by the 'unprecedented' demand for tickets.[22] As *Washington Post* journalist Molly Hensley-Clancy tweeted, the fact that FIFA would suggest such a thing in 2022—a year when women's sports attention and success had skyrocketed— is telling.[23] The scenario is particularly curious given that FIFA had in the preceding weeks knocked back major media organisations' sub-par offers for broadcast rights. It has suggested that the offers, some of which were more than 100 times lower than the offers for the men's equivalent, were insulting.[24] The organisation urged broadcasters to pay what women's football was worth. It seems FIFA is on the ball when it comes to extracting broadcast deals, but is caught off guard when it comes to providing fans with tickets to support their teams. (Fortunately, FIFA heeded the ticket sales demand and later moved the match to Stadium Australia, which has an 83,500-spectator capacity. The venue change did some reputational repair and marked a win for both fans and revenue.)

Still, the agency and autonomy presented by social media aren't without complexity, not least relating to athletes navigating grey areas of what is socially acceptable in terms of being feminine, athletic and empowered.[25] That's even before you consider the largely unpaid labour involved.

As a savvy and prolific social media user, New Zealand Football Fern Ali Riley is happy to leverage the various platforms to grow the game. At the same time, she acknowledges that while she finds it fun, she also considers it a 'responsibility'. She's trying to help grow women's football and its opportunities to a point where players use social media 'because they like to and not because they feel they need to'. She illustrates this with an example of English Premier League team Chelsea. Male players will post something because they're proud to play, she says. 'But everyone knows they're playing at 9 p.m. on Sunday. They don't have to do it for their followers to know there's a game in the Premier League.' So social media is another job the women players have to do. 'Oh, absolutely. It's a side hustle,' Riley agrees. (One upside is that new US National Women's Soccer League (NWSL) club Angel City FC, of which Riley is the inaugural captain, is paying players 1 per cent of ticketing revenue, so her social media match promotion is beginning to earn her some additional income. It bodes well given that Angel City sold out its first home game. That's 1 per cent of 22,000 ticket sales.)

It's a double-edged sword. Women athletes are exposed to more mostly unpaid work and mental load as they engage in the 'digital labour' of promoting themselves through social media.[26] As Danielle Warby notes, social media 'puts the work onto athletes when promotion should be something driven by the sports, media and sponsors as well. I see how hard it is for athletes in less-well-promoted sports.' But the flipside is that it represents invaluable, powerful promotional opportunities. As Warby says, 'controlling the narrative can't be underestimated'.

Then there's the body image interplay—another sharp edge for players to navigate. A 2020 Healthy Women in Sport: A Performance

Advantage (WHISPA) study in New Zealand laid bare some stark but foreseeable stats: 80 per cent of elite female athletes said social media affected their body image, with 15 per cent reporting disordered eating to attempt to conform to said image.[27] While social media is raising players' profiles and potentially attracting fans and sponsors, it also exposes them to sexism, homophobia and trolling.[28] We catch glimpses of it when players such as Kerr elect to call it out. Mostly, though, we are oblivious to the stream of abuse and 'feedback' players receive daily on their bodies, sexuality and abilities. So players endure the downsides to access the vital upsides. That's something 2023 and beyond need to be conscious of.

Related to that, we need to be realistic about the Matildas' chances of winning the tournament and the mental health pressure that being the much-hyped co-host nation heaps on them. The Matildas are a good team. They're a solid team. They're an inspiring team packed with the best role models you could ask for. But they're not yet a top-two team. They're worthy of being in and around the top 10, but are they likely to win the final, or even be in it? Probably not. Not yet. Just four teams have won the Women's World Cup (United States in 1991, 1999, 2015 and 2019; Norway in 1988 and 1995; Germany in 2003 and 2007; and Japan in 2011), so it would be yet another first for the Matildas, a team that has achieved a lot of firsts, if they were to achieve this. We need to be realistic that the tournament is not about whether or not the Matildas win. *Hosting* is the win.

Perry agrees that the tournament's success should not hinge on the Matildas' advancement. Speaking of her 2020 ICC Women's T20 World Cup hosting experience, she references the enormous gains it brought, including having more than 86,000 people fill the Melbourne Cricket Ground to support women's cricket: 'It was just so important for highlighting that female global sporting events are worth attending and worth investing in. It highlighted that you can make a great show of it and it can be a wonderful thing for a host country. I guess we were really lucky in terms of the fairytale ending of it [Australia won], but I don't necessarily think that needs to be the definition of tournament success. There are so many stories along the way. I think the Australian public doesn't really know the stories of other countries who play around the world—definitely cricket, but I think even more so for football.' Indeed, uncovering and disseminating the individual and collective stories is where some mighty wins are to be had.

In addition to alleviating the pressure on the Matildas, we need to edge New Zealand's results forward. The team has never won a game or progressed past the group stage in its five previous Women's World Cup attendances. Whether New Zealand needs to follow Australia's lead and leave Oceania is the perennial question. It would mean a harder qualifying route and failing to qualify for some tournaments, but it would also raise the bar. Ultimately, is it better to qualify easily but get pummelled at a tournament, or fail to qualify through tougher opponents and not get to a tournament at all?

When this question is put to him, Tom Sermanni agrees that it's fair to say New Zealand is the team Australia was and could have stayed. 'In saying that, the team is still competitive. The couple of challenges we need to fix with New Zealand are being a bit more consistent and being able to see out and win games.' With the competition expanded to thirty-two teams, it's possible New Zealand will have a chance to test itself against countries whose trajectories are similarly developmental. Snagging its first Women's World Cup game win would do wonders for this team. (That said, its group-stage draw makes that less likely. New Zealand will face heavyweights Norway (boosted by the aforementioned Ada Hegerberg), the increasingly strong Switzerland, and first-timers but up-and-comers the Philippines, who will be buoyed by a breakout 2022 AFC Women's Asian Cup campaign under former Matildas coach Alen Stajcic.) Likewise, we'll need to applaud, contextualise and educate around the new teams' entry to the tournament. Given their likely early development, there may be a few Eric the Eels[29] among them.

★ ★ ★

Requisite to mitigating some of the uninvited pressure and feedback delivered through social media channels is providing women with the tools they need to feel confident and excel. Uniforms are a central but often overlooked component of this. In 2019 Nike released women-specific kits that incorporated recycled bottles and, for the Matildas, featured splotches of yellow, green and white reminiscent of the Socceroos' 'Spew' jersey of decades before.[30] The kits were memorable, yes, and an advancement as the first women-specific fit, but the Spew 2.0 patterning was a missed opportunity.

Yellow spew shirts aren't flattering on anyone who's not an elite athlete. It's also unoriginal to create uniforms that reference men's kits instead of carving out an inimitable, women-specific identity. But the relevance of kit in which players feel comfortable isn't just a matter of aesthetics and ego. It's as much about overcoming another, often unacknowledged sports participation hurdle. A Victoria University study focusing on girls aged twelve to eighteen years confirmed what most girls and women already knew intuitively: done well, uniforms imbue comfort and confidence; done poorly, they cause discomfort and self-consciousness and act as a participation barrier.[31]

The study demonstrated that girls and women are clear about what they want: flexibility and self-determination in uniform selection, with a priority on shorts and T-shirt options rather than skirts or dresses. Also, breathable dark material that masks sweat. White shorts, traditionally worn for away kits, were singled out as something to be rethought (read: permanently banned). This is something we're starting to see movement on, with professional teams such as Manchester City moving away from white shorts.[32] Administrator Helen Tyrikos called bullshit on white shorts at a grassroots level a while back. Her response to male administrators' statement 'But we've got daughters, and the supplier has one' was 'OK, but have you ever had a period? In the rain?'

Appropriate cut and sizing is up there, too. While women in other sports have had to push back on inappropriately skimpy uniforms, women footballers have weirdly had the opposite problem: men's hand-me-down uniforms that have been way too large. 'When you're a little player like me … I'm only a metre sixty and fifty kilos,' former Matilda Angela Iannotta says, 'when you're wearing a long T-shirt and long shorts, it can be heavy on you.'

Such uniform considerations need to extend beyond the players, with match officials, for example, equally affected by assumptions of there only being male wearers. Just having a women's-cut referee uniform would make an enormous difference, Jacewicz says: 'We're still coming up against that barrier for young girls for whistling. It's such a simple fix.'

The women-specific kit needs to extend to shoes, to provide boot offerings that don't assume women are just men with small feet. Australian physics major and STEM advocate Laura Youngson co-founded Ida Sports after identifying this gap in the market while climbing Tanzania's Mount Kilimanjaro. (Fittingly, Youngson was trying to set a Guinness World Record for a football match played at the highest altitude and climb a physical mountain to draw attention to the metaphorical mountains women have to scale to overcome sports inequality.) After 'reading medical journals like a boss', she and her collaborators developed an affectionately titled 'Frankenshoe' prototype in her Melbourne kitchen. The response they received to the launched product validated Youngson's instincts, research and business approach. 'We've had so many players (and their parents) say to us, "It's like we exist in the sport for the first time",' she tells me.

★ ★ ★

While we're considering the less-considered aspects, it's imperative to look beyond the lustre of the Starting XI. Within each team there are multiple experiences for each tournament, depending on where a player is on their playing journey: first World Cup vs last World Cup; core player or cusp; fully fit or overcoming injury. Indeed, for a collective experience, it's also incredibly individual and layered. The players experience their own tournaments; the referees and assistant referees and event staff and fans experience their own tournaments, too.

To make a World Cup as a player, a whole bunch of things predominantly outside of your control need to perfectly align. First, you need to be able to be given the opportunity to play football, and in a country that qualifies for a World Cup. Second, you need to have been born in a particular few years to coincide with a

narrow age window considered to align with peak sporting performance. Third, you have to not be injured. Fourth, you have to have a
coach determine that you are the best possible player for a position.
Fifth, you have to be able to afford to pursue your sport, be it
through earning an income from it or from jobs unrelated to it, or
through familial or partner support. So not everyone who aspires
to make a World Cup makes it—talent alone doesn't get you across
the line.

For cusp players—players whose career does not perfectly align
with all of the above five categories—2023 will be tricky. For
example, if you narrowly miss out—if you're the twenty-fourth
player when the squad can only comprise twenty-three—are you
going to be able to watch the tournament? Broadcaster Stephanie
Brantz picks up on this line of thinking: 'When you do watch it,
you have to pretend to be so, so happy. Which, you know what, to
your credit you are. You're happy for your teammates. But part of
you must be dying inside, you have to think.'

There's a lot to unpack with this. 'I've always thought it must be
so hard for players who travel and sit on the bench. You've made
it, so you are at the top of your sport. You've made the team going
to the World Cup. But if you don't play, where does that sit in
your memories? Do you count that?' Brantz asks. 'Or even the one
who's just outside the XI.'

There are countless equivalent examples. Say you get injured: the
better your replacement does in your absence, the less likely you'll be
able to reclaim your spot once rehabilitated. Perhaps the most acute
example of selection vs non-selection challenges is when the first-
choice goalkeeper is injured and the understudy excels. Who gets the
gig when that injured keeper is back to being fit? As Brantz says, 'It's
not like, "You're both great, you can both play."'

'There's so many stories of exactly that,' Sacha Wainwright says.
'Your family travels to another country for the World Cup and you
don't get on the pitch. Your parents and extended family turn up
at the Olympics and you don't get on. The coach has picked one
of your good mates over you. The list goes on and on. And because
you've invested so much and it means so much, they're raw, those

experiences.' But those players' contributions are integral and valid: cusp players and competition for spots propel the team forward.

Still, it's difficult to know when it's worth persevering. Aivi Luik got the fairytale finish, but her story could have gone the other way: she could have always been the player who was in the World Cup mix but never quite got over the line. For every Luik, there are thousands of players whose careers were curtailed by equivalent scenarios. Their efforts and influence should not be overlooked.

'It's imposter syndrome' is how former Matilda Ellen Beaumont describes being on the cusp of making, then narrowly missing out on being selected for, the 2007 Women's World Cup. 'There's that element of self-doubt when you're only just in the squad … You always feel like there's a "but".' The other 'but', she notes, is the rich, irreplaceable friendships and experiences she had as a direct result of her football career. She might not have got to play in a World Cup, but those friendships and experiences were, and continue to be, life-changing.

Indeed, we often focus on the top-tier Matildas' feats to the exclusion of the surrounding benefits football at any and all levels brings. Former players including Alison Leigh Forman, Wendi Henderson and Shelley Youman have called for a focus and funding shift to inclusivity and prioritising enjoyment and the health of the 99 per cent of average athletes rather than steering money and opportunity towards the elite 1 per cent. So if the 2023 tournament's legacy should do anything, it should balance the celebration of the 1 per cent with celebrating the contributions of the players who sit outside—or even just outside—that. Likewise, keeping them in and around the game beyond their elite playing careers.

At the time we spoke, former Matilda Kate McShea was on her way to arrange uniforms for her children, who were about to start playing their first football season, fittingly at the same club where her own entry to the game began. Julie Murray was coaching her son's under-6 team, no doubt with the kids careening about oblivious to the fact that they were in the presence of football royalty. Beaumont had returned to the pitch to play in a Brisbane Roar legends showcase game. Vedrana Popovic, who was in contention but wasn't selected for the 2015 Women's World Cup, has been playing–coaching the previously underrepresented women's team at community football club St George in Brisbane. In the process, she's been experiencing renewed love for the game. Recent respective knee reconstruction and pregnancy notwithstanding, former Matildas and Brisbane Roar teammates Brooke Spence and Amy Chapman, who also didn't get to have the Women's World Cup fairytale finish, have similarly convened in the National Premier Leagues Women's (NPLW), the tier below the A-League Women's.

Peer Ellie Brush, who was in contention for the 2011 Women's World Cup, has returned to the A-League Women's team Canberra United after a detour via the AFLW and a knee reconstruction. Former teammates Michelle Heyman and Ash Sykes, who played in the 2015 Women's World Cup but who later stepped away from the grind of trying to stay in contention at the national team level, also returned to the game generally and Canberra United specifically.

Larissa Crummer, whose 2019 Women's World Cup hopes were dashed by sustaining a broken leg and complications so severe that there was only a remote chance she'd ever play football again, has, like Kellond-Knight, returned against the odds and regained Matildas call-ups. So too has Alex Chidiac, friend of Aivi Luik and fellow Common Goal member, with the two donating a percentage of their playing fees to sustainability measures. After an initial start polar opposite to Luik's—Chidiac was called into the Matildas as a teenager and was consistently in the mix until she suddenly wasn't—she narrowly missed out on 2019 Women's World Cup selection while Luik finally didn't. But as she alluded to in a Matildas video released in early 2023, Chidiac subsequently adopted a strategy similar to Luik's, concentrating solely on enjoying her football. She has since been recalled to the Matildas squad and is appreciating whatever opportunities that, or other football experiences, may bring.

Meanwhile, Renaye Iserief, who narrowly missed out on the 1988 Women's World Cup through injury, has played in three World Masters Games with former Matildas where the benefits exceeded the gold and two silver medals they won. ('It was great to reconnect with former teammates from the Matildas days. Playing in those tournaments really gave me a sense of why I played football—the many friendships and endless memories I made in all of my years playing,' Iserief says.) That's substantially relevant because the time subsequent to stepping away from elite football can see players out in the football wilderness.

A 2021 PFA report published as part of the organisation's retired and transitioned players program stated that 70 per cent of players said they found transition to the next phase of their life difficult; 57 per cent said their retirement was involuntary. Just 7 per cent of players reported being financially stable as a result of their careers.[33] That largely invisible post-playing transition and its long-lasting effects must be especially bumpy for women given that women footballers were and are paid a fraction—if that—of what male footballers were and are paid.

Former player turned commentator Grace Gill (who recently became the first Australian footballer to level up from delivering expert commentary to lead commentary in the A-League Women's) is one of the PFA's program ambassadors. 'This is a part of the game I've always felt really strongly about,' she says. 'As a player, it became apparent to me during my career that the support I was given on my pathway into the elite game was nothing like the support I was given at the other end of that.' Gill wasn't alone in experiencing this. 'Personally I was in what you would consider a "good" position—I had a strong support network, a stable job, and income outside of football, and I made the decision to retire on my own terms, not allowing my body, or anyone else, to decide this for me. Despite all of that, the adjustment during that period of my life was really tough. It's something that's hard to explain unless you've fumbled your way through it, but I know in speaking with many other women who I played alongside that this transition was and is a really difficult time.'

Sykes' experience is indicative of many elite women footballers', with the pressure to realise her representative dreams compounded by the financial pressures and lack of other support. 'At the end of the week if I hadn't made it through to the next [2015 Women's

World Cup] camp, I didn't have a job and had no way to pay rent or any of my bills from that point. I wanted to succeed and be a regular member of the Matildas squad so much I put a lot of pressure on my own performances, which just added to the stress. When I took a step back from the national team it felt like a massive weight off my shoulders and I think I started playing better football from that point on. Unfortunately, at that time we didn't have as good access to the support programs they do now, like psychological support, which I think would have helped a lot in prolonging my career. Not to mention better wages or being able to consider it a full-time profession so you don't have to worry so much about making ends meet! Anyway, living like that eventually just wore me down and took a lot of the enjoyment out of playing football so I chose to start the next phase of life with a stable income and football [as] just a social activity.'

Sykes adds: 'It's fantastic there are more resources available for the players now. I hope less and less of the players in Australia have to experience what we did. That will enable more players to stay in the game for a longer period of time and just increase the player pool for the A-league Women's or Matildas to choose from. If I look back at all the talented players from the early W-League or my Young Matildas generation who had to make a similar choice to me and walk away from the game, there is a wealth of talent there that could still be underpinning our national league.'

'Finishing a career is difficult,' Ferguson agrees. 'I feel like my transition was a bit easier because I was ready mentally, and also I went straight into helping out with coaching, so I was still involved to some extent, and doing the co-comms [on the ABC] as well. So you're still involved, you're still part of it. It's not just "Right, that's it. You're gone now. See you later. Go and find a new career."' But, she adds, 'Unfortunately, elite-level sport is like that. If you're not aware of the fact that you can fall out of favour with the coach, you can get injured and everything can come crashing down very quickly, then you're in for a very big fall when those things happen. Because that's the reality of being an elite sportsperson generally, and the majority don't make the final decision about ending their career. Either someone else makes it for them or injuries make it for them, and it's out of their control.'

Lisa De Vanna, one of the last players who bridged the previous and current generations and the absence of pay and decent conditions and now equal pay and conditions, could testify to that. Rather than being able to call time on her career and go out on a high, she had to try to prove she was still worth selecting and saw her national-team dream fade with a succession of non-selections all but determining her retirement fate.

Describing herself as a 'pre–World Cup' player, Sue Monteath would recognise that experience, too. She continuously represented Australia for ten years (1978–87 inclusive), but her national team career ended just shy of the 1988 tournament courtesy of a coach change. 'I was surprised that in 1988, with a new national coach, I wasn't selected,' she says. 'It was a tough pill to swallow, but it happens. One can only speculate as to why/how it happened. I felt gutted at the time.'

Iserief was similarly anguished to miss the 1988 tournament. Hers was one of the injury experiences Ferguson speaks of. Iserief made the squad but suffered a serious ankle injury. She had two weeks to prove her fitness, culminating in a final game. 'Everything hinged on that two weeks,' she explains. 'I did everything I possibly could to recover and went into that game knowing everything was on the line, hoping like hell I would get through unscathed.' The injury was nasty; the recovery time needed was long. But with the World Cup fast approaching, time was the thing Iserief didn't have. 'I made a split-second decision during the game to make a tackle [that] would change the trajectory of my playing days as a Matilda. I made that decision because I needed to test if my ankle would hold. It was like time had stopped. My ankle gave way and I went down in a heap, gutted. I knew that was it for me.'

So while their teammates headed to China, Iserief underwent an ankle reconstruction and both she and Monteath mothballed their careers. 'It was hard to get into the team and even harder to stay in, so I knew with this much time out of the side my national playing days were possibly over,' Iserief explains. 'It was tough, and it certainly wasn't how I wanted to go out. I often wonder how much further I could have gone in the game.'

Monteath's recollections of Australia's progress in that pilot World Cup are vague, possibly, she thinks, because she was trying to move on. 'It was also a lot harder to follow then, without the social media and increased publicity present today,' she explains. That may have been some salve compared with the ubiquity of coverage contemporary players not selected have to contend with.

Monteath notes that in some ways the unpaid career status also softened her transition away from playing. It was never a viable career in the sense of professional pay, so she turned her focus to her paid job, teaching, and took advantage of teacher exchange programs to expand her experience but perhaps also to seek out new international adventures that football could no longer provide. Fortunately, decades on, Monteath's contribution is rightly being accorded its place in Matildas history: in 2004 she was inducted into the Football Australia Hall of Fame, and in 2009 she was belatedly presented with cap #9. In 2019 the Queensland Academy of Sport Player of the Year award was named in her honour.

Karly Pumpa, too, is a player who acutely understands how careers can be cruelled. She's due a knee replacement now as the three ACL injuries and related structural damage she sustained continue to make their presence known. She says, 'I kind of had to separate myself from the sport emotionally and physically for quite a while because it was really hard [to be around the game without being able to play].'

Ferguson is one of the exceptions to the retirement scythe that slices through so many elite players' careers. 'I could see the pace of the game was getting away from me,' she says. She informed Sermanni that she wouldn't go on any tours in 2008 as she started transitioning out of her playing career. He later extended an offer for her to return, but she told him, 'No, I'm going to make the decision for you before you have to make it for me ... Thanks, but I'm done. I'm quite happy to move aside.'

Other than De Vanna, Clare Polkinghorne is perhaps the last remaining player to have been part of the team's unpaid, then partially paid, then fully paid trade. Now officially, but humbly, the most-capped Matilda, having surpassed Lisa DeVanna's 150 caps and equalled Cheryl Salisbury's 151, Polkinghorne's also the last of the players who were part of that 2007 breakout success. Polkinghorne's retirement, whenever it happens (hopefully not soon—if profession-alism of the game is enabling one thing, it's that players can continue much longer without the lack of pay or opportunity, for example, that would previously have curtailed their careers), will likely look like experiencing Women's World Cups as her family has. 'We've always joked that after Clare's retired, she's going to come and sit in the stands and do another Women's World Cup,' her brother Tom says. 'That's probably the thing she misses out on. I mean, she gets to play the games and have all the fun, but she always says, "I've travelled to all these places in the world, but my family's seen much more of them than I have."'

'We spoke about it, how I've been lucky enough to have my family along to most of the World Cups,' Clare confirms. 'The first one was just my dad, and then the whole family came to the second one and third one. Tom and a few others came to the fourth. So I've been lucky enough to have a lot of support with me at these major tournaments and we always speak about how different our experiences are as a player compared to a supporter ... As a player, you're pretty much in a bubble. [You go] from the hotel to the training ground, back to the hotel, to the match stadium ... I feel like it would be a much different experience, well I *know* it's a much different experience for the fans and the families that come along, so it's something that I definitely want to experience from the other side of things and [I'm] really looking forward to hopefully doing that with Tom.'

Polkinghorne's retirement will also be a retirement of sorts for her family—the end of an era or an evolution for a family on whose lives women's football has left an indelible imprint. 'I probably enjoy it just as much as Clare does,' Tom says. 'I would probably go back to 2007 and start again—and I haven't even kicked a ball.'

12

BEYOND GREATNESS

THERE'S A SOCIAL media meme where people post two photos side by side with the tagline: 'How it started. How it's going.'

Were you to post one for the Matildas, you'd likely juxtapose images akin to what the bid team projected on the Opera House. On the left would be an image of a first-generation Matilda such as Julie Dolan wearing a billowing second-hand uniform on a poor-quality pitch in front of few fans and even fewer media. In contrast on the right would be an image of a modern Matilda such as Sam Kerr, clad in tailored, sponsored kit and custom boots, celebrating scoring a hat-trick with a backflip that was photographed, filmed, broadcast and forever preserved. Or perhaps the left would feature Dolan and her teammates making lamingtons in a mini production line, then selling them alongside raffle tickets to fund their pay-to-play endeavours. Offsetting that image would be Kerr, the first Matilda making serious bank from her football career and related sponsorships, seated in front of a console and playing an animated version of herself as she and her teammates achieve representation on the traditionally male-only, multimillion-dollar-grossing FIFA EA Sports game. (Kerr herself now lays claim to being not just one of the first women to be featured in the game but the actual first woman to grace its cover, which she achieved with the release of FIFA '23.)

Viewed this way, it's easy to appreciate just how meteoric women's football's trajectory has been in Australia in the space of forty years, even if it felt glacial while we lived it. It's also easy to dust off your hands as if the job is done. Really, though, it's only just begun.

The 'Beyond Greatness' 2023 tournament theme is a natural build on 2019's 'Dare to Dream'. Reminiscent of the cultural and confidence shift Expo '88's 'Together We'll Show the World' ethos invoked, with women (and some men) showcasing and going beyond greatness on and off the pitch, it's a recognition of women's football's abundant actualised achievements, from players to administrators to referees. It marks stepping out of men's football's shadow. But 2023 won't be a coda. It will again be a litmus test for women's football's development and wider social and cultural progress, in light of and in spite of the plot twist that has been the COVID-19 pandemic.

The event will be a palimpsest, too, of previous generations' efforts and the first of many peaks for women's football—an appropriate moment to appreciate and acknowledge the gains made to date. There are few women better placed to do that than the women who were instrumental in its beginnings.

'Initially, back in '75, nobody knew,' Dolan says. 'I think I've still got the newspaper that says, "Look what our girls are doing." No one could believe that we were playing football. It did obviously progress from there, but in those days it seemed to be a slow progression. When I look back and compare it to seeing my image on the Opera House, which was representing all the pioneers, and then seeing Sam Kerr's, I thought, *Look how far we've come in that time*. That really put it into perspective for me. In forty years, or what most people would see as the forty-year history of the Matildas, gee, that's a long way.'

It's a really short long time. 'When you look at it in that sense, it *is* really short,' Dolan agrees. But, she notes, in other respects it's problematically long: 'For the players at the time, given that your career might be four, five, six years, ten years at most, forty years is a lifetime. If you were plugging away in those pioneering years and leaving jobs because there was nothing to come back to, then you could possibly think that was a hard road. There wasn't really such a thing as unpaid leave for women who wanted to go off and play football.'

No. Not then. But there's starting to be now.

'I knew this was going to be important at some stage,' Heather Reid says, surveying the assemblage of artefacts she's kept and carted between different homes and even different states: brochures, minutes, reports, images, notebooks, the plush toy mascot. 'I shake my head at where we're at now. But it's taken ... In all of the history, if we hadn't had that fifty-year hiatus where women were banned, we would have been at this point a lot earlier, obviously. But from 1988, when FIFA finally gave women a pilot Women's World Cup, through to where we're at now, in the space of those thirty years we have a Women's World Cup, a Youth World Cup, an under-17s World Cup and Olympic status.'

Not to mention a World Cup tournament that is as high-profile and esteemed as the Olympics it once leveraged off.

★ ★ ★

It's incredibly fitting that Australia and New Zealand secured the rights to host a Women's World Cup before they secured the rights to host a Men's World Cup. Their resources have been scant, but women in both countries have been quietly succeeding for years. It's fitting, too, that the bid was combined. Australia and New Zealand's entwined, symbiotic football relationship has ensured that they have as often been friends as foes as they forged their footballing paths. The countries' small sizes and relative newness to football, as well as their geographic isolation, have meant they have looked across the ditch to organise friendlies when other countries have been less interested in travelling to play against them. Both countries have grappled with lack of infrastructure, visibility and funding. Both have found their women's football association absorbed into their men's football association. In spite of this, both have been more successful than their male counterparts, and both have punched above their weight on the world stage.

For both countries, and for their counterparts around the world, the tournament's legacy needs to be the lasting effect it has on professionalism and visibility and the nuts and bolts of infrastructure. The change rooms it will invoke funding for, but also the social and cultural awareness shift it will inspire to move women from an afterthought to an equal thought. Where if there's one set of change rooms we have a problem, and those change rooms are something that must be shared equally, not something with default male occupancy and obliviousness to the fact that the women are getting changed in the car park. Where if there's only one good pitch and one good set of lighting, the women's and men's teams alternate using it and work together to obtain funding to improve facilities overall. Where irrespective of the quantity of the physical or fiscal resources and opportunities, they're divvied up equally. Where the legacy in women's football isn't viewed as a corporate social responsibility initiative but a viable, profitable, sought-after business.

That legacy involves normalising and inspiring participation at every level so the conversation is no longer about someone being 'the first woman to [insert action and role here]'. Where dedicated, proper seats are reserved at tables so women aren't needing to constantly live the adage that if they don't give you a seat, you need to bring a folding chair. That includes normalising women playing, coaching, refereeing, commentating, administrating, photographing, filming, writing, and more, and in an authentic sense rather than a 'binders full of women'[1] sense or a 'there are no suitable women applicants' sense without any acknowledgement of the glass and grass ceilings that have prevented there being suitable women applicants. Without any acknowledgement that women are having to lug around said folding chairs and find ways to politely unfold them and take up space, perpetually perched on the edge of such tables, acutely aware their chair is flimsy and their attendance largely uninvited or at least unaccounted for.

Amid the spectacle of 2023 that will mark the injection of professionalism and women's football advancement, we'll also be witnessing the last of the players who were the only girls on the boys' team; the last of the players who didn't have anyone to look up to;

the last of the players who had to forgo pay and many life milestones to pursue a career when it wasn't yet a career; the legends of the game who span the before and after who knew what it was like to self-support to play, then to receive nominal pay, and to have to fight and be grateful for every incremental improvement—in particular, the standouts who raised our awareness of the game and the bar on what women footballers could and can achieve, such as the Martas, the Rapinoes, the Sinclairs. But we need to balance acknowledging and appreciating the advances they made with ensuring that no one has to make those advances again; that no one should have to carry such a load alone or, worse, have to withstand the onslaught of conservative outrage or imperil their careers by speaking out about inequity. In short, no more firsts. No more tokenism. No more novelty. Just normality. If 2023 delivers us anything, it should be the backstop policies and parity that ensure we are seeing the absolute last of the firsts.

Of course, it's imperative not to overplay what the tournament will bring. In writing about AFLW, but in a sentiment equally applicable to football, journalist Sam McClure noted that the normalisation of women playing football means that one day the concept of women not being able to play football or their playing being seen as a novelty will be as foreign a concept as women not being allowed to vote.[2] But, as researcher Fiona McLachlan points out, breaking through the 'grass ceiling' is a much less clear and linear process. We've heard such optimism and hype around women's sport and its gender-equality-advancing ability before (like, 100 years ago and roughly once every decade since).[3]

At the 2021 Women Onside football collective conference, Moya Dodd spoke of how she is ambitious for women's football and we're in the current fairly enviable position because women before her were ambitious for women's football. So what do such bastions as Dodd want to see come from hosting the tournament? In short, lots. Their hopes sit on the spectrum from uplifting to pragmatic, and extend far beyond the tournament itself.

On former Football Fern Wendi Henderson's part, she hopes the tournament 'is the beginning of winning the hearts of the New

Zealand public for women's football'. As she notes, the Football Ferns have had few opportunities to showcase their skills at home. 'If the public can firstly see for themselves the level and standard of play that the women's game has got to, I hope they then see the commitment and dedication that the Football Ferns have to be part of it all.'

PFA co-CEO Kate Gill will be concentrating on extending the A-League Women's foundations to ensure growth and longevity. The addition of Wellington Phoenix in 2021 is an excellent move—if there were ever a time to give a New Zealand A-League Women's team the tick, it was in the lead-up to the co-hosted 2023 Women's World Cup. Yet the A-League Women's competition length and design are too short, too static. 'The A-League Women's is the most visible product and asset we have within the chain for taking our players from the grassroots to the national team and then beyond to big, influential clubs,' Gill explains. 'How do we continue to develop the pathway? The league has stayed so stagnant in terms of its competition design. Yes, we've improved the working conditions and the contractual requirements that wrap around the league, but we need to shift focus to how we really transform the competition.' The goal: a year-round program that enables players to be full-time athletes. Gill believes that collaborating with the NPLW might be a viable option, combined with a tailored broadcast deal to sit behind it. *Not* shoring up these domestic foundations will be problematic after 2023. As Gill notes, 'You'll have a halo effect, a lustre that shines for a little while. Then it will fade and all will be lost.'

For Rebecca Price, it's ensuring that the accelerated growth we've seen at the elite level filters down to the grassroots. 'I think we have some work to do to raise the tide and float all the boats, all those little clubs. They have to benefit from this. If we don't leverage the World Cup to do that, it would be an awful waste. It would be like the Athens Olympics, where they built all of this infrastructure and then two years later it was all decrepit and falling apart. That's the equivalent, I think, to finish the metaphor.'

'A bubble-free tournament. No border closures. No transport strikes. If the sun could shine, that would be an advantage,'

Stephanie Brantz says. 'The one thing that does concern me is the time zone, although we are good for Asia so that's a lot of numbers through the Asian countries. But, you know, other people are about to experience how crap it is to watch a World Cup on the other side of the world,' she laughs.

For Ali Riley, it's about figuring out how New Zealand can leverage where Australia's at. The noise and gains Australia makes, be it in terms of lengthening the A-League Women's season, increasing exposure or improving conditions, is something New Zealand players can point to: 'Because we're able to say, look, we need all of those things too—we're ten years behind all of this.' As she acknowledges, the inclusion of the Wellington Phoenix team in the A-League Women's means that the countries are linked not just by proximity but by the mutual beneficence of growing the game. Given the entwined nature of their football development, she says, 'where Australia benefits, we're a little bit pulled along behind'.

Riley cites 2015 host country Canada as a cautionary example. Despite exemplary tournament running and results, and a victory tour with crowds of fans in love with the sport, there hasn't been a huge ascendancy post-hosting. Canada still doesn't have a domestic league even after winning 2020 Olympic gold (one was only announced in December 2022 and it won't kick off until 2025), so there's a diaspora of players necessarily plying their trade in the US league or even further afield. 'So it's these contrasting feelings and images of how far the game has come but how far we still have to go,' she says.

Like everyone else embedded in and driving women's football, Riley views 2023 as the next step, not the pinnacle. 'I'm happy to have been a part of it from 2007 until now, and I'm so excited to experience the next level.' She views 2023 as a level in women's football's necessary upward trajectory: 'Again, not the top, but the next level where we can go with it.'

For Clare Polkinghorne it's a chance to both look forward and look back, as well as global and local across the four—hopefully soon to be five—World Cups in which she's played. 'I think what stands out for me [across the World Cups] is the improvements in all facets of the game, whether it's technical, tactical, physical … Everything has just taken off in terms of the quality of players and teams, and I think the difference between world number one and even world number twenty has been reducing over that time.'

She notes that elements wrapping around the game have also climbed. 'The interest in the game has definitely continued to improve and we're getting to the point where teams are selling out stadiums, and big stadiums,' she says. (Exhibit A: the Matildas' recently moved the opening 2023 tournament match, which will now act as an 83,500-fan cauldron of women's football fandom and support.) 'That's only a positive for the game moving forward, and I think if we continue to grow that, the game is heading [to] a really good place.'

Of that domestic potential, Polkinghorne says, 'Obviously from a playing perspective, we're focusing on preparing ourselves as well as possible and doing the best we can as a group. But I think the bigger picture from that is continuing to grow the game in Australia. Having a home World Cup is going to be something that we can really leverage to drive interest in the game and drive the next generation of footballers in the country, and just having the world's best players playing on Australian and New Zealand soil is going to be a really good opportunity for us to showcase how far the game has come. I think it'll be a good opportunity to continue to inspire the next group of athletes coming through and get people not only interested in the Matildas but interested in women's football and just get as many people involved as we can—not only fans, but also supporters and sponsorship and all that sort of thing. So it's going to be a big year for women's football, especially in Australia, and hopefully the success on the field can help to drive that as well.'

Fascinatingly, many of the interviewees said they hoped, through increased visibility, that there are—or soon will be—many boys and men who have women football heroes, and are imagining the cultural shift that such a change will entail. Sam Kerr has already reached that crossover—there's a now-famous photo of brother-and-sister fans who used electrical tape to modify Socceroos jerseys to turn them from (Lucas) Neill's 2 to Kerr's 20. Megan Rapinoe and Ellyse Perry have, too. ('I'll never forget the time I went to the shopping centre in Brisbane and I saw on the outside of the Nike store the massive Sam Kerr poster,' Karly Pumpa says, referencing a recent major ad campaign. 'I just got goosebumps and almost got emotional because it's the best thing that I've ever seen in women's football. You never thought you'd see that. In America, yes ... but not over here. I remember thinking, *Wow, good on her* and *How good is this for the sport?*')

Dolan nominates recognising contributions of former Matildas beyond her era. Pioneers like her have been well recognised, she says, as are the current generation, but there's a lost generation of players in between that includes players such as Julie Murray. 'She's my hero,' Dolan says. 'She was an absolutely amazing player, and had so many firsts in her career. I don't think we've recognised that generation enough. Cheryl Salisbury, yes, but not the [other] players at the time, even up to Sally Shipard. We've missed a whole lot of fantastic players there. We'll have to rectify that.'

Pumpa might well be considered one such player from that era. She recalls, for example, being asked to pen a message of support for the Matildas as the team progressed through a major tournament. The letters from Pumpa and her peers would be pinned up around the hotel corridors the current players traversed. Writing the letter invoked a range of thoughts and emotions in Pumpa, given that she played at a time of greater anonymity and that she necessarily spent some time away from the game in the intervening years. 'When you're writing some of these things, you wonder if any of them will even know who I am,' she says, perhaps referencing that imposter syndrome Beaumont speaks of. 'But it's nice to think that they might read it and see it.' She's happy to contribute how she can. 'Honestly, they do us proud all the time. I really love watching how well they're doing. I love seeing how much the game and team's progressed.'

Having transitioned from player to administrator tasked with ensuring worldwide player welfare, Sarah Gregorius is spurred on by both the accelerating growth and the opportunity for 2023.

Momentarily forgetting she'll probably have to fit some work in between enjoying the tournament, akin to how her family did, she points to how supremely fun it's going to be. So for 2023, her hopes are uncomplicated: 'It's like, let's go. Things are really starting to ramp up. I'm dead keen.'

'I'm hoping that the Matildas will go deep, deep, deep, deep, deep into the tournament,' Brantz says. But, like Gregorius, she nominates higher priorities than the Matildas' success: 'As far as the actual tournament itself, I'm just hoping it puts on the best inclusive display of women's football we've ever seen.' Tangentially related, announcing the formation of the ParaMatildas and bringing the Afghanistan national team into the Australian domestic fold are good early signs of such inclusive progress.

For Karen Menzies, whose return to the game and legacy and meaningful contribution is continuing and expanding with her appointment to the NIAG, it's about acknowledging and better facilitating the valuable contribution Aboriginal players and Torres Strait Islander players can make. 'I'm not suggesting we want to elevate Indigenous over non-Indigenous players. That's never where we come from,' she says. 'I just want to see that there's true equity among all players, regardless of their cultural heritage. The reality for Indigenous players is that we often come from families and communities who have weathered the devastation of colonisation and forcible separation and assimilation, and now we're dealing with the resulting historical, collective and intergenerational trauma. So Indigenous players do need additional support around them to feel like, "Yes, you're valued and you're worthy and you can do this." If I can be a part of that, that's my goal.'

Fatima Flores nominates the practical, starting with the fact that there needs to be beer. Stadium-side, the 2019 tournament was, much to Flores's and many others' consternation, a dry event. 'That was the biggest load of crap I've ever heard,' she says. 'Australia had better get that right, because that will not go down here.' (For the record, after overcoming her initial surprise at my question about this, Jane Fernandez says she hasn't heard there *won't* be beer. Still, Flores's is not an unrealistic concern given that 2022 Men's World

Cup host Qatar banned alcohol at the last minute.) Although amusing, the beer observation also speaks to the need to understand and cater to the audience. 'But also, don't make it so corny for or so suited for family friendly,' Flores says. 'Yes, we love families and all that. But you can't just put on games for kids, because you lose a massive chunk of people if you don't cater to the adults in the room … [Exhibit A: The Wiggles performed at a Matildas 2022 friendly against the USWNT.] With women's, it's "Let's make sure there's no swearing and no drinking and everyone's well-behaved", but we're not hooligans even if we do drink. Calm down. And we don't want a 4 p.m. or 6 p.m. kick-off just to suit families.'

Little things (like beer and kick-off times) become big things in execution. Take, for example, the security pat-downs fans have had to pass through to make it into the stadiums. In 2019, if you identified as a woman—or, rather, if security identified you as one—you were required to queue up to be patted down by a woman security guard. The issue was that the fans were mostly women and the security guards were mostly men. If a woman walked up to a male security guard, she was shooed towards the women's line, which often involved a long and frustrating wait. (Dodd noted the practice also often split up people attending together who were not necessarily easily able to find each other in the sea of bodies on the other side: a dad and daughter, for example.) Notably, if someone who was non-binary or not stereotypically 'feminine' walked up, the guards were unsure of protocol and often completed the pat-down. It was fascinating. And frustrating, and arguably an allegory for wider problems afflicting women's football: thoughtlessness, insufficient resourcing, men not being especially challenged, women working double time.

Bundle in with that the need for a decent number of women's toilets. 'I always have a laugh when I go to the women's game and there's three cubicles for women and the men's toilets are very large and have urinals,' Rebecca Price says. 'It's like, "Has there been no forethought that at a women's sporting event they need to increase the capacity of the female-only bathrooms?" I cannot believe this is a recurring problem. I think it's funny because if you don't laugh you'll be angry all the time.'

Speaking of being angry, with the USWNT's pay-parity woes no longer providing distraction, it's fair to say that most players and administrators will be singularly focused on tipping the FIFA prize-purse domino. With two host countries that have enacted progressive pay-parity CBAs, FIFA has a superb opportunity to earn some excellent PR by significantly closing the prize-purse gap. Failing that, the PFA and Jennifer Robinson will no doubt be considering whether they need to resurrect the 2019 case, and Kerry Harris might have to start thinking about how she can top her 'equal pay' chant. Neither players nor fans nor administrators will allow FIFA to forget that. With Australia's sex discrimination commissioner joining the ambassadorial mix, it's fair to say the firm but fair pressure to do better will increase. Jenkins is, after all, a woman whose intellect, gravitas and diplomacy will make it difficult for FIFA officials to unabashedly trot out unsubstantiated lines about supporting gender equity (*cough cough* Visit Saudi sponsorship).

Said commissioner Kate Jenkins' ambitious but achievable hope is twofold. First, that Australia, which has hosting not only the Women's World Cup but also the Olympics and Commonwealth Games in its near future, models and normalises completing human-rights assessments for major sporting events. 'Certainly that would be my hope for Australia as an example of it being possible to think about these issues in advance and to plan and prepare to avoid them rather than deal with them after,' Jenkins says. She aspires, too, to there being a 'quantum shift' in terms of gender equality, including through better facilities, participation and pay. 'From my role more broadly, I would like that to flow to other sports, but more than that across our community so that there's greater respect for women participating in whatever they want to participate in. That would be my objective, which is a big one, and it's not just going to be the Women's World Cup, but in the context of a whole lot of other things that are happening at the moment, I think it has extra weight.'

Mostly, though, administrators and fans are acutely aware of just how enormous and enormously uplifting the tournament is going to be. Australians and New Zealanders don't quite know what's about to hit them, especially the event's infectiously enthusiastic, inspiring and truly global nature. 'People don't understand that the Women's World Cup is one of the top five major events in the world [and women's sports' largest[4]],' Eugenie Buckley explains. 'I have this conversation with people all the time because I've worked on Rugby World Cups as well. This is actually bigger than the Rugby World Cup, because the eyeballs on it are different. The audience in the US, Germany and China alone is massive. When I tell them how big it is, people look at me and go, "What?!" Over a billion people watched the Women's World Cup in 2019 in France. That's not bad.'

For their part, the Croissants are already planning for 2023. 'We'll have a lot more resources available in Sydney,' they tell me, adding, 'We know where the Spotlight is.' For starters, the group has set up a spreadsheet and a shared bank account to pool costume-creating resources and ideas. It's safe to say that the tradie-outfit-clad Croissants and their crocodile will be out, striding out and supporting women's football in full force.

No doubt the Croissants will be among the more gregarious and recognisable of the women weaving their way through the tournament crowds and lending their visual and vocal support to the Women's World Cup. (It should be noted Australians and New Zealanders know how to get behind sporting events, so the Croissants will likely be joined by a bunch of inflatable-kangaroo-wielding peers. And probably two women resurrecting their random but hit 2019 tournament brown felt 'Duff Beer' costumes.) No doubt they'll also again be crossing paths with, weaving among and perhaps even posing for photographs with women who are also edging women's football forward: human-rights lawyers, admin-istrators, volunteers, former and aspiring Matildas, existing and future Berrys, Dodds, Walshes, Dolans, Watsons and Reids. Except this time, they and we may better know those women's names. We may better know their contributions and stories. With ample media coverage and exemplary tournament delivery highlighting and hailing their contributions and skills, we may even counter—or, in a football context, give new meaning to—the Matilda Effect.

AFTERWORD

OVER THE YEARS I tried to write this book, to be a woman was at times thrilling and buoyant and heartening, at others frustrating and difficult and exhausting. We experienced the highs of the Matildas achieving pay parity and Australia and Aotearoa New Zealand winning the 2023 Women's World Cup bid—two things that had us resetting our expectations and imaginings about what might be possible—but those highs were tempered (undermined, even) by wider social and cultural reminders of just how far women are from achieving true equality.

That women's sports remain secondary to men's sports was evidenced during the COVID-19 pandemic, when funding and playing opportunities for women's sports were the first to go and the last to be factored into budget and logistics, and when men's sports continued to dominate media coverage even when no sport was being played. Beyond sport, women lost their lives in the most shocking and brutal of circumstances—Hannah Clarke at the hands of an abusive former partner who set fire to her and her children in their car on a quiet suburban Brisbane street, Sarah Everard murdered by a police officer despite 'doing everything right' as she walked home at night from a friend's place on busy, well-lit London streets. On news of Everard's death, women world-wide reeled in palpable grief. 'Text me when you get home', an ingrained phrase women know all too well and use regularly to ensure their friends' welfare, went viral. Perhaps most telling of all was how mystified men were to discover that women had to use such a safety mechanism at all.

Worldwide, women bore the brunt of the domestic, caring and remote-learning workloads during COVID-19 lockdowns. In the middle of that, the Intergovernmental Panel on Climate Change released a damning report declaring 'code red for humanity'—a bleak outlook made bleaker when you consider that women and children are, and will continue to be, most vulnerable to the volatility and disadvantages wrought by climate change. And the Taliban, a regime known to actively impede women's education and human rights, regained control of Afghanistan, erasing twenty years of 'progress' in a matter of a few wrenchingly devastating, fear-filled days. In particular danger were the Afghanistan women's national team players who had not only fought to be able to play football but also to expose and address sexual abuse perpetrated by male football administrators.

At a popular-culture level, Britney Spears had to fight to regain control of her uterus and her money. At a sporting level, NWSL coach Paul Riley was accused of engaging in a pattern of predatory sexual coercion and emotional abuse. Reports that administrators knew about the abuse but had failed to act to protect the players were simultaneously shocking and unsurprising. Domestically, Fox Sports sacked reporter Tom Morris over inappropriate remarks he made about fellow Fox Sports journalist Megan Barnard. Meanwhile, transgender athletes, and specifically trans women athletes, copped transphobia writ large amid a sickening federal election campaign predicated not on policy but on punching down—again, both utterly shocking and wearyingly unsurprising.

At cultural, activist and legal levels, we lost scintillatingly intelligent, iconic women such as US Supreme Court justice Ruth Bader Ginsburg, writer and essayist Joan Didion, and actor and activist Betty White. All three had unapologetically and unwaveringly used their intellect and actions to dismantle conventional gender stereotypes.

In a hammer blow, a regressive US Supreme Court overturned *Roe v Wade*, a decision that had protected women's bodily autonomy from men who so frequently, so unnervingly try to subvert it. In an equally distressing move closer to home, Sussan Ley, the Australian environment minister embedded in a climate-change-denying, coal-promoting government, successfully appealed the ruling that she owed a duty of care to children when considering and approving new mines. This came while thousands of people—me included—endured the visceral trauma of cleaning up their home in the aftermath of flooding that politicians told us 'no one could have predicted' (read: climate scientists have long predicted).

Somewhere in the haze of those wearying months, women had to take to the streets and march to parliament while the male prime minister demonstrated bewilderment and an out-of-touch worldview that seemed to be oriented through the lens of having a wife and daughters rather than what was moral, ethical, right. That's before he even mentioned that the women marching were fortunate not to have been met by bullets.

Around that time, we discovered what we could not unknow: that a former male government staff member had been sacked for masturbating on a female MP's desk. Tangentially, the term 'big swinging dicks', a reference to male politicians who tried to thwart former Liberal MP Julie Bishop's leadership ambitions, entered the lexicon. That was long before the same government released a Women's Network logo that resembled a penis and testicles; media headlines had to clarify that it was *not* satire. The kicker among kickers was that we discovered that the *Sex Discrimination Act* doesn't apply to parliament. Worse, despite one in three parliamentary staff telling investigators they had been sexually harassed, the government did its best to ignore the *Respect@Work Report* and its recommendations designed to address sexual harassment in said workplace.[1]

Frankly, with that laundry list it was difficult not to be completely worn down and despondent. But in those months, too, we had young women—traditionally some of the least powerful in society—such as Brittany Higgins and Grace Tame challenging perceptions of what it is to be a sexual assault survivor and advocate.

This was despite having to relive their trauma, contend with intense media scrutiny and social media trolling, and navigate the toll it took on their mental health. We had Chanel Contos who, a year to the day from when her social media advocacy commenced, succeeded in having mandatory consent training implemented in schools. We had a succession of intelligent, educated, pragmatic women reluctantly but powerfully stepping into the political realm to shift the gears from political point-scoring statements lacking policy substance, and gotcha journalism. Those accomplished 'teal independent' women unseated incumbent conservative politicians who had for too long failed women and failed to enact crucial policies to tackle corruption and climate change.

We had women like ABC investigative journalist Louise Milligan and former Adelaide Festival director Jo Dyer, who fought for allegations against Christian Porter, at the time the highest-ranking legal officer in the land, to be investigated in the public interest even when the government declined to. We had journalist Annabel Crabb and current and former women politicians shining a compelling, conversation-changing (and hopefully culture-changing) spotlight on the challenges women face in politics through the television and podcast series *Ms Understood*. Through that, we learned that women entering politics (which started in 1921, the same year Australian women started playing organised football) experienced decades of the absence of women's bathroom facilities. It took until 1975 for a dedicated women's toilet to be set up in Parliament House; many women footballers are still waiting for such a thing to be funded and built at their clubs.

During this time, Megan Rapinoe visited the White House and testified about systemic gender discrimination with such eviscerat-ingly direct statements as 'Despite all the wins, I am still paid less than men who do the same job that I do. For each trophy, of which there are many, and for each win, for each tie and for each time we play, it's less.'[2] Her point, among many salient points, was that if it can happen to literally the best and highest-profile women's football team in the world, it can happen to any person who is marginalised because of their gender. There is, she said, 'no level of status, accomplishments or power that will protect you from the clutches of inequality. One cannot simply outperform inequality of any kind.'[3]

Issuing equivalently eviscerating statements to equally great acclaim, we had climate activist Greta Thunberg. Her unperturbed social media response to goading internet personality Andrew Tate so infuriated him that he comprehensively doxed himself with a pizza box, of all things. Thunberg's owning of Tate, who was arrested in Romania on suspicion of human trafficking, inspired countless fist pumps, social media shares and memes.

In this time, we also had Lucy Small, who won a longboard surfing competition in Curl Curl in Sydney in April 2021 and received $1500 while the male winner received $4000. Small politely thanked sponsors for the contributions but noted that it was 'bittersweet' that the women's prize pool was half the men's. She subsequently co-founded the Equal Pay for Equal Play campaign to lobby the New South Wales Government to make gender equality a determining factor for sports organisations that wished to obtain funding. We had women such as human-rights lawyer and former Olympian Nikki Dryden and force-of-nature advocates such as former Socceroo Craig Foster leveraging their networks and skills to obtain humanitarian visas and evacuate the Afghanistan women's football team to safety, and the Women Onside football network and Melbourne Victory football club supporting those players as they navigated their way through grief and stress and homesickness and quarantine.

We had girls such as eleven-year-old sports fan Abbie, who created *Her Way*, a monthly magazine intended to redress the dearth of women's sports media coverage. We had women like Sedona Prince, who used social media to call out the stark difference between the weights rooms provided by the National Collegiate Athletic Association (NCAA) for the women's and men's basketball tournaments. (The men's set-up was a fully stocked, professional-standard room; the women's was a single small stack of free weights.) And we had women like Parramatta Eels sports scientist Tahleya Eggers, who said not a single word but whose body language spoke volumes: arms crossed, unimpressed, she was absolutely done with a prime minister who turned up to a rugby league team's change room to celebrate a win but would not attend a march or a meeting to address ingrained, life-threatening issues women face.

It was surprising—although also unsurprising—just how many times interviews for this book veered into the above topics and more. How, despite how much has changed for women in society and sport, so much hasn't. But what was encouraging was just how done women are with these issues—exhausted, angry, reeling, despairing, yes, but also rallying: determined to make collective progress no matter how non-linear and at times difficult and frustratingly circuitous the path. While the men in leadership positions who had the power to change the conversation and the legislation, policy, policing and services to address these issues were remarkably absent, silent, punching down or treating the issues as pesky PR or legal problems to be managed away, women around the world continued working alone and as one to address and overcome them. Although gruelling, it was an appropriate backdrop against which to write a book highlighting and celebrating women's too often overlooked or underappreciated football contributions.

ACKNOWLEDGEMENTS

This book wouldn't have been possible without the munificence of the current and former players, administrators and coaches who entrusted me with their experiences and stories and patiently helped me piece together timelines and details. Some seriously talented and tenacious women (and some men) have steered women's football through decades of scarcity and precarity; it's thanks to them that women's football is now so extraordinarily successful in the face of overwhelming challenges and odds.

In attempting to ever so incrementally shift the needle on the recognition women receive for their contributions to football, this book aims to help spotlight such previously unknown or under-valued contributions and stories. But a lot happens in and around World Cups; there are also lots of people involved. Administrator Maria Berry aptly noted there are twenty-three players on any given tour, which means there are twenty-three different tours—even within a single team, no two people's experiences are the same. I have tried to include a range of moments and stories that were illustrative, but none could ever be definitive.

Notably, not all Matildas have remained in the game. Some who were burned by the lack of opportunity or pay, or worn down, have retreated. Women's World Cups are illuminating and awe-inspiring. The women who feature in them perform remarkable feats on the pitch and often, through their accidental but necessary advocacy to create circumstances for women to succeed, edge women's football towards ever greater accomplishments. But not every Women's World Cup experience is wonderful, whether through injury or missed opportunity or non-selection; not everyone who aspires to make a Women's World Cup makes it. Some make the squad but never make it onto the pitch. Some leave the game through injury or exclusion or the grinding reality of unaffordability. Because for all the hype, opportunity, and glory Women's World Cups can bring, they also bring pressure and competition and players whose inclusion in the squad propels their teammates' on-pitch performances to their peaks. For every on-camera moment that sparks admiration, there are plenty of tough off-camera moments we'll never see.

But players' (and administrators' and referees' and coaches') contributions are invaluable and extend far beyond the Starting XI. Without them, the Matildas wouldn't be the groundbreaking team they are today. My hope is that the 2023 Women's World Cup, and the small part this book plays in it, enable current, former, retired, future and cusp players to experience the antithesis to the Matilda Effect, where their contributions are recognised, validated and feted. (What also wouldn't go astray are some reparations and some wraparound services to, for example, give them greater access to top healthcare to better manage injuries sustained while playing that may now be chronic. Likewise some innovative superannuation top-up policies similar to dollar-matching available to low-income earners. Such policy inventiveness might help redress some of the superannuation and compound interest former players missed out on throughout their unpaid football careers.)

★ ★ ★

Unparalleled thanks must go to the people who provided constructive feedback on copious numbers of chapter drafts, often with incredibly short, unforewarned turnaround times full of my wobbly emotions because: deadlines.

Special mention must go to my parents, Jill and Alan, and my siblings, Weesie (Louise) and BC (Bryan), who lived the unglamorous book-writing experience with me—every draft, every moment I'm in goblin mode and grumpy. As family, they didn't get to opt out, and I'm very grateful they chose to opt in.

Thanks must also go to Michelle Gillett, whose suggestions improved this book exponentially and who regularly recommended excellent true crime and football podcasts to de-frag my brain. Maybe, between us, we'll solve the T-Rex mystery one day.

Geoff Wilson, too, is one of the unsung heroes of getting this book across the line through his precise feedback. Sorry I nearly gave you a heart attack with sizeable chapters.

Claire Smiddy, Julie Dalling, Elizabeth Livingstone, Lise Schreiber, Clare Murphy, Victoria McCreanor and Rebecca Leeks checked in with the best environmental, cycling, legal, election, climate change and current affairs conversations, memes, and moral support. You'll never know how much and how often they absolutely made my day.

Thanks must go to Baden Appleyard, John McGuire, James Lamb and Katherine Capper, who provided technical counsel and acted as sounding boards. I hope to one day be skilled enough in an area useful enough to repay the favour. In the interim, I promise to bring you questions that are at least colourfully left-field.

A huge thankyou to Duncan Fardon, Nathan Hollier and the MUP team for championing and advocating for this book and for me every step of the way, and to Katie Purvis and Cathy Smith, for whipping my wordy sentences into succinct shape.

Thanks, too, to my indoor and outdoor football teams, who provided me with regular reminders of the transformative power playing football can have (and also, let's be clear, plenty of banter).

Finally, my eternal gratitude to every interviewee who was so incredibly generous with their time and stories amid constantly shifting sands (I 11/10 don't recommend writing a book in the middle of a multi-year pandemic punctuated by a climate-change-exacerbated flood), especially those (particularly Heather Reid, Maria Berry, Moya Dodd and Tom Sermanni) who patiently answered my questions, then my follow-up questions, then clarified information and chronology and more. As I've told many of the giants on whose shoulders women's football stands, you're my absolute heroes. I sincerely hope the next books I get to read are yours.

The following people provided invaluable assistance in helping me pull this book together:

Alex Adsett
Kevin Airs
Di Alagich
Kim Anderson
Baden Appleyard
Rachel Bach
Melissa Barbieri
Helen Barrow
Nerissa Bartlett
Ellen Beaumont
Kate Beerworth
Maria Berry
Pam Bignold
Helena Bond
Steve Bond
Shauna Bouel
Stephanie Brantz
Laura Brock
Eugenie Buckley
Catherine Cannuli
Katherine Capper
Evie Chamberlain
Bree Chesher
Lauren Colthorpe
Tris Cotterill
Barbara Cox
Michele Cox
Alan Crawford
Bryan Crawford
Jill Crawford
Louise Crawford
The Croissants (Maddy Bart,
  Lucy Friend, Lucy Gilfedder,

Libby Graham, Ciara O'Sullivan,
  Amanda Skellern, Kimberley
  Skellern)
Julie Dalling
Darebin Women's Sports Club
  (Darebin Falcons), including
  Jasmine Hirst
Theresa Deas
John Didulica
Moya Dodd
Julie Dolan
Rae Dower
Alex Duff
Alicia Ferguson
Jo Fernandes
Jane Fernandez
Fatima Flores
Alison Leigh Forman
Heather Garriock
Sonia Gegenhuber
Grace Gill
Kate Gill
Michelle Gillett
Joe Gorman
Daniel Greentree
Sarah Gregorius
George Halkias
Lauren Hanna
Kerry Harris
Megan Harris
Wendi Henderson
Jacqui Hurford
Angela Iannotta

Renaye Iserief
Kate Jacewicz
Andy Jackson
Kate Jenkins
Mark Jensen
Tal Karp
Elise Kellond-Knight
Alanna Kennedy
Helen Klaebe
James Lamb
Meredith Lawley
Rebecca Leeks
Elizabeth Livingstone
Joanna Lohman
Aivi Luik
Victoria McCreanor
John McGuire
Terry McPherson
Kate McShea
Joseph Mayers
Karen Menzies
Bonita Mersiades
Sue Monteath
Rosie Morley
Ashley Morrison
Clare Murphy
Julie Murray
Jane Oakley
Ann Odong
Bridie O'Donnell
Amanda Olsen
Catherine Ordway
Aidan Ormond
Jane Patterson
Ellyse Perry
Clare Polkinghorne
Tom Polkinghorne

Vedrana Popovic
Rebecca Price
Tara Pryor
Karly Pumpa
Heather Reid
Ali Riley
Jennifer Robinson
Karly Roestbakken
Anneliese Rubie-Renshaw
Tara Rushton
Jackie Scott
Tom Sermanni
Sally Shipard
Thea Slatyer
Pete Smith
Vitor Sobral
Callum Stebbing
Marion Stell
Rebecca Stott
Ash Sykes
Kasey Symons
Ellen Thompson
Helen Tyrikos
Amanda Vandervort
Sacha Wainwright
Sarah Walsh
Danielle Warby
Elaine Watson
Gillian Watson
Tracey Wheeler
Monique Williams
Geoff Wilson
Candace Wright
Kirsty Yallop
Tameka Yallop
Rebecca Yolland
Shelley Youman

NOTES

Introduction

1 Matilda Joslyn Gage, 'Woman as Inventor', *North American Review*, 136(318), 1883, pp. 478–89.

2 Canadian Association of University Teachers, 'The Matilda Effect', *CAUT Bulletin*, 2019, p. 10.

3 Margaret Rossiter, 'The Matthew Matilda Effect in Science', *Social Studies of Science*, 23(2), 1993, pp. 325–41; Margaret Rossiter, *Women Scientists in America: Volume 1: Struggles and Strategies to 1940*, Johns Hopkins University Press, Baltimore, MD, 1984; Susan Dominus, 'Women Scientists Were Written Out of History. It's Margaret Rossiter's Lifelong Mission to Fix That', *Smithsonian*, October 2019.

4 Rossiter, 'The Matthew Matilda Effect in Science'.

5 Ibid.

6 The Nobel Prize, 'Nobel Prize Awarded Women', 26 October 2022, Nobel Prize website.

1   1988: Be so good they can't ignore you

1 FIFA, 'Ellen Wille: Mother of Norwegian Football', FIFA website, date unknown. The webpage was live at the time of writing but has since been unpublished. An article dated 26 June 2019 on the France 24 website by Sophie Gorman, 'Ellen Wille, the Mother of Women's Football', covers similar territory.

2 FIFA Football Museum, *The Official History of the FIFA Women's World Cup: The Story of Women's Football from 1881 to the Present*, Carlton Publishing Group, London, 2020, p. 28.

3 Marion Stell & Heather Reid, *Women in Boots: Football and Feminism in the 1970s*, Australian Scholarly Publishing, Melbourne, 2020.

4 FIFA Football Museum, p. 41.

5 Alexander Abnos, '4: Start of Something Big', in 'The 10 Most Significant Goals in US Soccer History', *Sports Illustrated*, n.d.

6 FIFA Football Museum, p. 41.

7 Ibid., p. 42.

8 Elaine Watson, 'Tournament Report', Brisbane, 1988. I viewed this unpublished report in Heather Reid's private collection in October 2021.

9 Ibid.

10 Elaine Watson, *Australian Women's Soccer: The First 20 Years*, AWSA, Canberra, 1994.

2 1991: Legit now

1 FIFA, 'Tournament Report (Medical Report)', FIFA, 1991, p. 45.

2 FIFA Football Museum, *The Official History of the FIFA Women's World Cup: The Story of Women's Football from 1881 to the Present*, Carlton Publishing Group, London, 2020, p. 54.

3 Alexander Abnos, 4: Start of Something Big', in 'The 10 Most Significant Goals in US Soccer History', *Sports Illustrated*, n.d.

4 FIFA Museum, '"The Future of Women's Refereeing Is in Your Hands"', 8 March 2021, FIFA Museum website.

5 Gregory Quin, Elodie Wipf & Fabien Ohl, 'France: Media Coverage of the Athens Olympic Games by the French Press: The Olympic Games Effect in *L'Équipe* and *Le Monde*', in Jorid Hovden, Toni Bruce & Pirrko Markula (eds), *Sportswomen at the Olympics: A Global Content Analysis of Newspaper Coverage*, Sense, Leiden, 2010, pp. 103–14 (quote p. 106); Barbara Ravel & Gina S Comeau, '"Le Moment De Briller"?: Examining France's Media Coverage of Les Bleues and the FIFA Women's World Cup France 2019', in Molly Yanity & Danielle Sarver Coombs (eds), *2019 FIFA Women's World Cup: Media, Fandom, and Soccer's Biggest Stage*, Palgrave Macmillan, London, 2021, pp. 9–25 (quote p. 11).

3 1995: Great expectations

1 Hillary Clinton, 'Women's Rights Are Human Rights', *Women's Studies Quarterly (Beijing and Beyond: Toward the Twenty-First Century of Women)*, 24(1/2), 1996, pp. 98–101.

2 Janene Mar, 'SBS-TV Comes to the Party', *Australian and British Soccer Weekly*, 9 May 1995, p. 18.

3 Janene Mar, 'Matilda-Fax', *Australian and British Soccer Weekly*, 6 June 1995, p. 18.

4 1999: There's something to this

1 FIFA Football Museum, *The Official History of the FIFA Women's World Cup: The Story of Women's Football from 1881 to the Present*, Carlton Publishing Group, London, 2020, pp. 89, 91, 100.

2 Ibid., p. 100.

3 FIFA Fair Play Day is an annual day dedicated to encouraging and exemplifying ethical, respectful play and good sportspersonship around the world.

4 Joanna Lohman, 'You Can't Win Without the Gays', *Gay & Lesbian Review*, 28 April 2021.

5 Toni Bruce, 'New Rules for New Times: Sportswomen and Media Representation in the Third Wave', *Sex Roles*, 74(7–8), 2016, pp. 361–76 (quote p. 366).

6 Katherine Harman, 'Kelley O'Hara and Lesbian Rule: "[H]umdrum, Everyday Postwin Kiss, and That's What Makes It Monumental"', in Molly Yanity & Danielle Sarver Coombs (eds), *2019 FIFA Women's World Cup: Media, Fandom, and Soccer's Biggest Stage*, Palgrave Macmillan, London, 2021, pp. 201–22; William Cassidy, *Sports Journalism and Women Athletes: Coverage of Coming Out*, Palgrave Macmillan, London, 2019.

7 See, for example, Catharine Lumby, Helen Caple & Kate Greenwood, *Towards a Level Playing Field: Sport and Gender in Australian Media, January 2008 – July 2009*, Australian Sports Commission, Canberra, 2014.

8 Australian Senate, 'The Senate: Matters of Public Interest—Sport: Australian Women's Soccer Association—Speech [by Senator Kate Lundy]', 28 August 2002.

6 2007: A tournament of firsts

1 Cheryl Cook et al., 'One and Done: The Long Eclipse of Women's Televised Sports, 1989–2019', *Communication & Sport*, 9(3), 2021, pp. 347–71.

2 Jenesse Miller, 'News Media Still Pressing the Mute Button on Women's Sports', *USC News*, 24 March 2021.

3 Helen Caple, Kate Greenwood & Catharine Lumby, 'What League? The Representation of Female Athletes in Australian Television Sports Coverage', *Media International Australia*, 2011, pp. 137–46; Catharine Lumby, Helen Caple & Kate Greenwood, *Towards a Level Playing Field: Sport and Gender in Australian Media, January 2008 – July 2009*, Australian Sports Commission, Canberra, 2014; Women in Sport et al., *Where Are All the Women? Shining a Light on the Visibility of Women's Sport in the Media*, Women in Sport, London, 2018.

4 Suzanne McFadden, 'Here's the News: Kiwi Sportswomen Still Lag Behind', *Newsroom*, 29 April 2021.

5 Jenna Price with Blair Williams, '2021 Women for Media Report: "Take the Next Steps"', Women's Leadership Institute Australia, Melbourne, 2021, pp. 6 and 8.

6 Carrie Dunn, *Female Football Fans: Community, Identity and Sexism*, Palgrave Macmillan, London, 2014, pp. 2–3.

7 Kasey Symons, Sam Duncan & Emma Sherry, 'Brief Research Report: "Nothing About Us, Without Us": A Case Study of the Outer Sanctum Podcast and Trends in Australian Independent Media to Drive Intersectional Representation', *Frontiers in Sport and Active Living*, vol. 4, 2022, pp. 1–7 (esp. pp. 1–2).

7 2011: The golden generation

1 Kim Toffoletti, Ann Pegoraro & Gina S Comeau, 'Self-Representations of Women's Sport Fandom on Instagram at the 2015 Women's World Cup', *Communication & Sport*, 9(5), 2021, pp. 696–9.

2 Mildred F Perreault & Gregory P Perreault, '"I Stand by the Comments I Made": The 2019 FIFA Women's Soccer Championship: Images, Commentary and Narratives Made with Memes', in Molly Yanity & Danielle Sarver Coombs (eds), *2019 FIFA Women's World Cup: Media, Fandom, and Soccer's Biggest Stage*, Palgrave Macmillan, London, 2021, pp. 111–29 (esp. pp. 125–6); Meredith M Bagley & Mary Anne Taylor, 'Being There, Being Here: What Critical Field Methods Can Tell Us about WWC 2019', in Yanity & Coombs (eds), pp. 133–58 (esp. pp. 133–6).

3 Holly Thorpe, Kim Toffoletti & Toni Bruce. 'Sportswomen and Social Media: Bringing Third-Wave Feminism, Postfeminism, and Neoliberal Feminism into Conversation', *Journal of Sport and Social Issues*, 41(5), 2017, pp. 359–83 (esp. p. 361).

4 IFAB, *Laws of the Game: 2018/19*, International Football Association Board, Zurich, 2018, pp. 55–8.

5 Michele Cox, Geoff Dickson & Barbara Cox. 'Lifting the Veil on Allowing Headscarves in Football: A Co-Constructed and Analytical Autoethnography', *Sport Management Review*, 20(5), 2017, pp. 522–34 (esp. p. 524); Vincent Gessler, 'Islamophobia: A French Specificity in Europe?', *Human Architecture: Journal of the Sociology of Self-Knowledge*, 8(2), 2010, pp. 39–46 (esp. p. 43).

6 Cox, Dickson & Cox, p. 527.

8 2015: It's not about the grass

1 Kelley O'Hara (@kelleymohara), '@sydneyleroux You Should Probs Tweet That to FIFA ... #WWC2015 #realgrassplease', [Tweet], 15 April 2013.

2 Full disclosure: Airs commissioned me to write that 2015 Women's World Cup article.

3 FIFA Football Museum. *The Official History of the FIFA Women's World Cup: The Story of Women's Football from 1881 to the Present*, Carlton Publishing Group, London, 2020, p. 196.

4 Grant Wahl, 'USA Finds Inspiration in Supreme Court Ruling for WWC Win over China', *Sports Illustrated*, 28 June 2015.

5 Garriock is now an FA board member and as such potentially has some power to help change policies.

6 Catherine Ordway & Hayden Opie, 'Integrity and Corruption in Sport', in Nico Schulenkorf & Stephen Frawley (eds), *Critical Issues in Global Sport Management*, Routledge, Abingdon-on-Thames, UK, 2017, pp. 38–63 (esp. p. 48); Catherine Ordway & Richard Lucas, 'Restoring Trust in Sport: Corruption Cases and Solutions', in Catherine Ordway (ed.), *Restoring Trust in Sport: Corruption Cases and Solutions*, Routledge, Abingdon-on-Thames, UK, 2021, esp. p. 6.

7 Meg Watson, 'The Matildas Have Gone on Strike Because, Oh My God Can We Just Pay Them Properly?' *Junkee*, 9 September 2015.

8 Sam Squiers, 'Editorial: Don't Let the Matildas Strike Be in Vain', *Sportette*, 14 September 2015.

9 AFL, 'AFL, AFLPA Announce New CBA for AFLW Season Seven', Womens.AFL website, 19 May 2022.

9 2019: Time's up

1 Michela Musto, Cheryl Cooky & Michael A Messner, '"From Fizzle to Sizzle!" Televised Sports News and the Production of Gender-Bland Sexism', *Gender & Society*, 31(5), 2017, pp. 573–96 (quote p. 573).

2 Kathryn Gill, 'In My Words: Former Matilda Kate Gill on the AFC Asian Cup', Professional Footballers Australia website, 21 January 2022.

3 Eileen Narcotta-Welp & Anna Baeth, '"You Come at the Queen, You Best Not Miss": Post-Colonial Representations of the US Women's National Soccer Team during the 2019 World Cup', in Molly Yanity & Danielle Sarver Coombs (eds), *2019 FIFA Women's World Cup: Media, Fandom, and Soccer's Biggest Stage*, Palgrave Macmillan, London, 2021, pp. 73–91 (esp. p. 74).

4 Aimee Lewis, 'Women's World Cup: "It's Way More Than Football"—Jamaica's Remarkable Journey to France 2019', *CNN*, 3 June 2019.

5 Sarah Carrick, Alex Culvin & Ali Bowes, 'The Butterfly Effect? Title IX and the USWNT as Catalysts for Global Equal Pay', *Journal of Legal Aspects of Sport*, 31, 2021, pp. 289–311 (esp. pp. 289–90).

6 Joanna Lohman, 'You Can't Win Without the Gays,' *Gay & Lesbian Review Worldwide*, 28 April 2021.

7 Professional Footballers Australia, 'From "No Play" to "Equal Pay": The Empowerment of Women in Australian Professional Football from 2015 to 2019', PFA, West Melbourne, n.d., p. 14.

8 Ibid., p. 15; Professional Footballers Australia, 'Dispute over Unequal Prize Money: Request for Mediation' letter, 2019. This letter was sent to FIFA directly so is unpublished.

9 Fédération Internationale de Football Association, *FIFA Financial Report 2018*, FIFA, Zurich, 2019, p. 14.

10 John Didulica & Kathryn Gill, 'Changing the Game', *Law Institute Journal*, 94(5), 2020, pp. 30–3.

11 *Frontiero v. Richardson*, 411 US 677, 1973.

11 Levelling up

1 Susan Harris Rimmer, *Independent Human Rights Context Assessment: Australia & New Zealand*, Griffith University, Nathan, Qld, 2019; Eddie Ngaluafe, 'Human Rights Lawyer Contributes to the Winning Women's World Cup Bid', *Griffith News*, 30 July 2020.

2 Australian Human Rights Commission, *FIFA 2023 Women's World Cup Human Rights Risk Assessment*, AHRC, Sydney, 2021, pp. 24–5.

3 Ibid., p. 26.

4 L Stewart et al., 'Developing Trans-Athlete Policy in Australian National Sport Organizations', *International Journal of Sport Policy and Politics*, 13(4), 2021, pp. 565–85.

5 Australian Human Rights Commission, p. 49.

6 Ibid., pp. 52, 54–6.

7 Ibid., p. 58.

8 Actor Johnny Depp had sued ex-wife Amber Heard for defamation in both the United Kingdom and the United States in relation to an op-ed in UK paper *The Sun*. Depp claimed the article, which made reference to domestic violence claims, damaged his reputation. Depp was unsuccessful in the UK case, but successful in the US one. Burke's comment references the US trial decision.

9 In March 2022, film producer Harvey Weinstein was sentenced to twenty-three years in prison after being convicted of sexual assault and sexual abuse dating back decades. His crimes were first reported in the *New York Times* and the *New Yorker* in October 2017; Jenkins was appointed Sex Discrimination Commissioner in 2016.

10 Michelle K Ryan & S Alexander Haslam, 'The Glass Cliff: Evidence that Women Are Over-Represented in Precarious Leadership Positions', *British Journal of Management*, 16(2), 2005, pp. 81–90.

11 Suncorp, *Suncorp Australian Youth & Confidence Research 2019*, Suncorp, Brisbane, 2019.

12 Football Australia, *Legacy '23: Exciting and Enduring Outcomes for Our Game Beyond the FIFA Women's World Cup 2023™*, FA, Sydney, n.d., pp. 3–4.

13 Emma Nobel, '*The X-Files* and the Scully Effect: Fake Aliens, Real-World Phenomenon for Women in STEM', *ABC News*, 19 August 2020; 21st Century Fox, The Geena Davis Institute on Gender in Media, and J Walter Thompson Intelligence, *The 'Scully Effect': I Want to Believe … in STEM*, New York & Los Angeles, n.d.

14 Amelia Heathman, '*Hidden Figures*: The True Story Behind the Women who Changed NASA's Place in the Space Race', *Wired*, 28 February 2017.

15 YouGov, *Women in Sport Report 2021: The Growth in Women's Sport—and What It Means for Marketers*, YouGov, London, 2021, p. 12.

16 Cheryl Cooky & Dunja Antunovic, *Serving Equality: Feminism, Media, and Women's Sports*, Peter Lang, Bern, Switzerland, 2021, p. 44.

17 Kasey Symons et al., 'The (Un)Level Playing Field: Sport Media During Covid-19', *European Sport Management Quarterly*, 22(1), 2021, pp. 55–71.

18 FIFPRO, *Flash Report: Player Workload and Impact During the Emergency Calendar*, FIFPRO, Hoofddorp, The Netherlands, 2021.

19 Chantal Brunner et al., 'WSLA: Improving the Media Coverage of Our Sportswomen', New Zealand Women's Sport Leadership Academy, Auckland, n.d. [2021]. Available at https://www.olympic.org.nz/assets/Uploads/WSLA-Visibility-Report-2018.pdf.

20 Symons et al., pp. 68–9; Kim Toffoletti & Holly Thorpe, 'Female Athletes' Self-Representation on Social Media: A Feminist Analysis of Neoliberal Marketing Strategies in "Economies of Visibility"', *Feminism & Psychology*, 28(1), 2018, pp. 11–31.

21 Isobel Cootes, 'The 2023 Women's World Cup Sells More Tickets in One Day than It Did in a Week for France', *Optus Sport*, 13 October 2022.

22 Samantha Lewis, 'FIFA Admits It Was Caught Off Guard by "Unprecedented" 2023 Women's World Cup Ticket Demand as Aussie Fans Are Left Empty-handed', *ABC News*, 1 November 2022.

23 Molly Hensley-Clancy (@mollyhc), 'The fact that FIFA would, in the year 2022, claim to be "caught off guard" by the demand for Women's World Cup tickets tells you basically everything you need to know', [Tweet], 2 November 2022.

24 Isobel Cootes, '"We Are Not Going to Accept Those Offers": FIFA President Gianni Infantino Rejects Lowball Women's World Cup 2023 Broadcast Bids', *Optus Sport*, 25 October 2022; Rory Jones, 'Study: 70% of Australians Watch More Women's Sport Now than Before Pandemic', *SportsPro*, 8 March 2022.

25 Toffoletti & Thorpe, p. 28.

26 Zoe George, 'How Social Media Is Taking a Toll on Elite Athletes', *Stuff*, 23 May 2021, pp. 1–9.

27 Alison K Heather et al. (WHISPA), 'Biological and Socio-Cultural Factors Have the Potential to Influence the Health and Performance of Elite Female Athletes: A Cross Sectional Survey of 219 Elite Female Athletes in Aotearoa New Zealand', *Frontiers in Sports and Active Living*, 3, 2021 (esp. pp. 5, 7).

28 George.

29 Eric Moussambani (a.k.a. 'Eric the Eel') is a swimmer from Equatorial Guinea who became a worldwide sensation for his performances at the 2000 Sydney Olympics. He had been granted a wildcard entry to the 100 metres freestyle race and had never swum in an Olympic-sized swimming pool before competing. He completed the race in a record slow 1:52.72, but became a huge crowd favourite for his efforts.

30 In the 1990s, the Socceroos famously wore a kit dubbed 'Spew' for its mishmash of colours. The release of the Matildas' kit drew immediate comparisons, such as in Anna Harrington's article 'Nike Unveils the Matildas' New Kit for the 2019 Women's World Cup', *Fox Sports*, 12 March 2019.

31 Victoria University, *What Girls Want in Sport Uniforms to Make Them Feel Comfortable and Confident to Participate in Sport: A National Study*, Victoria University, Melbourne, 2021, pp. 2, 4, 5, 8.

32 Meredith Cash, 'A Top European Women's Soccer Club Is Changing Its Uniforms so Players Don't Have to Wear White Shorts While on Their Periods', *Insider.com*, 29 October 2022.

33 Professional Footballers Australia, *Retired and Transitioned Players Report 2021*, PFA, West Melbourne, 2021, pp. 10, 12.

12 Beyond greatness

1 Garance Franke-Ruta, 'Binders Full of Women: A Meme that Means Something', *The Atlantic*, 18 October 2012.

2 Sam McClure, 'Television Boom for Women's Football', *The Age*, 31 March 2016.

3 Fiona McLachlan, 'It's Boom Time! (Again): Progress Narratives and Women's Sport in Australia', *Journal of Australian Studies*, 43(1), 2019, pp. 7–21.

4 YouGov, *Women in Sport Report 2021: The Growth in Women's Sport—and What It Means for Marketers*, YouGov, London, 2021, p. 5.

Afterword

1 Australian Human Rights Commission, *Set the Standard: Report on the Independent Review into Commonwealth Parliamentary Workplaces, November 2021*, AHRC, Sydney, 2021; Australian Human Rights Commission,

Respect@Work: National Inquiry into Sexual Harassment in Australian Workplaces, AHRC, Sydney, 2020.

2 Madeline Hislop, '"Devalued, disrespected, dismissed": Megan Rapinoe Speaks on Equal Pay at White House', *Women's Agenda*, 25 March 2021.

3 Ibid.

INDEX